CONSTRUCTING IDENTITIES
IN LATE ANTIQUITY

CONSTRUCTING IDENTITIES IN LATE ANTIQUITY

Edited by Richard Miles

London and New York

First published 1999
by Routledge
11 New Fetter Lane, London EC4P 4EE

Simultaneously published in the USA and Canada
by Routledge
29 West 35th Street, New York, NY 10001

Routledge is an imprint of the Taylor and Francis Group

Typeset in Garamond by
BC Typesetting, Bristol
Printed and bound in Great Britain by
Biddles Ltd, Guildford and King's Lynn

British Library Cataloguing in Publication Data
A catalogue record for this book is available from the British Library

Library of Congress Cataloging in Publication Data
Constructing identities in late antiquity/edited by Richard Miles.
p.   cm.
Includes bibliographical references and index.
1. Civilization, Classical.   2. Rome–Cultural policy.
3. Identity in literature.   4. Christianity–Rome–Influence.
5. Rome–History–Germanic Invasions, 3rd–6th centuries.   I. Miles,
Richard, 1969–
DG78.C585   1999
937–dc21   98-37614
                                                         CIP

ISBN 0–415–19406–7

CONTENTS

CONTENTS

LIST OF FIGURES

NOTES ON CONTRIBUTORS

Gillian Clark is a Senior Lecturer in Classics at the University of Liverpool.

Pat Easterling is Professor of Ancient Greek at the University of Cambridge and a Fellow of Newnham College.

Jill Harries is Professor of Ancient History at the University of St Andrews.

Simon Harrison is a Research Fellow at St John's College, Cambridge.

Peter Heather is a Reader in History at University College, London.

Janet Huskinson is a Lecturer in Classical Studies at the Open University.

Paula James is a Lecturer in Classical Studies at the Open University.

Richard Miles is a Research Fellow at the Open University and a Teaching By-Fellow at Churchill College, Cambridge.

Helen Morales is a Lecturer in Classics at the University of Reading.

Peter Stewart is a Lecturer in Classics at the University of Reading.

Tim Whitmarsh is a Research Fellow at St John's College, Cambridge.

ACKNOWLEDGEMENTS

The editor would like to thank all those who attended the two-day colloquium at the Open University, Milton Keynes, where the individual papers were discussed. Their contributions undoubtedly improved all aspects of this volume. Particular thanks are due to our excellent chairpersons, Kate Cooper and Christopher Kelly, who through inspired interventions and careful diplomacy kept the discussion flowing. The Faculty of Arts Research committee of the Open University very generously met the cost of the two days. Thanks are also due to Richard Stoneman for his initial encouragement and Kate Chenevix Trench for seeing the book successfully through the publication process. Undoubtedly, the editor's greatest debt is to Janet Huskinson, without whose hard work, encouragement and good humour this project would not have come to fruition.

1

INTRODUCTION

Constructing identities in late antiquity

Richard Miles

The past decade has seen a proliferation of scholarly work on collective identity, especially among political scientists and historians (as well as psychologists, anthropologists and archaeologists). As one social scientist has observed: 'Whereas in the 1970s and 1980s, conflict was explained and discussed in terms of conflicting ideologies, that terrain of contestation is now more likely to be characterised by competing and conflicting identities' (Woodward 1997: 18–19).

This academic trend has usually been explained in terms of a posited 'crisis of identity' in the 1990s, on the grounds that identity becomes an issue only when something assumed to be fixed, coherent and stable is displaced by the experience of doubt and uncertainty (Mercer 1990: 4, Woodward 1997: 15–20).

Various explanations have been put forward for this late twentieth-century 'crisis of identity': globalisation and migration of labour, the disruptions following the break-up of the USSR and the Eastern European bloc and the emergence of new social movements concerned with the politics of personal and sexual identities have all been pointed to as potential catalysts (Woodward 1997: 15–29).

However, although it is certainly correct to say that academics have in the past few years turned to identity and difference as a main organising principle, identity, by its very nature, is always at issue. Identity has always given us a location in the world and presents the link between us and the society in which we live. Identity is there to answer that fundamental question 'Who am I?' The academic world might have rediscovered identity, but men and women have never ceased thinking about and articulating themselves in these terms.

Recent scholarship on the ancient world has mirrored wider academia's concern with identity and difference.[1] The past fifteen years have seen the gradual development of a more sensitive attitude towards text and image, which are no longer regarded simply as mines of empirical data that will help the classical scholar to reconstruct the 'reality' of the ancient world, or as an isolated literary exercise, but rather as dynamic cultural forces that create their own 'imaginaire' and meanings. A significant number of cultural historians of the ancient world have also been influenced by the post-colonial school of writers whose primary concern has been to investigate cultural imperialism and responses to it under the rubric of identity.[2]

This volume is the product of a two day seminar held at the Open University on 28 February and 1 March 1997. The focus of the meetings was on how identity was constructed and represented in late antiquity. The essays that resulted from these seminars centre on two interrelated themes:

1   Identity. How is the theme of identity, whether it be geographical, ethnic, religious, status- or sex-based, used in late Roman texts and images to create and organise particular visions of late antique society and culture?
2   Periodisation. How do constructions of identity and culture contribute in the fashioning of 'late antiquity' into a discrete historical period?

In the past twenty years scholars of the later Roman empire have perhaps been too successful in resuscitating what was until then a much-neglected field of study. Thanks to the efforts of scholars such as Peter Brown and Averil Cameron, late antiquity is now recognised as an exciting and important area of the ancient world.[3] As Cameron points out,

> It is a mark of the dramatic change that has taken place in our historical perceptions of the ancient world that when the new Fontana series was first launched, the later Roman Empire, or, as it is now commonly called, late antiquity, was not included in it; now, by contrast, it would seem strange to leave it out.
>
> (Cameron 1993: 1)

It is useful, for heuristic purposes, to portray late antiquity as a discrete historical period, as undoubtedly in religious, economic, social and political terms the period spanning from the late third to the sixth centuries was very different from what came before and after it. However, by portraying late antiquity as a 'world' which is worth studying in its own right, scholars have perhaps been guilty of 'ring-fencing' the period in a way that suggests self-containment. It is perhaps worth pointing out the obvious, namely, that the term 'late antiquity' is a modern construction. Although in many ways the inhabitants of the Roman empire during this period perceived themselves as being different from those who had come before them, they certainly did not think of themselves as being 'late antique'.[4] What becomes clear in this collection of essays is that there is no unitary 'late antique' identity, just as there is no single 'late antique' culture in which these identities are created. Identity and culture are both in a constant state of flux and development.

Several of the contributors to this volume highlight the dangers of seeing late antiquity as a discrete cultural time span. Peter Stewart points out that the riot of the statues at Antioch, contrary to what some historians of the later Roman empire would have us believe, 'are neither so surprising nor so novel as they may at first seem' (p. 160). Indeed, he argues that fourth- and fifth-century Christian sources relating to the destruction of pagan images 'resist our efforts to identify cultural change between the conventional periods of the Principate and the later Roman Empire. They defy evidence for social, cultural and artistic transformation with symbols of continuity' (p. 182). Morales argues that the constructions of gender and vocality in Musaeus' *Hero and Leander* 'are symptomatic of an ideology which has a long tradition in Greek and Roman literature' (p. 55).

The term 'late antique' can also lead to other dangerous assumptions. Janet Huskinson warns against labelling images on third- and fourth-century sarcophagi as 'Christian' or 'non-Christian' or the 'snap identifications of female praying figures as "souls", of philosophical-looking men as "apostles"' (pp. 191–2). Huskinson concludes her chapter on a cautionary note arguing that although the intellectualisation of female images on these sarcophagi might indicate 'empowerment of some kind' brought about by the gradual Christianisation of Roman society in the fourth century, the last images of the biblical story of Susannah on the fourth-century sarcophagi 'close off the image in the time-honoured way', where it is a male figure, Daniel, whose wisdom and decisiveness eventually vindicate her (pp. 209–10).

What needs to be asked is whether there are any general organising features in the construction of identity that the scholar can identify as being particular to this period. To argue that identity becomes an important concern in the later Roman empire is of no particular use, because identities are being constructed and dissolved in all historical periods. Even to argue that new labels of identification come into existence is not really correct. Christians and barbarians might become more prominent in late antique texts, but both had existed as important constructs well before late antiquity. Nor is there any universal meaning that can be attributed to such terms as 'Roman', 'Greek', 'Christian' and 'barbarian'. Therefore, if one is to look for any unificatory aspects it is in how identity was discussed in late antique texts and images. Here a general, although tentative, consensus seems to emerge that the sample texts and images under consideration display an increased openness and mobility in realigning and reappropriating older paradigms. There is a novel, self-consciously revisionist perspective to constructions of identity and culture. For Whitmarsh, Heliodorus' great romance, the *Aethiopica*, reveals 'the open and mobile cultural patterns of late antiquity' (p. 32), where terms such as Hellene seem to be more self-consciously questioned. Clark sees similar phenomena in neo-Platonist discourses on alien or barbarian *sophia* (pp. 122–3). Huskinson detects a willingness to elide and confuse existing gender differentiations, reflecting an 'ambivalence to closure' (p. 210). James shows how the most 'Roman' of cultural locations, the arena, is converted into an impressive 'literary metaphor for the Christian victory' (p. 89) in Prudentius' text. Harrison (chapter 7) argues that Augustine's *De Libero Arbitrio* is a text in which the Christian thinker formulates the question of his cultural identity as part of a complex set of philosophical questions in order to force the reader to confront his own education and cultural identity. Easterling and Miles (chapter 5) contend that the Church fathers' construction of their own and their audiences' identities in their diatribes against the theatre points to a new malleability in the discussion of such issues.

Although many of these cases should perhaps be viewed as provocative and playful rhetorical poses, manifestations of the enduring sophistication of literary *paideia*, this does not negate their importance (pp. 123, 31–2). For what we are witnessing is a significant change in acceptable rhetorical strategies and discourse amongst the intelligentsia of late antiquity. The construction of identity is, at its heart, a matter of an *imaginaire* rather than a fixed *reality*.

What brought about these changes? There can be no doubt that there was a profound transformation in the political, bureaucratic and religious institutions in the late third and early fourth centuries. Three particular developments seem to stand out, namely, the changes in imperial self-representation and ideology, the influx of 'barbarians' and their growing importance in the military and civil structures of the empire, and the emergence of Christianity as a powerful force. Each of these developments has been well documented elsewhere, but part of our task in preparing this volume has been to look at how the different responses to these changes (i.e. resentment, approval and indifference) affected the way individuals and groups constructed themselves in late antiquity.

All the chapters in this volume are concerned with how identities are constructed in image and text rather than as a 'fixed' reality. Identities, both individual and collective, are not a set of essential characteristics, but are the ascribed or recognised characteristics which a person or group is agreed to possess. Benedict Anderson's description of the nation as an 'imagined community' can be applied to all group identities in that members of even the smallest identity group 'will never know most of their fellow members, meet them, or even hear of them, yet in the minds of each lives the image of their community' (Anderson 1991: 6). Part of the contributors' task in this project has been to examine what kind of communities were imagined in late antiquity.

It is possible to have an overarching single identity, but it will always be made up of several, if not myriad, separate identities, some of which may be contradictory (Smith 1991: 4–7). Some will be stronger than others and the pattern will change over time. One has only to look at the choices open to Porphyry and those who wrote about him: Phoenician, Hellene, Roman or philosopher (Clark, chapter 6)? The multifarious nature of identity is also in evidence in Harries's essay (chapter 10) on the representations of the *iudex* in late antiquity, according to which the same individuals who are portrayed as bloodthirsty tyrants in the acts of the martyrs in their role as persecuting judges are portrayed in a completely different light, as generous patrons and leaders in their communities, in epigraphic material.

The formation and contestation of identity are fundamentally about *power*, the power to represent. In late antiquity the barbarians were barbarised, the East orientalised, non-Christians paganised because they *could be* subjected to such categorisations without their voices being heard or their ideas known. In late antiquity, as both Clark (chapter 6) and Whitmarsh (chapter 2) point out, this allowed Neoplatonic debates about the origins of *sophia* to flourish. Writers such as Heliodorus and Porphyry could create and represent 'non-Greek', alien wisdom. Meanwhile, the Roman emperor, through his control of the production and dissemination of laws, could construct a particular image of his provincial officials (chapter 10).

It is within this context that the image of the 'barbarian' in late Roman texts is so important. No identity can exist by itself and without an array of opposites or negatives. The 'barbarian' is an important conceptual pole in late antique texts and images. Rather than thinking about these images in terms of a history of the 'barbarian', it is perhaps more fruitful to think in terms of what light the 'barbarian' as a literary construct throws on our authors' attitudes to their own identities. Hence, the discussions recorded from the seminars of Plotinus and exchanges between Iamblichus and Porphyry on the languages, traditions and religions of the Near East and India will tell us little about the actuality but rather raise questions about Roman citizenship and Greek culture. As Clark argues, 'Any "Oriental" inheritance in these texts has been filtered through Greek ethnography and philosophy, and different beliefs about the soul have more to do with philosophical debates about Plato and Aristotle than with Egyptian or Iranian theological tradition' (p. 123). Similarly, as Heather points out, in the fourth century 'It is no surprise, therefore, that the more precise connotations of the image of the barbarian, as it had evolved by late antiquity, served to underline what was good and important about being Roman' (pp. 235–6). Huskinson in her chapter shows how the images of women on third- and fourth-century sarcophagi establish a rhetoric about women that is 'defined in terms of a male society, as potential reinforcements or as threats to its values' (p. 192).

This does not mean, however, that such organising constructs are nothing more than an idea or a creation with no corresponding social reality: they are a created body of theory and practice in which, for many generations, there has been a considerable material investment (Said 1995: 6). As Heather describes in chapter 11, the ideologically inspired image of barbarians in the fourth century helped create Roman imperial foreign policy. But it should not be inferred that it was only the creators of this image who had considerable material investment in these stereotypes. These 'barbarians', as the culturally subjugated 'other', had a highly articulated set of relationships with *Romanitas*. Indeed, the cultural experience of one overlaps and depends on the other. Each is articulated on a largely common although disputed terrain provided by culture (Said 1993: 78–9, 1995: 230–1). Consequently, we find the kings of the barbarian successor states of the fifth century using the ideologically inspired images of *Romanitas* to legitimise their own rule.

The different constructions of a particular identity can reflect wider changes in the cultural framework of a society. Harries points out that the changing representations of the provincial *iudex* in the imperial law codes reflect 'The Janus-like qualities of late Roman autocracy' (p. 231), on the one hand ritualised, and, on the other, reflecting the evolution of complex strategies for the assertion and expression of power. This 'culture of criticism' allowed the assertion of the emperors' authority by repeatedly stressing the accountability of their own officials. But this is not to say that all political upheavals necessarily mean a change in how certain identities are constructed. For instance, Heather (chapter 11) shows how despite the establishment of the barbarian kingdoms in the Roman West in the fifth century, the fourth-century construction that pitched civilising *Romanitas* against uncivilised barbarians still held good. What did change was who aspired to, or represented themselves as belonging to, such groups. Theoderic uses his *Romanitas* as a weapon to portray other barbarian kings and even the eastern emperor as being decidedly un-Roman. Hence the Ostrogothic king could proclaim his equality with, and even his superiority over, contemporary rulers.

The geography of an area, like history, culture and its politico-economic manifestations, is disputed and ever-changing.[5] The idea of a geographical area has to be reified through images and text. So, in order to make the later Roman empire into any kind of political or cultural reality, or even to give it a geographical identity, significant numbers of people need to have had a concept of what the empire consisted of. A recurrent theme at the conference was how significant was geography in the construction of identity. What became clear was quite how arbitrary the geographical distinctions were. Such distinctions, while appearing to exist objectively, have only a fictional reality. This is borne out in Clark's (chapter 6) description of the seminar of the third-century neo-Platonist philosopher, Plotinus. On the surface, it was a cosmopolitan affair held in Rome and attracting students from all over the empire. But as Clark points out, its focus was completely directed towards Greece and the Near East. Its working language was Greek, and in fact Porphyry, an important member of the seminar, shows no sign in his writings of understanding Latin or any awareness of the Western philosophical tradition. It is a common practice to designate a familiar place which is 'ours' and an unfamiliar place beyond those boundaries which is 'theirs'. Those who live outside these boundaries are not required to acknowledge them. These geographic boundaries match the social, ethnic and cultural ones in expected ways (Said 1993: 52). What is more important than actual physical geography is the theoretical mapping and charting of territory that underlies the fiction, historical writing, art and philosophical discourse of the time (Fuhrman 1983: 1, Said 1993: 69).[6] Whitmarsh argues that geography is a crucial structuring device in the *Aethiopica*. The river Nile serves to structure the linear shape of the text: the journey up Egypt's great river mirrors the progression towards self-knowledge and becoming culturally other. By employing an unconventional 'linear' narrative, Heliodorus presents a different conceptual geography from the traditional Greek one.

Identities are produced, consumed and regulated within culture. The term 'culture' implies that there is such a thing as a homogeneous group, even though there is no need for consensus throughout that group as to the actual content of that culture (Wintle 1996a: 6). However, as Said has pointed out, 'all cultures are involved in one another; none is single and pure, all are hybrid, heterogeneous, extraordinarily differentiated and unmonolithic' (Said 1993: xix). 'Culture', in other words, is an ever-changing construct, a multifarious collective mental conditioning (García 1993: 67, Shelley 1995: 192). Culture as a descriptive, communicative and representative force is articulated through text. Each text creates its own 'world' with its own parameters and dynamic. Hence, as Harries points out in her chapter on the role of the *iudex* in late antiquity,

> The various representations of this both feared and indispensable figure in Roman society are therefore often more relevant to the creators of texts and the cultural perceptions of late antiquity than to the actual functioning both of *iudices* themselves and, more broadly, of the judicial system of the time.
>
> (p. 215)

What all these texts indicate is that culture and identity are produced *performatively* as narrative. This is well illustrated in Morales's study of *Hero and Leander* (chapter 3), where not only representations of vocality are shown to play a crucial role in distinguishing gender status, but also the omnipresent narrator frames and reinterprets Hero's words thereby creating a discrepancy between what she is reported as saying and how her speech is heard and understood by its audience. This leads to what Morales terms a 'discourse of distorted dissent' whereby if the female subject vocalises dissent to a sexual overture it is interpreted as consent and if she remains silent, it is interpreted as consent. Narrative is in a constant state of contestation, revision and reformation (Bhabha 1990: 296–7, 1994: 2). This is borne out in chapter 2 where he argues that the *Aethiopica*, in its reconfiguration of traditional narrative and geographical structures, represents the ever-changing and incomplete properties of cultural identity.

This is not to say that each of these texts should be studied in glorious isolation from one another. It is these texts that create knowledge and contribute to an accumulated tradition or discourse which further texts simultaneously gain authority from and add to. Such discourses are at the heart of all constructions of identity (Said 1995: 96). This is also well illustrated in Morales's reassessment of the dominant ideological interpretation of *Hero and Leander* as a social commentary on civic identity: a discourse which serves to validate socially sanctioned marriages and stigmatise the indulgence of individual desire outside of the institution of marriage (chapter 3). Through the study of late antique texts it is possible to trace the development of certain discourses relating to different identities. As Whitmarsh argues in the case of Heliodorus' *Aethiopica*, the

> narrative structure engages with and reconfigures a widespread narrative pattern which was fundamental to the construction of cultural identity in the archaic and classical periods. Heliodorus' active transformation of this pattern . . . articulates a new conception of cultural identity.
>
> (p. 18)

In the same way, Heather in his chapter has been able to show the importance of text in the construction of a dominant discourse concerning *Romanitas* and barbarians in the fourth and fifth centuries. Indeed, Morales reminds us of the tenacity of a 'gendered discourse of distorted dissent' (p. 55) through which women's speech, paradoxically dismissed, socially disavowed and overdetermined 'continues to manifest itself in the attitudes of judges and jurors and in the thinking of every modern-day Marilyn and Don Juan' (p. 56).

9

It could be objected that, as this material was created and consumed by the small group who were literate in late antique society, this collection of studies reflects only what might be called 'elite culture'. However, the 'imagined community' is moulded by both 'top–down' initiatives from the centre and by more or less spontaneous 'bottom–up' movements (Gellner 1983: 35–8). Discourse interconnects these two developments. It is important that the literate in society create the narrative for an identity and make the community imaginable. The mediatory role performed by the elite is well illustrated in Easterling and Miles's chapter where they show how tragedy was part of a cultural language and identity shared by all social strata of the late antique 'Greek' city. Consequently we find the Church fathers using images from tragedy to instruct their congregations in the Christian way of life. In addition, Stewart's chapter with its discussion of mass participation in statue destruction emphasises that images are not just restricted to the literate elite.

The rise of Christianity as a powerful force in the fourth century is an important theme. Christianity had provided identity within the Roman empire for the previous three centuries, but with the advent of the first Christian emperor, Constantine, and the gradual process of Christianisation that took place in the fourth century, the term 'Christian' becomes increasingly problematic and complex; if we accept that such terms are indicative of a collective notion identifying 'us' against 'them', it is important to see what effects this process has on other identificatory constructs.

The question of what it actually meant to be a Christian was of central importance in late antiquity. An identity cannot exist without an array of opposites, negatives and oppositions; this means that the debate centred as much on what it meant to be Roman, Greek, woman or man as it did on what it was to be Christian. For example, Huskinson (chapter 9) argues that with the advent of Christianity as a serious religious force in fourth-century Rome there is a corresponding change in the iconography of women on sarcophagi, including the emergence of the 'female intellectual' as a popular motif. Her suggestion is that the emergence of a Christian society, with its emphasis on the renunciation of worldly power, allowed women to portray themselves and be portrayed as acting out qualities which had previously been denied to them.

Important late antique definitions such as 'Roman', 'Greek', 'Barbarian', 'Christian' and 'pagan' are all deeply problematic: each has a myriad of potentially different and often contradictory meanings. In all our essays we are dealing with perception rather than a fixed 'reality'. Consequently, although these texts display agreement about group identities *vis-à-vis* outsiders, seldom is there any internal concurrence in their self-representation (Wintle 1996a: 5–6). Within surviving late antique texts and images it has become clear that there were widely divergent views on what being a Christian meant. If one were to take the two poles of this debate, one might be tempted to turn, on the one hand, to Eusebius writing his panegyrics and histories at the court of Constantine, advocating the indivisibility of *Romanitas* from Christianity, and, on the other, to the holy men of the deserts of Syria and Egypt whose power was expressed through a conscious rejection of the temporal world. But as Heather (chapter 11) points out, by the end of the fourth century, it was not just inarticulate ascetics but also the highly educated Christian intelligentsia who felt increasingly ill at ease with the ideology of the Christian empire.

Harrison's chapter shows what important issues identity and culture had become amongst the great thinkers of the Christian church. Augustine's self-conscious rhetorical strategy of removing the identities of the interlocutors and all references to the philosophical past reflects the struggle between Christian *simplicitas* and the huge debt which the Church fathers owed to their non-Christian education. As Harrison points out, 'This was tension felt, and felt very strongly, by others across the late antique world' (p. 135). Similarly, the Church fathers, at the same time as condemning tragedy and other forms of theatre, utilise them as a locus for internal debate within Christianity between classical heritage and Christian *simplicitas* (pp. 103–7).

The past is integral to identity constructed as it is as being tangible and secure, as fixed, unalterable and indelibly recorded. The representation of the past validates present attitudes and actions by affirming their resemblance to former ones (Lowenthal 1985: 4 and 40). However, the past, like the present, is a contested area. There is a continuous debate between individuals and institutions about what does constitute the past, and an ever-present tension between tradition and innovation (Said 1993: 1).[7] Every generation must reach a *modus vivendi* that simultaneously embraces and abandons precedent (Lowenthal 1985: 72). In the writings of the Christian intelligentsia of the fourth and fifth centuries one witnesses such a debate going on.

The chapters in this collection emphasise the presence of this tension in all sorts of different shared cultural locations. For Stewart, the iconoclastic tradition is a 'cultural language shared by pagans and Christians' (p. 160). Easterling and Miles in their chapter illustrate how tragedy, and theatre in general, were a locus for both the Christian Church and the later sophists in the construction of their own self-images. Cultural congruity between these two groups is evident in that both are interested in tragedy as a performance genre, and the Church fathers' virulent condemnations of the theatre mirror the more qualified rhetorical and even playful disapproval on the part of the sophists. It is the theatre's role as a vehicle of civic identity especially in the Greek East which makes it such an important locus for Christian debate. Church and theatre are consciously put together as rival contenders for the centre of the late antique Greek city. James, in her study of Prudentius' *Psychomachia*, regards the 'cultural space' of the poem to be the spectacles, a public place associated with Roman civic identity and cultural life. The poem creates an intellectual locality in which the hierarchy of reception mimics the hierarchy of the seating at the amphitheatre: this is a 'theatre of punishment produced for the delight and edification of a Christian audience' (p. 72). The arena with its programme of public punishment 'was a major means of sustaining community identity' (p. 74). Consequently, the *Psychomachia* helps elucidate 'areas of correspondence between pagan and Christian consciousness' (p. 89).

But one wonders how apt is the word 'appropriation', so favoured by post-colonial thinkers such as Said, in this context. 'Appropriation' gives the rather misleading impression that Christian writers could in some way distance themselves from their own cultural heritage. What Stewart has to say in connection with the Christian destruction of pagan statues must hold for all areas of cultural life in late antiquity, namely that although Christian writing in its use of the language of *damnatio memoriae* in a Christian context 'declares the perceived novelties of the times in which they lived' (p. 182), it in no way indicates 'an aggressive appropriation of "secular", pagan imagery' (pp. 182–3) but rather that 'the language of *damnatio* would have come easily to the minds of Roman Christians who thought about the place of statues and images of power in their imperial world' (p. 183).

In different ways the contributors to this collection have all been trying to explore what they see as an important area of late antique studies. Although several excellent books on gender, identity and the late antique Christian church have been published recently, much remains for the historian, literary critic and archaeologist to investigate regarding the construction and representation of identity in late antiquity.[8]

Acknowledgements

I would like to thank Michael Alderton, Paul Cartledge, Camilla Chaudhary, Pat Easterling, Peter Garnsey, Janet Huskinson, Christopher Kelly, Antony Lawson, Peter Stewart and Tim Whitmarsh, whose generous criticisms and suggestions did much to improve this introduction.

Notes

1 See, for example, Cartledge 1997a, Gill 1996, Hall 1997, Laurence and Berry 1998 and Goldhill forthcoming.
2 For three particularly successful examples see Alcock 1993, Cartledge 1997 and Hall 1989. Probably the most influential of the post-colonial works have been Edward Said's *Orientalism: Western Conceptions of the Orient* and *Culture and Imperialism*. There are however a significant number of post-colonialist scholars who question the validity and usefulness of any academic study of 'identity'. See, for instance, Chanady 1994: ix; Radhadkrishnan 1987.
3 For two of the best examples see Brown 1972 and Cameron 1993. The paucity of literary studies of late antique texts indicates that in some areas of classical scholarship prejudices are still strong (see Morales, chapter 3, this volume).
4 For the convincing argument that *all* periodisation is more or less artificial see Morris 1997.
5 See Burke 1980: 21 and García 1993: 10 on Europe as a collective social fabrication.
6 Maps are the most obvious means for this kind of visualisation. See Wintle 1996c for how maps reflect the ever-changing and disputed nature of the geographical place.
7 Hobsbawm's distinction between 'invented' tradition and tradition must surely be a false dichotomy, as in essence all traditions are constructed. Nevertheless, his definition of an 'invented' tradition is a valuable one:

> a set of practices, normally governed by overtly or tacitly accepted rules and of a ritual of symbolic nature, which seeks to inculcate certain values and norms of behaviour by repetition, which automatically implies continuity with the past. In fact, where possible, they normally attempt to establish continuity with a suitable historic past.
>
> (Hobsbawm 1990: 1)

8 For two particularly interesting studies on this subject see Burrus 1995 and Cooper 1995.

RICHARD MILES

Bibliography

Alcock, S.E. (1993) *Graecia Capta: The Landscapes of Roman Greece*, Cambridge: Cambridge University Press.

Amin, S. (1989) *Eurocentrism*, New York: Zed.

Anderson, B. (1991) *Imagined Communities: Reflections on the Origin and Spread of Nationalism*, revised edition, London: Verso.

Bhabha, H.K. (1990) 'Introduction: Narrating the Nation', in H.K. Bhabha (ed.), *Nation and Narration*, London: Routledge.

—— (1994) *The Location of Culture*, London: Routledge.

Brown, P. (1972) *The World of late antiquity from Marcus Aurelius to Muhammad*, New York: Harcourt Brace.

Burke, P. (1980) 'Did Europe Exist before 1700?', *History of European Ideas* 1: 21–9.

Burrus, V. (1995) *The Making of a Heretic: Gender, Authority, and the Priscillianist Controversy*, Berkeley: University of California Press.

Cameron, A. (1993) *The Later Roman Empire*, London: Fontana.

Cartledge, P. (1997a) *The Greeks: A Portrait of Self and Others*, revised edition, Oxford: Oxford University Press.

—— (1997b) 'Historiography of Ancient Greek Self-Definition', in N. Bentley (ed.) *Companion to Historiography*, London: Routledge.

Chanady, A.B. (1994) 'Latin American Imagined Communities and the Post-Modern Challenge', in A. Chanady (ed.) *Latin American Identity and Constructions of Difference*, Minneapolis: University of Minnesota Press.

Cooper, K. (1995) *The Virgin and the Bride: Idealized Womanhood in Late Antiquity*, Cambridge, Mass.: Harvard University Press.

Fuhrman, M. (1983) 'L'Europe: Contribution à l'histoire d'une idée culturelle et politique', *History of European Ideas* 4: 1–15.

García, S. (ed.) (1993) *European Identity and the Search for Legitimacy*, London: Pinter Publishers.

Gellner, E. (1983) *Nations and Nationalism*, Oxford: Basil Blackwell.

Gill, C. (1996) *Personality in Greek Epic, Tragedy, and Philosophy: The Self in Dialogue*, Oxford: Clarendon Press.

Goldhill, S. (ed.) (forthcoming) *Being Greek under Rome: The Second Sophistic, and the Development of Empire*, Cambridge: Cambridge University Press.

Hall, E. (1989) *Inventing the Barbarian: Greek Self-Definition through Tragedy*, Oxford: Clarendon Press.

Hall, J.M. (1997) *Ethnic Identity in Greek Antiquity*, Cambridge: Cambridge University Press.

Hobsbawm, E.J. (1983) 'Introduction: Inventing Traditions', in E.J. Hobsbawm and T. Ranger (eds) *The Invention of Tradition*, Cambridge: Cambridge University Press.

—— (1990) *Nations and Nationalism since 1780*, Cambridge: Cambridge University Press.

Jones, E.L. (1981) *The European Miracle: Environments, Economies and Geopolitics in the History of Europe and Asia*, Cambridge: Cambridge University Press.

Laurence, R. and Berry, J. (eds) (1998) *Cultural Identity in the Roman Empire*, London: Routledge.

Lowenthal, D. (1985) *The Past is a Foreign Country*, Cambridge: Cambridge University Press.

Mercer, K. (1990) 'Welcome to the Jungle', in J. Rutherford (ed.) *Identity, Community, Culture, Difference*, London: Lawrence and Wishhart.

Morris, I. (1997) 'Periodization and the Heroes: Inventing a Dark Age', in M. Golden and P. Toohey (eds) *Inventing Ancient Culture: Historicism, Periodization and the Ancient World*, London: Routledge.

Radhadkrishnan, R. (1987) 'Ethnic Identity and Post-Structuralist Difference', *Cultural Critique* 6: 199–220.

Said, E. W. (1993) *Culture and Imperialism*, London: Chatto and Windus.

—— (1995) *Orientalism: Western Conceptions of the Orient*, new edition, London: Vintage.

Smith, A.D. (1991) *National Identity*, Harmondsworth: Penguin.

—— (1992) 'National Identity and the Idea of European Unity', *International Affairs* 68, 1: 55–76.

Wintle, M. (1996a)'Cultural Diversity and Identity in Europe',

—— (1996b) 'Cultural Identity in Europe: Shared Experience',

—— (1996c) 'Europe's Image: Visual Representations of Europe from the Earliest Times to the Twentieth Century', in M. Wintle (ed.) *Culture and Identity in Europe: Perceptions of Divergence and Unity in Past and Present*, Aldershot: Avebury.

Woodward, K. (1997) 'Concepts of Identity and Difference', in K. Woodward (ed.) *Identity and Difference*, London and Milton Keynes: Routledge and the Open University Press.

Zetterholm, S. (ed.) (1994) *National Cultures and European Integration: Exploratory Essays on Cultural Diversity and Common Policies*, Oxford: Berg.

2

THE WRITES OF PASSAGE

Cultural initiation in Heliodorus' *Aethiopica*

Tim Whitmarsh

The novel represents the single most important literary innovation of Greek culture under the Roman empire.[1] Although the writers of this period were certainly not as derivative and uncreative as an older generation of scholars liked to suggest, nothing (not even Lucian's satire) can match the range and sophistication of the novel, or its influence upon subsequent literary traditions. Within this genre, Heliodorus' *Aethiopica* stands out for a number of reasons. It is by far the longest of the extant texts, the most narratologically sophisticated, and almost certainly the latest;[2] there are, as we shall see, a number of other reasons why it deserves special consideration.

Whilst the literary qualities of the novels are now readily appreciated, there still remains considerable debate as to how they may be related to their social and cultural context. All the texts in question focus on the adventures of an idealised, young (heterosexual) couple, in a world which is, more or less specifically, set in the Classical past. Heliodorus allows his readers no doubt that his is the world of the fifth century: Athens is run democratically, and Egypt is occupied by Persia. How do we link this 'imaginary' space to the 'real' space of social interaction? Ancient historians have responded in a number of ways. First of all, surveys of papyrus finds and internal evidence have provided evidence as to the composition of the readership of the novels: these are not (as once was thought) 'bourgeois' but élite texts, written for a wealthy and sophisticated audience (Bowie 1994; Stephens 1994).[3] Other scholars have mined the novels for evidence of contemporary *realia* (e.g. Rougemont 1992; Bonneau 1992; Cauderlier 1992). This approach can yield important results, but inevitably involves a certain violence to the internal dynamics of the text; moreover, the distinction between 'fictional' and 'historical' phenomena is extremely difficult (if not impossible) to locate, both at the abstract, philosophical level (Pavel 1986) and at the level of historical practice.

More attractive than such 'realist' approaches are attempts to get inside the *imaginaire* of the novel, to understand the reasons for its orientation, structuring and privileging of certain elements. The novels have been successfully linked to the Atticist tendencies of imperial Greek literature: the attempt to re-create the dialectical and lexical patterns of Classical Athens was accompanied by a more general archaism of subject-matter, a phenomenon which has a wider socio-cultural importance (Swain 1996: 101–31, building on Bowie 1974). A still more explicit link between text and society has been developed by scholars who, following the lead of Michel Foucault (Foucault 1988: 228–32), have analysed the novels' projection, manipulation and parody of sexual ideology (Konstan 1994; Goldhill 1995; Cooper 1996: 20–44) – and sexual practice, as Peter Brown and Foucault in particular have demonstrated, was the site of continually renewed social and institutional conflict in later antiquity (Foucault 1988; Brown 1988).

This chapter is an exploration of the relationship between Heliodorus' *Aethiopica* and its social context from a different perspective (this is not, of course, to deny the importance of, for example, either Atticism or sexual ideology to the economy of the text). What I want to consider here is how Heliodorus presents and manipulates the theme of cultural identity, and how his treatment intersects with patterns of identity in late imperial Greek society. This topic has received some brief treatments in the course of more general treatments of Greek literature during the principate (Bowersock 1995: 48–53; Létoublon 1993: 126–36; Swain 1996: 118; Kuch 1996: 218);[4] it remains to be shown, however, just how actively and creatively Heliodorus reflects upon it. Indeed, the thematic centrality of cultural identity to the *Aethiopica* can be discerned from the most schematic summary of the plot:

> The *Aethiopica* is the tale of a girl born white to black parents, the queen and king of Ethiopia. Fearing suspicion, Queen Persinna instructs one of the court philosophers, the Gymnosophists, to hide the child. This Sisimithres passes the child on to a priest at Delphi, Charicles, who is wandering in Egypt. Charicles rears the child as his own at Delphi.

Time passes, and the child, now named Charicleia, learns to exalt virginity as she enters adolescence. An Egpytian priest, Calasiris, arrives at the same time as a deputation from Thessaly, led by the handsome Theagenes. The two fall in love, and Calasiris engineers their escape from Delphi. Calasiris has read a band which was exposed with Charicleia, signalling in Ethiopian royal script the provenance of Charicleia, and explaining that her white skin was due to Persinna's having looked upon a painting of Andromeda at the moment of Charicleia's conception. Gradually, despite trials and separations (including Calasiris' death from old age and a dangerous brush with the wife of the Persian satrap of Egypt), the pair make their way to Ethiopia, where Charicleia is eventually acclaimed as the daughter of the royal couple. Charicleia and Theagenes are both tested for their virginity on a magical 'grid', and their marriage is approved.

To set out the plot in this fashion is to misrepresent Heliodorus' complex narratological technique. He starts his narrative in the middle (beginning *in medias res*, as scholars, following Horace, put it); part of the account is related by an omniscient narrator, and part (after the fashion of the *Odyssey*) by Calasiris in a lengthy 'flashback'. Further elements in the plot are recovered through various signs and traces (oracles, secret messages and so forth). Nevertheless, despite the simplification, this outline demonstrates just how important the theme of identity, including cultural identity, is to the narrative of the *Aethiopica*: as much as a tale of sexuality mastered and successfully translated into legitimate marriage, it is also an account of the recovery of an identity concealed by the illusion of cultural difference. Heliodorus, as we shall see, is most attentive to issues concerning the acquisition, display and reshaping of cultural identity. I want to argue, indeed, that Heliodorus' narrative structure engages with and reconfigures a widespread narrative pattern which was fundamental to the construction of cultural identity in the archaic and classical periods. Heliodorus' active transformation of this pattern, I shall conclude, articulates a new conception of cultural identity.

The narrative pattern to which I refer is that of the mythical journey which accompanies an adolescent *rite de passage*. As Arnold van Gennep argued in his fundamental work on the subject, rites of passage are generally accomplished through three stages: separation, marginalisation and aggregation, or reaggregation (van Gennep 1960).[5] It was observed long ago that various Greek myths can be said to correspond to this pattern, and can profitably be discussed as 'initiation myths': tales of Jason (Segal 1986: 56–60; Moreau 1994: 117–42), Orestes (Zeitlin 1978: 160–74) and Telemachus (Moreau 1992), notably, dramatise the separation of the male adolescent from his community, his 'marginalisation' (expressed through images of ambivalence, disfigurement and liminality, as well as more obviously through his relocation from the central space of the *polis* to the marginal space of the sea, mountains or the edge of the earth), and his re-entry into community life as a full member of society. A corresponding set of myths exists for female transition: figures such as Callisto and Io are used to represent and explore the marginal phase of female transition, and their metamorphoses express metaphorically the absolute transformation of *parthenos* (virgin) into *gunê* (woman) (Dowden 1989).[6] The extent to which these myths reflect practices of ritual seclusion has been debated (Vidal-Naquet 1986a: 106–28; see also 129–56; Vidal-Naquet 1986b; Calame 1997: *passim*, esp. 89–206); what interests me here, however, is not social reality but the patterning of narrative.

There is much to be said about the novels' use of initiatory patterns. Despite the reputation and authority of Walter Burkert, scholarship has been little inclined to pursue his observation that 'there is an initiation structure in the plot of most ancient romances' (Burkert 1987: 66–7).[7] This neglect may well be the result of the strong reaction provoked by Merkelbach's theory that the novels developed from ritual texts for use in mystery religions; yet we should not allow our response to his undeniably overstated ideas to blind us to the importance of religious thought in the novels (Merkelbach 1962). It is crucial, in this context, to distinguish the deeply ingrained narrative patterns of mythical thought from ritual practice: I am not about to argue that the *Aethiopica* reflects any real religious behaviour. More importantly, however, I suspect that resistance to analysis of mythical patterns in the novels reflects an assumption that post-classical literature is divorced from, indeed to be opposed to, mythical thought – although, as Veyne points out, Pausanias, the Greek traveller of the second century CE, comes much closer to mythical thought than is often imagined (Veyne 1988: 95–102). Although few would express it in such terms, the assumption that later Greek society did not think in terms of myth reflects a crudely progressivist conception of human history, one which links 'myth' with an archaic naïveté (Hunter 1992: 33, and esp. Beard

1993). Not that the novels *are* myths:[8] they are, of course, individually authored literary *texts*, both ironic and sophisticated, and need to be approached as such. It would, however, be odd, given the central role of myth in the conceptualisation of (even imperial) Greek society, not to find mythic narrative patterns forming part of the novels' intertextual weft.

It is not my intention here to discuss exhaustively the initiatory aspects of the *Aethiopica* (although a number inevitably emerge during the course of the discussion). Rather, I wish to focus upon Heliodorus' use and manipulation of the narrative pattern of the mythical journey, the *voyage initiatique*, to give structure and sense to the world. 'The world', of course, refers here not to a physical mass, but to a conceptual construction, invested with symbolic, ideological and (most important for the present project) cultural meaning.[9] I propose to interpret the acculturation of Charicleia and Theagenes (and, concomitantly, of the reader, who 'travels' with the protagonists) as an acquisition of cultural identity, and thus to interpret the *Aethiopica* itself as an exploration of this theme.

In order to clarify my point, I propose now to consider briefly the two narratives which are consistently evoked throughout the *Aethiopica*. The first is the myth of Perseus and Andromeda, which is alluded to at several points (most notably in the painting which causes Charicleia to be born white: 4.8.3–5; 10.14.7; see also 10.6.3; see further Billault 1981). The most famous account of the story in antiquity was that of Euripides in his (lost) *Andromeda*. In the absence of this version of the story, the fullest extant version is that of Apollodorus in his *Library* (2.4.1–5). According to Apollodorus, Acrisius, king of Argos, tried to do away with his grandson Perseus who, according to an oracle, was destined to kill him, by placing him and his mother Danae in a chest. The chest was washed up on Seriphus. 'When Perseus had grown to manhood' (ἡνδρωμένου Περσέως) Polydectes, the king's brother, who had fallen in love with Danae, contrived a pretext to send Perseus off to fetch the head of the Gorgon (whose beauty is later stressed: 2.4.3). This Perseus accomplished (after his well-known encounters, and with the help of Athena and Hermes); then he travelled to Ethiopia, rescued Andromeda from a rock by killing the sea-monster who menaced her, married her and produced a son, Perses. Returning to Seriphus, he killed Polydectes who was now pursuing Danae with vigour. On return to Greece with Danae and Andromeda, Perseus attempted to avert the fated death of Acrisius by avoiding Argos, but killed him accidentally with a discus at the games at Larissa.

Ashamed of what he had done, he then went to king Megapenthes and exchanged Argos with Tiryns, and founded a dynasty.

This narrative is clearly initiatory, as indicated by Apollodorus' reference to Perseus' newly acquired manhood at the start of the journey[10] (indeed, it clearly recalls other initiatory narratives, notably the myths of Jason, Odysseus and Oedipus). Manhood is signified by the acquisition of political power and a woman. It is not necessary to restrict oneself to psychoanalytic criticism to interpret this account of maturation (although the monstrous females, the crones and the beautiful but terrifying Gorgon might tempt adepts at Freudian or Lacanian interpretation). Indeed, the narrative is not so much a reflection of a universal psychological truth of familial conflict and resolution as a legitimation through myth of values specific to Greek culture: one crucial aspect missed by a narrowly psychoanalytic interpretation is the spatial organisation of the narrative, which is both crucial and culture-specific. Perseus is sent on his initiatory journey from Argos, in the centre of Greece, to the edge of the world (and the location of Ethiopia at the margins of the world is crucial to the *Aethiopica*, too, as we shall see). The myth, by mapping the privileged narrative phases of beginning, middle and end (or, to use van Gennep's terminology, separation, marginalisation and reaggregation) onto the spatial model of centre, margins and centre, serves to construct the world as conspicuously Hellenocentric.[11]

The *Odyssey* is also evoked throughout the *Aethiopica*.[12] This is most clearly signalled in Calasiris' dream on Zacynthus, in which the priest receives a visitation from Odysseus himself. The hero castigates the priest for his failure to pay honours to him, and warns that 'you will suffer the same troubles as me' (τῶν ὁμοίων ἐμοὶ παθῶν αἰσθήσηι), before passing on Penelope's best wishes to Charicleia, since she holds 'chastity' (τὴν σωφροσύνην) above all (5.22.3). The divagations of the *Aethiopica* are 'the same as' (or perhaps 'similar to') those of the *Odyssey*. Indeed, in some respects, the 'shape' of the *Aethiopica* recalls very closely the model of the *Odyssey*. Both begin with the protagonists on the shores of distant countries; in either case, the events leading to this situation are narrated in flashback, and in either case the narrative progresses through divagations to reach a 'home' at the end, where patrilineage and royal privilege are re-established. In other ways, however, as we shall see, the narrative of the *Aethiopica* presents a crucially different cultural paradigm to the *Odyssey*.

The transitional aspects of the *Odyssey* have been ably interpreted by Charles Segal in a pair of important articles on the subject (Segal 1962; Segal 1967).[13] The poetics of the epic, he argues, suggest that Odysseus' 'journey is a continual separation from the casual and the fortuitous, through which the wanderer finds his way back to the essential and lasting' (Segal 1994: 36), and 'a return to humanity in its broadest sense' (Segal 1994: 37). The *pôthos* (desire) of Odysseus is always for the home he knows, the familiar patriarchal *oikos* (home) which not only accords with his conception of civilisation and humanity but also provides his very *identity*, as 'Odysseus son of Laertes'. It is not my intention here to assert or contest the validity of this approach to the *Odyssey*, although in some senses it surely does underplay the complexity and deviousness of the text (see e.g. Goldhill 1991: 23–4). What matters to me is that Heliodorus may be 'misreading' (in Harold Bloom's sense: see Bloom 1973: 19–45)[14] Homer in this way, that is to say, strategically oversimplifying his 'parent' text in order to construct and represent his own literary difference (see further Whitmarsh 1998).

In a literal sense, Charicleia is returning home, back to her biological parents: although Calasiris' dream matches her up with Penelope and Calasiris with Odysseus, it is clear that she is the most important of the several 'Odyssean' figures in this text. Like Odysseus, Charicleia and Theagenes find in the conclusion to the text an end to their 'wandering' (the source of a continually reaffirmed anxiety in the *Aethiopica*).[15] Again like the *Odyssey*, the *Aethiopica* concludes with a series of exercises in recognition (Cave 1988: 17–20), ending with a powerful assertion of identity and royal privilege. Yet whereas the *Odyssey* emphasises the *recovery* of Odysseus' place in Ithacan society (what van Gennep would call the 'reaggregation' of his identity), in the *Aethiopica* both Theagenes and Charicleia are entering a strange and unfamiliar world. The language barrier (stressed at e.g. 9.1.5; 10.9.6; 10.15.1; 10.35.2) is exemplary of a larger gap between Greek and Ethiopian mores (see further Winkler 1982: 104–5). This gap is doubly stressed: Ethiopia is 'idealised' as a perfect community, characterised by the justice of the Ethiopian royal advisers (see especially 10.10.3-4); but it is also the site of culturally inferior phenomena, such as the ignorant wrestler Meroebus who is defeated by Theagenes' Greek cunning (10.31.5) and the definitively barbaric[16] practice of human sacrifice (which is, however, finally abolished in the *Aethiopica*). Ethiopia is not, however, entirely 'other': the important Ethiopians speak Greek (10.9.6; 10.38.3), the gods honoured are Helios, Selene and

Dionysus (2.2.7; 10.2.1; Pan is mentioned at 10.4.1), and the heroes are Perseus, Andromeda and Memnon (10.6.3). Although these features in no way define the Ethiopians as Greek (Dionysus is a paradigmatically 'Oriental' god, for example), they serve to portray Ethiopia in terms assimilable to a Greek, or at least Hellenised, readership. Heliodorus' Ethiopia is an odd, culturally hybrid place. What I want to stress, however, is Heliodorus' crucial innovation in finishing his journey at the edge of the (Greek) world. Whereas the *Odyssey* could be taken as a narrative of cultural consolidation, fulfilling the desire for 'home' by rejecting the monstrous excess of 'abroad', the *Aethiopica* is a 'utopian' tale, passing from the familiarity (to a Greek reader) of Delphi and mainland Greece to a (previously) unknown kingdom at the edge of the world.[17] Since Homeric times, the Ethiopians had been the 'most distant of men' (ἔσχατοι ἀνδρῶν, Hom. *Od.* 1.23; on the traditionally marginal siting of the Ethiopians, see Romm 1992: 49–54), and indeed Homer's words are echoed by the necromantic corpse who prophesies that Charicleia will end up 'at the most distant limits of the earth' (γῆς ἐπ' ἐσχάτοις ὅροις, 6.15.4). Heliodorus, however, reverses the perspective: from Ethiopia, *Greece* is the edge of the world (10.16.6). Whereas the *Odyssey*'s narrative might be taken to reinforce a sense of 'self' and 'other', the *Aethiopica* sites its joyous, celebratory ending on the side of the 'other'.

To an extent the *Aethiopica*'s teleology (what scholars have called its 'linear' narrative: see Szepessy 1957: 244–54; Létoublon 1993: 108–9; Fusillo 1989: 29) replicates the patterning of the *Odyssey*: for the readers of either text, the narrative 'travels' from wandering to conclusion, by way of a 'flashback'. Yet the two texts have very different cultural meanings: whereas the spatial organisation of the *Odyssey* could be said to underscore the reader's Hellenocentric world-view, that of the *Aethiopica* compromises, indeed problematises, such Hellenocentrism. To a limited degree, this anti-circularity is paralleled in Achilles Tatius' novel of the second century CE, *Leucippe and Cleitophon*. Whereas the novels of Longus, Xenophon of Ephesus and Chariton see their protagonists return at the conclusion of the text to their original provenances, Achilles' narrative, which begins in Sidon and 'flashes back' to Tyre, concludes with a sea voyage to Byzantium. This supposed inconsistency has sometimes led critics to assume either that Achilles has been careless or that the text is incomplete, but it is more likely that Achilles is deliberately spurning the 'circularity' of traditional 'initiatory' narratives. *Leucippe and Cleitophon*, however, differs crucially from the *Aethiopica*, in that Achilles' narrative is as anti-linear as it is anti-circular. In the *Aethiopica* anti-circularity is not simply an act of defiance, but a vehicle of literary and cultural meaning, a means of defining a new paradigm of identity.

I want to turn now to consider in greater detail this narrative of acculturation, and the cultural values with which it is imbued. Charicleia and Theagenes travel away from Greece, from the 'familiar' centre of religious inspiration in Delphi (on Heliodorus' presentation of Delphi, see Rougemont 1992), through the relative familiarity of Egypt to the unknown, to the Ethiopian Gymnosophists and their perfect justice. This pattern, Greece–Egypt–Ethiopia, creates not just a linear 'shape' but also a sacred hierarchy for the text, as it progresses through ascending stages of wisdom, represented in turn by the dim Greek priest Charicles, the cunning Egyptian priest Calasiris and the supremely just Ethiopian priest Sisimithres (see most recently and fully Dowden 1996: 280–3). Within the 'real-time' narrative (as opposed to the 'flashback' narrations), however, Greece plays no part: the text opens in Egypt on the southernmost shores of the Mediterranean, at the Heracleotic mouth of the Nile. The narrative then progresses down through Egypt to Ethiopia. The Nile, thus, constitutes the spine of the narrative, and Heliodorus conspicuously and, as we shall see, self-consciously organises his text around it; it is to the narrative role of the Nile that I now turn.

The Nile and its marvels exert an enormous fascination upon Greek writers: 'which of its elements is not a marvel?', writes Aelius Aristides (τί δ' οὐ τῶν ἐκείνου θαῦμα; 48.119). Two questions in particular baffled Greek writers, concerning its aestival inundation[18] and the location of its sources.[19] These came to represent the philosophical questions *par excellence*; and, conversely, the answers represented absolute *sophia* (wisdom). An important intertext here is Philostratus' *Life of Apollonius*, the importance of which for the *Aethiopica* has often been noted (see esp. Rohde 1914: 466–73; Bowie 1978: 1664–5; Anderson 1986: 230–1; 234). In the *Life of Apollonius*, the holy man Apollonius travels to the sources of the Nile in the quest for wisdom (6.17; 6.22–6: the secrets of the tides of the Atlantic on the coast of Spain (5.2) and the mysteries of the Indian Brahmans (3.13–50) represent analogous phenomena at the edge of the world). Damis, the mysterious figure upon whose eyewitness account Philostratus claims to have based his narrative, finds the noise from the cataracts 'difficult and intolerable to perceive' (χαλεποῦ ... καὶ οὐκ ἀνεκτοῦ αἰσθέσθαι), and so cannot proceed to the sources. Only Apollonius and his Egyptian 'Sherpas' continue, and even they can only behold the sources: the road up is 'impossible to travel, impossible to be conceived of' (ἄπορον μὲν ἐλθεῖν . . . ἄπορον δὲ ἐνθυμηθῆναι, 6.26). Is it simply impossible to contemplate making such a difficult journey? Or is there something more mysterious, more conceptually 'inconceivable' about the place itself? The protective shroud which Philostratus weaves around the sources of the Nile gives them an air of sacred taboo, like an intensified version of the points in the travel-narrative of Pausanias where the author refuses to describe sacred centres on the grounds of their sanctity (see Elsner 1992: 22–5; 1995: 144–50).[20]

Heliodorus' narrative does not reach the sources of the Nile, but as the narrative processes up the Nile we might be expecting it to: the text hints that southern Egypt and Ethiopia constitute the end of a sophic journey. Charicles journeys to Catadoupy 'to research (*kath' historian*) the cataracts of the Nile' (καθ' ἱστορίαν τῶν καταρρακτῶν τοῦ Νείλου, 2.29.5), and the emphasis upon 'research' (*historia*) recalls the fascination which the Nile held for the founding father of 'history' (*historia*), Herodotus (Hdt. 2.34). Calasiris, going one step further than Greek philosophers such as Pythagoras who travel to Egypt for wisdom,[21] travels to Ethiopia 'out of desire for the wisdom (*sophia*) which they have' (ἐπιθυμίαι τῆς παρ' ἐκείνοις σοφίας, 4.12.1): similar phrases are used of Greek wise men who travel to Egypt.[22] This sense that Ethiopia is for the Egyptians what Egypt is for the Greeks is an important means of structuring the tripartite sacred/philosophical hierarchy of the text, mentioned above; it also suggests an allegorical interpretation of Ethiopia as a state of supreme enlightenment (I shall return to this point).

Heliodorus is well aware that the lands of the Nile exercise a fascination upon Greeks. In a key passage, Calasiris comments upon the interest which the Greeks have in Egyptian matters: 'for every Egyptian tale and narrative (*diêgêma*) is most seductive (*epagôgotaton*) to Greek ears' (Αἰγύπτιον γὰρ ἄκουσμα καὶ διήγημα πᾶν Ἑλληνικῆς ἀκοῆς ἐπαγωγότατον, 2.27.3). It is characteristic of this playfully self-referential author that this sentence works on several levels: the Delphic priests, Cnemon and we the readers are (presumably) all Greeks attracted by Calasiris' Egyptian tales. The metatextual interpretation of this phrase is strongly suggested by *diêgêma* ('narrative'), used self-reflexively in the other novels;[23] and by *epagôgos* ('seductive', used elsewhere by Heliodorus in erotic contexts: 1.9.2; 1.9.4; 3.4.1; 7.19.8),[24] a word appropriate to the lures of the *Aethiopica*. Calasiris then immediately proceeds to elucidate the mystery surrounding the flooding of the Nile, using the secrets inscribed in the sacred books which it is only permissible for priests to consult (2.28.2). This insight increases the air of the sacredness of the phenomenon, but also through the reference to reading reinforces the link between the Nile and textuality. Even the explanation itself further underlines the connection. Heliodorus tells us of the springs of the Nile in the mountains of Ethiopia, but denies that the Etesian winds cause the flooding in the way described by Herodotus' explanation: in fact, the winds drive the clouds south, until they burst over Ethiopia, causing the floods. Calasiris thus signals to his audience (both intra- and extratextual) that, although Greeks are fascinated with the Nile, the origins of its mysteries – like the origins of Charicleia and the narrative itself – lie not in Egypt but in Ethiopia.

Heliodorus' (and Calasiris') presentation of the Nile thus (playfully) illustrates the virtues of the text itself: sexy, serene and sacred, the Nile, like Heliodorus, lures Greeks down through Egypt to Ethiopia. Egypt, then, is represented as a place of transition.[25] In particular, the marginality of the territories between Egypt and Ethiopia is emphasised: Philae is represented as 'contested' ($\grave{\varepsilon}\pi\acute{\iota}\mu\alpha\chi o\nu$, 8.1.1) and the subject of dispute ($\grave{\alpha}\mu\phi\acute{\iota}\beta o\lambda o\nu$, 8.1.2), and Syene is the site of a major siege. The narrative's transition from Egypt to Ethiopia is prolonged, through a drawn-out territorial disputation; and this great emphasis given to the borders suggests that there is something 'initiatory' about the transition from one country to another. Boundary-crossing is always a highly symbolic act (see e.g. van Gennep 1960: 15; Hartog 1988: 61–111; Jacob 1991: 13–18), but in the hieratic context of the *Aethiopica* it seems to emblematise (albeit playfully) something 'higher', a journey from one state to another. Unlike some 'circular' narratives of youthful initiation, where the frontier zones represent the peripheral space in which the adolescent must spend time before returning to the centre, Egypt in the *Aethiopica* represents a liminal space (in Victor Turner's terms)[26] which must be crossed *en route* to another place.

There is a strong sense in the *Aethiopica* that the Ethiopian episodes constitute a kind of privileged epilogue to the text, an 'after-life' to the Egyptian episode. The metaphor is not idle. The 'false death' (*Scheintod*) of Charicleia in the cave in the second book (2.1; 2.3.3–5.2), and which recurs in other novels (Charit. *Chaer. & Call.* 1.5.1; Ach. Tat. *Leuc. & Cleit.* 3.15), recalls not only the symbolism of death which accompanies transition (which is in a sense a death of the old self and a birth of the new) in many cultures but also the conceptual association of the two in Greek thought.[27] Persinna's assumption that Charicleia is dead, only to find that she has returned, finds parallels in initiatory patterns elsewhere (van Gennep 1960: 188). The crone's consultation of her dead son near the village of Bessa underlines the association between Egypt and death: the word used (7.1.1) for this consultation, *nekuia*, was the name regularly given in antiquity to the eleventh book of the *Odyssey*, and so the link between this scene and epic *katabasis* (descent into the underworld, a death of sorts: see Hom. *Od.* 12.21–2) is signalled. The death of the priest Calasiris, the pair's surrogate 'father', precedes the assumption by Charicleia and Theagenes of priesthoods themselves at the end of the text: they cross from a state of dependence on their father, through a period of 'wandering', to a state of identity in their own rights.[28] Death, then, plays an important metaphorical role for Heliodorus in the establishment of patterns of transition to adulthood and identity. From the very outset, the lands of the Nile are associated with death (Charicleia assumes that the black Egyptian pirates are ghosts, 1.3.1; ancient ghosts were black, see Winkler 1980: 160–5), and Theagenes interprets an oracular mention of Ethiopia as referring to Hades (8.11.4; Ethiopia is also associated with death at Plut. *Brut.* 48.2). If Egypt is the land of *Scheintod*, then Ethiopia represents the true death and rebirth of initiation.[29] This imagery must be taken in the playful spirit of the *Aethiopica* as a whole, of course, but playfulness should not automatically be taken for triviality.

Geography, then, is a crucial structuring device for this text. Indeed, this is reflected in the larger architectonics of the narrative. The majority of the action – eight books, the 'standard' length of a novel[30] – is set in Egypt. The text is not, however, an 'Egyptian story' but an 'Ethiopian story' (*Aethiopica*). This is stated by Hydaspes in a classic case of Heliodoran self-referentiality (not yet commented upon, to my knowledge). Hydaspes has been observing the Syenians' activities during the festival of the Nile, and replies that, since the river has its sources in Ethiopia, they should be celebrating not Egypt but Ethiopia: 'these pieties are not Egyptian things (*Aegyptia*) but Ethiopian things (*Aethiopica*)' (ἀλλ' οὐκ Αἰγύπτια ταῦτα . . . ἀλλ' Αἰθιοπικὰ τὰ σεμνολογήματα, 9.22.7). In this most self-reflexive of texts, this can surely be read as Heliodorus' witty play with the title of his own text.[31] The *Aethiopica* is not just a tale of Egypt, the land which was traditionally perceived by Greeks as the origin of philosophical wisdom. It goes beyond an *Aegyptia*: it is an *Aethiopica*, the ultimate philosophical narrative.

The Nile, then, takes us down through Egypt, through the contested territories, towards its sources; it is the narrative thread which unites the Mediterranean world, Egypt and Ethiopia. In a sense, the Nile itself represents the *Aethiopica*, and I wish now to consider further the implications of this correspondence between text and river. Winkler has already pointed to various correspondences between the tale of Charicleia and Heliodorus' account of the ebbs and flows of the Nile (Winkler 1982: 151–2). We could think of more ways in which this text resembles the Nile. Certainly, there are elements which Calasiris praises in the Nile which could apply equally well to this text. Firstly, 'it is the sweetest (*glukutatos*) to drink'³² (πιεῖν . . . ἐστι γλυκύτατος). 'Sweetness' (*glukutês*) was deemed by rhetoricians to be a quality of a certain literary style, and it has been argued persuasively that another novel, *Daphnis and Chloe*, self-consciously aligns itself with this ideal (Hunter 1983: 92–8). The second element of the Nile which Calasiris praises is its tenderness to the touch: 'it is most gentle to the touch, since it is not as hot as it was when it started, but is still tepid, since it began there' (θιγεῖν προσηνέστατος, οὐκέτι μὲν θερμὸς ὡς ὅθεν ἤρξατο ἔτι δὲ χλιαρὸς ὡς ἐκεῖθεν ἀρξάμενος, 2.28.5). The 'temperature' of the text, too, might be said to avoid the extremes of frigidity and the other, 'red-hot' novels (Achilles Tatius for example writes that an 'erotic tale' (λόγος ἐρωτικός) provides the 'fuel of desire' (ὑπέκκαυμα . . . ἐπιθυμίας), 1.5.6). Calasiris also praises the Nile in that it is the only river not to emit vapours (μόνος ποταμῶν αὔρας οὐκ ἀναδίδωσι, 2.28.5): could this be a playful way of suggesting that this text will produce The Truth, whereas other novels give us only hot air . . . ?

This text is enormous like the Nile, produces the unexpected (as does the Nile in summer), and is prone to digression (as Hydaspes diverts the Nile). What is more, the *Aethiopica* (again like the Nile) has a suppositiously religious aura: 'the Egyptians falsely call the Nile a god, and consider it to be the mightiest of the gods, asserting pompously that it is a counter-imitation (*antimimon*) of heaven' (θεοπλαστοῦσι τὸν Νεῖλον Αἰγύπτιοι καὶ κρειττόνων τὸν μέγιστον ἄγουσιν, ἀντίμιμον οὐρανοῦ τὸν ποταμὸν σεμνηγοροῦντες, 9.9.3). The Nile is mimetic (*antimimon*) of the heavenly, suggesting both a Platonic chain of supplements to an original essence and the artifices of a literary composition. Indeed, the Nile is even 'textual' to the extent that it is open to allegory: the 'vulgar' (δημοσιεύουσι) and the 'initiated' (μύστας) read its divinity in different fashions (9.9.4). There are elements in the text which suggest that the *Aethiopica*, too, is constructing itself (playfully) as if it were open to allegory: the air of religious solemnity which pervades the text adds a mock-religious suggestiveness to many details (Winkler 1982: 151–5; Sandy 1982: *passim*; Dowden 1996: *passim*). There is even extant a later allegorisation of the text by a certain 'Philip the philosopher', although perhaps this should be taken in the same playful vein as the text itself.[33] Like the *Aethiopica*, the Nile is a kind of text, open to (indeed encouraging) 'mysteriosophic' readings.

The use of a river to represent a text is not new (it is a common image in the Alexandrian poetic tradition).[34] What is new, however, is Heliodorus' ingenious use of a river as a geographic template representing *narrative* structure. The *Aethiopica* opens *in medias res* at one of the many mouths of the river, with a famously aporetic scene in which readers are bewildered by the scarcity of data to help them interpret (Winkler 1982: 97–9; Bühler 1976). The indeterminacy of the opening of the text is figured by the multiple mouths of the Nile. Yet like the Nile as it flows south, the *Aethiopica* all comes together: the reunion of Charicleia and Theagenes, and of Calasiris, Thyamis and Petosiris at Memphis (in book 7) mirrors the confluence of the mouths of the river a little way to the north of the city. But this text will not make do with mere convergence of narrative threads: what it sets up is a grand revelation of the origins of the Nile, the fount of the divine, the essence of *sophia*. In fact, the text concludes with the discovery of the origin not of the Nile but of Charicleia: our anticipation of an astounding philosophical revelation is gratified by the extraordinary story of a black girl born white. The anticipation of wonders (θαύματα) which Heliodorus' text provokes by linking itself to the Nile is gratified by the wondrous story of Charicleia's birth.[35]

The Nile, then, provides the linear 'shape' of the *Aethiopica*, not simply as a narrative map but also as a means of structuring the meaning of the text. The *Aethiopica*'s self-representation as a (bogus) religious text is articulated partly through its assimilation to the sacred river which leads sophic pilgrims up to its mysterious sources. The revelation of the truth concerning Charicleia at the end of the tale – a revelation which is self-consciously prolonged, and treated with great care and self-consciousness by the text (see the excellent discussion of Cave 1988: 17–21) – is set up as a kind of mystical enlightenment, a pronouncement of *sophia*. The geographical structure of the text, then, expresses and explores, with varying degrees of irony, the 'message' of the text.

What are we to make of this linear geographic progression? All the novels (including, but in a different way, *Daphnis and Chloe*) present the transition to adulthood as occurring in marginal space, in which the novel's adventure-time is played out. There are crucial differences, however, in the organisation of space. The novels of Chariton and Xenophon employ the model of centre and periphery, the narrative of exile and return, which (as we have seen) was characteristic of classical and preclassical initiatory myth. Achilles Tatius disfigures the symmetry of the pattern, but this disfigurement is (brilliantly) petulant and inconclusive. The *Aethiopica*, on the other hand, constructs a very different patterning of the world, radically rewriting the narrative structure of the *Odyssey*. The marginal, transitional space of Egypt is not the periphery of a circular space (as it might be in another narrative) but a space between Greece and Ethiopia, between a prior and a subsequent state. Ethiopia, meanwhile, is constructed as a space beyond Egypt. To use van Gennep's language, Heliodorus replaces the 'reaggregation' of traditional initiatory narratives with an 'aggregative' model, whereby the paradigm articulates not a mere reincorporation in a different guise into the same society, but a transition to a wholly new state.

In fact, Heliodorus employs a related but profoundly different set of initiatory motifs, drawn not from adolescent acculturation but from religious ritual. In the *Aethiopica*, the protagonists do not effect a transition merely to adulthood, but also to a higher religious state. The text concludes with the appointment of Charicleia and Theagenes to priesthoods (10.41.1–2) – a clear index of religious initiation – but not before foretelling their marriage at Meroe, 'where the more mystic parts (*mustikôterôn*) of the wedding ritual were to be performed (*telesthêsomenôn*) with greater magnificence' (τῶν ἐπὶ τῶι γάμωι μυστικωτέρων κατὰ τὸ ἄστυ φαιδρότερον τελεσθησομένων, 10.41.3). The imbrication of the language of religious initiation and of sexual experience is not new in the Greek novel (compare Ach. Tat. *Leuc. & Cleit.* 1.9.7; 2.19.1 etc.; nor is this metaphor confined to the novels: see Burkert 1987: 104–6), but Heliodorus' association of religious initiation (*mustika*, *telos*) with marriage and the conclusion (*telos*) of the narrative is certainly a striking innovation.

What, in the context of our earlier conclusions, is the force of this new initiatory paradigm? In order to answer this, we must consider more generally the fragmentary evidence on ancient mystery cults. One dominant theme which emerges is the sense of an utter transformation to a new state, a complete and irreversible process. Aristotle (fr. 15) and Dio Chrysostom (12.33–4) write that the initiate is expected to 'experience' (παθεῖν) something, while Aristotle adds that he will be 'acted upon' (διατεθῆναι). The most telling comment, however, comes from Sopatros, the Atticising orator of the fourth century CE. He writes that 'I saw that initiatory rite, which all of you initiates understand, and emerged from the sanctuary a stranger to myself' (τὴν τελέτην ἐκείνην εἶδον, ἣν οἱ μεμυημένοι πάντες ἐπίστασθε, ἐξῄειν ἀπὸ τῶν ἀνακτόρων ἐπ' ἐμαυτῶι ξενιζόμενος, pp. 114.26–115.1 Walz).[36] The mysteries give birth to a new 'self': as Burkert puts it, 'mystery festivals should be unforgettable events, casting their shadows over the whole of one's future life, creating experiences that transform existence' (Burkert 1987: 89). The *Aethiopica*, similarly, uses the language of the mysteries to dramatise the *transformation* of the adolescents, and underlines the completeness of this transformation by grafting it onto a linear, 'aggregative' narrative. At the same time, of course, Heliodorus promises to transform us, the readers, for we too have now travelled to the ends of the earth. We have become 'other to ourselves', to use Sopatros' language, once we see the world from an Ethiopic perspective.

It is a complex question how to read the tone of the *Aethiopica*'s mysteriosophic language. At one level, Winkler must be right: this sense that the text will reveal The Mysterious Truth is both a means of figuring narrative closure, and one more aspect of the text's self-conscious and ironic play with the notion of revealed wisdom (Winkler 1982: 152–7; see Dowden 1996 for disagreement). But at another level, all metaphors are not alike, and intercultural travel cannot *simply* be a metaphor for narrative closure; or, at any rate, narrative closure is itself constitutive of symbolic meaning. Heliodorus figures the gradual revelation of (narrative) wisdom as a process of becoming culturally other: this wisdom is quite specifically alien. Since Plato at least, the origins of *sophia* – in Greece, Egypt, Persia or India – had been contested (see in general Momigliano 1974). The issue could become a matter of fierce cultural pride: Diogenes Laertius, for example, dismisses the claim that philosophy began with the barbarians, claiming that not only philosophy, but even the human race began in Greece (1 *praef.* 1–3)! Heliodorus' use of the notion of the revelation of alien wisdom as a narrative structure, then, could be interpreted as taking a highly marked position on a hot topic, linking the highly symbolically charged moments of narrative revelation and religious initiation to a pronounced cultural estrangement. By interacting with and

31

TIM WHITMARSH

reconfiguring the narratives of acculturation which undergird Greek claims to cultural hegemony, and which support a Hellenocentric view of the world, Heliodorus produces his own form of 'alien wisdom'. Although the *Aethiopica* does not betray a doctrinally coherent system of meaning, it can be said to have created, in its syncretic polyphony, a specifically counter-hegemonic, centrifugal, anti-Hellenocentric 'meaning'.

I have not attempted to discover Heliodorus' 'attitude' towards cultural identity, or the degree to which he reflects prevalent assumptions of his period (as other recent scholars have done: see Bowersock 1995: 48–50; Swain 1996: 117–18). This is because I consider the theme of cultural identity to be part of the literary fabric of the text, and as such fluid, playful and ironic: we need to consider how culture and acculturation operate as *narrative* devices, not as simple reflections of social reality or authorial intention. Yet I began this chapter by offering to contribute something to the current scholarly interest in the relationship between the novels and the society which produced them, and I believe that this mode of analysis can contribute much to an understanding of Hellenic and Hellenising cultural identity in the Roman empire. As I have stressed throughout, Heliodorus' engagement with initiatory myths does not (necessarily) mirror a corresponding ritual practice in the real world, but rather contributes to, and seeks to effect change within, an ever-evolving set of stories which have to do with cultural identity. Heliodorus revisits the paradigmatic narratives of Greek culture from a new, self-consciously revisionary perspective, appropriating the narratives which undergird traditional perceptions of the world and reconfiguring them in the 'open' and 'mobile' cultural patterns of later antiquity. The 'world' (in the non-physical, 'imaginary' sense which I have been employing) of Heliodorus is structured in an altogether different fashion to its traditional Greek counterpart: a non-Greek writing Greek at a time[37] when the very term 'Hellene' was persistently questioned,[38] he wilfully confuses the Hellenocentric, culturally consolidatory patterns of earlier Greek society. The 'world' is always already a literary concept, a notion constructed, contested and reconfigured through a series of narratives which are motivated by cultural and ideological pressures (or resistances to them). It is within such a matrix of competing, politically and ideologically charged, versions of 'the world' that this chapter has sought to site the *Aethiopica*.

I take 'cultural identity', then, to be not the expression through material culture of a preformed and self-evident social unit (a 'race'

32

or an *ethnos*, for example), but a locus of continually evolving and continually challenged patterns of thought and language. It is not a single entity which is refracted through a number of individuals, but an inherently multiple set of languages and discourses:[39] it comprises the vast mass of stories which are told either to give meaning and stability to the exterior world, or to challenge and transform that world.

Heliodorus' contribution to the discourses of cultural identity, it has been argued here, is of the latter variety: as an 'outsider', writing in the late and self-consciously 'bastard' genre of the novel,[40] he reorders, and seeks to transform, 'the world' of late antiquity.

Notes

This chapter has benefited immeasurably from the generous criticism of a number of scholars. In addition to the discussions of the seminar group chaired by Kate Cooper and under the direction of Richard Miles and Janet Huskinson, the specific comments of Pat Easterling, Simon Goldhill and Froma Zeitlin have been invaluable. Julie Lewis has given me indispensable assistance with the religious material. All unattributed references are to Heliodorus' *Aethiopica*, which is cited from the edition of Rattenbury and Lumb (1960).

1 The bibliography on the Greek novel is immense, and ever-increasing: for guidance, see Bowie and Harrison 1993, and, for a more comprehensive catalogue of relevant works, Schmeling ed. 1996: 815–64.

2 There is a notoriously vexed debate over the dating of the *Aethiopica*, into which I do not propose to enter here: for recent arguments, see Lightfoot 1988; Bowersock 1995: 149–60; Swain 1996: 423–4; Morgan 1996: 417–19. Suffice it to say that, while I am not wholly convinced by arguments based upon Heliodorus' supposed dependence upon Jul. *Or.* 1.27b–28d; 30a and 2.62b–66d (nor, for that matter, by Bowersock's additional arguments), I concur that the style, language and much of the subject-matter (e.g. Charicleia's 'martyrdom'!) suggest a fourth-century date of composition.

3 Brigitte Egger has advanced interesting arguments concerning the possibility of a female readership: see e.g. Egger 1994. This hypothesis (unfortunately) cannot be demonstrated either way, but it provides an important corrective to many over-hasty assumptions.

4 For a critique of these positions, see Whitmarsh 1998, which was written to complement the present project.

5 First published in French in 1908. Important developments of van Gennep's position are to be found in Gluckman ed. 1962; Turner 1967: 93–111; Turner 1969. Since the pioneering work of Gluckman and Turner, there has been an enormous quantity of literature on the subject: I have learned especially from Vizedom 1976, Droogers 1980 and the various essays in Bianchi ed. 1986, but see also the extensive bibliography (with a Graeco-Roman slant) in Moreau ed. 1992: II. 297–305. For a critical overview of the applicability of initiation theory to Greek culture, see Versnel 1990: 44–59.

6 I am aware that in what follows I have placed only slight emphasis upon the differences between male and female initiatory myths, although I acknowledge that social practice may have differed greatly along gendered lines.

7 Gual's observations on initiatory patterns in *Daphnis and Chloe* are an exception to this general neglect: see Gual 1992. The situation in scholarship on the Greek novel stands in obvious contrast to that on the Roman novel, where Apuleius' *Golden Ass* in particular is routinely considered as a *roman initiatique*.

8 *Pace* Reardon 1969: 308; 1991: 28–30, who does not explain what he means by the term.

9 On ancient notions of 'the world' see Romm 1992, a rich account. Other important modern works stressing the textuality of place and space include Nicolet 1988; Vasaly 1993; Edwards 1996.

10 The initiatory aspect of Perseus' travels is also emphasised by the Byzantine scholar John Tzetzes in his commentary on Lycophron, *ad* 838, 15: πρὸς ἥβην ἐλαύνοντος.

11 On the crucial opposition between marginal and central space in the classical and preclassical periods, see Vidal-Naquet 1986a: 138–9.

12 See Keyes 1922 on the structural similarities, although his theories concerning the composition of the *Aethiopica* are suspect. More generally, see Feuillâtre 1966: 105–14; Garson 1975; Fusillo 1989: 28–32.

13 These articles have been modified and reprinted as chapters 2–4 of Segal 1994, from which I cite them.

14 Esp. p. 30: 'Poetic influence . . . always proceeds by a misreading of the prior poet, an act of creative correction that is actually and necessarily a misinterpretation.'

15 Heliodorus' characters make frequent reference to their βίος ἀλήτης: see e.g. 2.24.5 (Calasiris, of Nausicles and himself); 5.16.2, 7.8.2 (Calasiris of himself); 5.2.7, 5.6.3–4, 6.15.4, 7.13.2, 7.14.7 (Charicleia and Theagenes of themselves).

16 Since at least Euripides' *Iphigeneia at Tauris*, as noted by Létoublon 1993: 133.

17 The term 'utopia' was, as is well known, coined by More, with a deliberate ambiguity as to whether it was 'eutopia' ('good place') or 'outopia' ('no place'). To attribute utopianism to the ancient world is, thus, strictly speaking anachronistic. The ancient world did, however, know of idealised societies, especially at the edge of the world; and Stoic and Cynic philosophy expressed an especial interest in such places. See, in general, Ferguson 1975 and esp. Dawson 1992 on ancient 'utopias'; for an interpretation of the *Aethiopica* as a utopian text, see Szepessy 1957: 244–51.

18 Ar. *De inund. Nil.* = frr. 246–8 Rose; Nearchus *apud* Strab. 15.1.25; Diod. Sic. 1.36.7; 1.38.1–41.10; Strab. 17.1.5; Luc. *Bell. Civ.* 10.219–331; Philostr. *VA* 2.18; 6.1.

19 Hdt. 2.34.1; Σ Ap. Rh. 4.269; Diod. Sic. 1.37; Strab. 17.4.1; Verg. *Georg.* 4.291–3; Sen. *Quaest. Nat.* 4a; Plut. *Mor.* 897f; Arr. *Anab.* 6.1; Ael. Ar. 48 *passim*.

20 The account of the Nile by Diodorus Siculus is comparable to that of Philostratus in the respects which I have highlighted: no Greeks even entered Ethiopia prior to the reign of Ptolemy Philadelphus (1.37.5), in

summer no one can ascend the large cataract separating the two states (1.32.7–11), and darkness and mystery surround the sources of the Nile (1.37.6–10).

21 E.g. Porph. *Vit. Pyth.* 11–12; Iambl. *Vit. Pyth.* 18–19. Pythagoras is sometimes said to have travelled to the sources of the Nile: see e.g. Diog. Laert. 9.36. On Egypt as the land of philosophical initiation, see André and Baslez 1993: 283–5.

22 E.g. ἵνα τῶν ἐνταῦθα νομίμων καὶ παιδείας μετάσχωσιν, of Homer at Diod. Sic. 1.96.2.

23 See Hunter 1994: 1066–7 on Chariton's self-reflexive use of the word διήγημα; for an analogous usage in Heliodorus, see Whitmarsh 1998.

24 The other two instances of the word's use in Heliodorus concern children: 2.31.1 refers to the attractiveness of the child Charicleia, 9.11.6 to the appealing gait of the Syenian children, instrumental in soliciting Hydaspes' pity.

25 Egypt is represented as a liminal territory from early in Greek literature: see Hdt. 2.16, where Egypt is seen as the land of transition between Asia and Libya (for this interpretation of the passage, see Hartog 1988: 17).

26 See *supra* n. 5.

27 See e.g. Turner 1967: 96 on the Ndembu, and Eliade 1966 for a general discussion of this association. The Greek passage linking death and initiation is Plut. fr. 178 Sandbach, esp. lines 6–7: 'For this reason the language and the reality of death resemble those of initiation' (διὸ καὶ τὸ ῥῆμα τῶι ῥήματι καὶ τὸ ἔργον τῶι ἔργωι τοῦ τελευτᾶν καὶ τελεῖσθαι προσέοικε). A fragment of the Lollianus romance (B1 *recto*: see Stephens and Winkler 1995: 337–41) seems to deal with a *Scheintod*, and refers to 'initiates' (line 14): see Winkler 1980: 171–5.

28 On the use of the language of 'wandering' to express the subject's state prior to initiation, see Tierney 1937: 18–21. In the Neoplatonic tradition, the soul 'wanders' through the phenomenal world, longing for its return to the noumenal world: see e.g. Plot. *Enn.* 1.6.8; 2.3.9; 5.9.1; 6.9.11, and further Merkelbach 1962: 247; Lamberton 1986: 106–7.

29 The association of Ethiopia with death also figures the defloration of Charicleia: Greek girls are often said to die twice, once on their wedding night and once at their death (Charicles' first daughter does actually die on her wedding night: see 2.29.3–4; Szepessy 1972; Knoles 1980–1). See further Lebeck 1971: 68–73; Rehm 1994.

30 In a forthcoming paper, E.L. Bowie suggests that generic expectations lead us to anticipate eight books of novel. In books 7 and 8, it appears as if Charicleia and Theagenes have been happily united for a wedding, and that *Egypt* is the end of the text.

31 It is not known with certainty whether Heliodorus' text was entitled *Aethiopica*, *Charicleia* or *Charicleia and Theagenes*. The *sphragis* at the conclusion of the text (τοιόνδε πέρας ἔσχε τὸ σύνταγμα τῶν περὶ Θεαγένην καὶ Χαρίκλειαν Αἰθιοπικῶν, 10.41.4) yields a description perhaps overly cumbersome for a title: comparative evidence would suggest that the text would have been entitled Αἰθιοπικά (cf. Φοινικικά, attested on the papyrus: Stephens and Winkler 1995: 318; Μιλησιακά, attested by Plut. *Crass.* 32.3). The earliest reference to the text calls it

TIM WHITMARSH

Aethiopica (Socr. *Hist. Eccles.* 5.22)). The reference by 'Philip the Philosopher' (*infra*, n. 33) to it as *Charicleia* is a metonymic conceit.
32 A well-known feature of the Nile: see e.g. Plut. *Quaest. Conv.* 725e.
33 On this allegorical reading, see Lamberton 1986: 148–56. Lamberton provides a translation of the text, which is itself most readily accessible in Colonna ed. 1938.
34 Call. *Hymn.* 2.108–9; 4.205–8 (with Bing 1988: 136–7); Hor. *Carm.* 4.2.1.5–8. Homer was from Hellenistic times conventionally linked with Ocean, in that all poetic 'rivers' spring from him: see esp. *CA*: 187–8; Dion. Hal. *De Comp. Verb.* 24 and Williams 1978: 88–9.
35 θαῦμα and cognates at 9.22.2; 9.22.4; 10.9.1; 10.9.4 (θάμβος); 10.9.4; 10.12.1; 10.13.2 (θάμβος); 10.13.3; 10.15.1; 10.16.6; 10.23.4; 10.30.5; 10.34.2; 10.35.2; 10.39.3; ἔκπληξις at 10.15.1; 10.30.7.
36 The suggestion of Innes and Winterbottom 1988: 95 that ξενιζόμενος ἐπ᾽ ἐμαυτῶι means 'surprised at myself' banalises the Greek.
37 On the problems of the dating of Heliodorus, see *supra* n. 2.
38 On the emerging complications with the term ῞Ελλην, see the (rather overschematic) account of Bowersock 1995: 29–53.
39 The bibliography on modern theories of cultural identity is predictably immense: see the introduction to this volume. My own ideas have been particularly influenced by Anderson 1983 and Bhabha 1994, both of whom consider the role of the modern novel in constructing cultural identity; Bhabha in particular considers how post-colonial novel-writing reveals the Janus-like aspect of culture.
40 I have discussed Heliodorus' self-representation in these terms in Whitmarsh 1998.

Bibliography

CA = Powell, J.U. (ed.) (1923) *Collectanea Alexandrina: Reliquiae Minores Poetarum Aetatis Ptolemaicae*, Oxford: Oxford University Press.

Anderson, B. (1983) *Imagined Communities*, London: Verso.
Anderson, G. (1986) *Philostratus: Biography and Belles-Lettres in the Third Century A.D.*, London: Croom Helm.
André, J.-M. and Baslez, M.-F. (1993) *Voyager dans l'antiquité*, Paris: Fayard.
Baslez, M.-F. *et al.* (eds) (1992) Le Monde du roman grec. Actes du colloque international tenu à l'École Normale Supérieure, Paris: Presses de l'École Normale Supérieure.
Beard, M. (1993) 'Looking (Harder) for Roman Myth: Dumézil, Declamation and the Problems of Definition', in Graf, F. (ed.) *Mythos in mythenloser Gesellschaft: das Paradigma Roms*, Stuttgart and Leipzig: Teubner.
Bhabha, H.K. (1994) *The Location of Culture*, London: Routledge.
Bianchi, U. (ed.) (1986) *Transition Rites: Cosmic, Social and Individual Order*, Rome: Bretschneider.
Billault, A. (1981) 'Le Mythe de Persée et les *Éthiopiques* d'Héliodore: légendes, représentations et fiction littéraire', *Revue des Études Grecques* 94: 63–75.
Bing, P. (1988) *The Well-Read Muse: Present and Past in Callimachus and the Hellenistic Poets*, Göttingen: Vandenhoeck & Ruprecht.

Bloom, H. (1973) *The Anxiety of Influence: a Theory of Poetry*, New York: Oxford University Press.

Bonneau, D. (1992) 'Les *realia* du paysage égyptien dans le roman grec: remarques lexicographiques', in Baslez *et al.* (eds) (1992).

Bowersock, G.W. (1995) *Fiction as History: Nero to Julian*, Berkeley: University of California Press.

Bowie, E.L. (1974) 'Greeks and their Past in the Second Sophistic', *Past and Present* 46: 3–41; revised and repr. in Finley, M. (ed.) *Studies in Ancient Society*, London: Routledge & Kegan Paul.

—— (1978) 'Apollonius of Tyana: Tradition and Reality', *Aufstieg und Niedergang der römischen Welt* 2.16.2: 1652–1699.

—— (1994) 'The Readership of Greek Novels in the Ancient World', in Tatum (ed.) (1994).

Bowie, E.L. and Harrison, S.J. (1993) 'The Romance of the Novel', *Journal of Roman Studies* 83: 159–78.

Brown, P. (1988) *The Body and Society: Men, Women and Sexual Renunciation in Early Christianity*, London: Faber & Faber.

Bühler, W. (1976) 'Das Element des Visuellen in der Eingangsszene von Heliodors *Aithiopika*', *Wiener Studien* 10: 177–85.

Burkert, W. (1987) *Ancient Mystery Cults*, Cambridge, Mass.: Harvard University Press.

Calame, C. (1997) *Choruses of Young Women in Ancient Greece: their Morphology, Religious Role and Social Functions*, Oxford: Rowman & Littlefield.

Cauderlier, P. (1992) 'Réalités égyptiennes chez Héliodore', in Baslez *et al.* (eds) (1992).

Cave, T. (1988) *Recognitions: a Study in Poetics*, Oxford: Oxford University Press.

Colonna, A. (ed.) (1938) *Heliodori Aethiopica*, Rome: Accademia dei Lincei.

Cooper, K. (1996) *The Virgin and the Bride: Idealized Womanhood in Late Antiquity*, Cambridge, Mass.: Harvard University Press.

Dawson, D. (1992) *Cities of the Gods: Communist Utopias in Greek Thought*, Oxford: Oxford University Press.

Dowden, K. (1989) *Death and the Maiden: Girls' Initiation Rites in Greek Mythology*, London: Routledge.

—— (1996) 'Heliodorus: Serious Intentions', *Classical Quarterly* n.s. 46: 267–85.

Droogers, A.F. (1980) *The Dangerous Journey: Symbolic Aspects of Boys' Initiation among the Wagenia of Kisangari, Zaire*, The Hague: Mouton.

Edwards, C. (1996) *Writing Rome: Textual Representations of the City*, Cambridge: Cambridge University Press.

Egger, B. (1994) 'Looking at Chariton's Callirhoe', in J.R. Morgan and R. Stoneman (eds) *Greek Fiction: the Greek Novel in Context*, London: Routledge.

Eliade, M. (1966) *Rites and Symbols of Initiation: the Mysteries of Birth and Rebirth*, New York: Harper.

Elsner, J. (1992) 'Pausanias: a Greek Pilgrim in the Roman World', *Past & Present* 135: 3–29.

—— (1995) *Art and the Roman Viewer: the Transformation of Art from Augustus to Justinian*, Cambridge: Cambridge University Press.

Ferguson, J. (1975) *Utopias of the Classical World*, London: Thames & Hudson.
Feuillâtre, E. (1966) *Études sur les Éthiopiques d'Héliodore*, Paris: Presses Universitaires de France.
Foucault, M. (1988) *The History of Sexuality. Vol 3: the Care of the Self*, Harmondsworth: Penguin.
Fusillo, M. (1989) *Il romanzo greco: polifonia ed eros*, Venice: Marsilio.
Garson, R.W. (1975) 'Notes on Some Homeric Echoes in Heliodorus' *Aethiopica'*, *Antiquité Classique* 18: 137–40.
Gärtner, H. (ed.) (1984) *Beiträge zum griechischen Liebesroman*, Hildesheim: Olms.
Gennep, A. van (1960) *The Rites of Passage*, London: Routledge & Kegan Paul.
Gluckman, M. (ed.) (1962) *The Ritual of Social Relations*, Manchester: Manchester University Press.
Goldhill, S. (1991) *The Poet's Voice: Essays on Poetics and Greek Literature*, Cambridge: Cambridge University Press.
—— (1995) *Foucault's Virginity: Ancient Erotic Fiction and the History of Sexuality*, Cambridge: Cambridge University Press.
Gual, C. (1992) 'L'Initiation de Daphnis et Chloé', in Moreau (ed.) (1992).
Hartog, F. (1988) *The Mirror of Herodotus: the Representation of the Other in the Writing of History*, Berkeley: University of California Press.
Hunter, R.L. (1983) *A Study of Daphnis and Chloë*, Cambridge: Cambridge University Press.
—— (1992) 'Writing the God: Form and Meaning in Callimachus, *Hymn to Athena'*, *Materiali e Discussioni per l'Analisi dei Testi Classici* 29: 9–34.
—— (1994) 'History and Historicity in the Romance of Chariton of Aphrodisias', *Aufstieg und Niedergang der römischen Welt* 2.34.3: 1055–86.
Innes, D. and Winterbottom, M. (1988) *Sopatros the Rhetor: Studies in the Text of the Διαίρεσις Ζητημάτων*, London: Institute of Classical Studies.
Jacob, C. (1991) 'Alexandre et la maîtrise de l'espace: l'art du voyage dans l'*Anabase* d'Arrien', *Quaderni di Storia* 17: 5–40.
Keyes, C. (1922) 'The Structure of Heliodorus' *Aethiopica'*, *Studies in Philology* 19: 42–51.
Knoles, J. (1980–1) '"The Spurned Doxy" and the Dead Bride: Some Ramifications for Ancient *Topoi'*, *Classical World* 74: 223–5.
Konstan, D. (1994) *Sexual Symmetry: Love in the Ancient Novel and Related Genres*, Princeton: Princeton University Press.
Kuch, H. (1996) 'The Margin of the Ancient Novel: "Barbarians" and Others', in Schmeling (ed.) (1996).
Lamberton, R. (1986) *Homer the Theologian: Neoplatonist Allegorical Reading and the Growth of the Epic Tradition*, Berkeley: University of California Press.
Lebeck, A. (1971) *The Oresteia: a Study in Language and Structure*, Washington, D.C.: Centre for Hellenic Studies.
Létoublon, F. (1993) *Les Lieux communs du roman: stéréotypes grecs d'aventure et d'amour*, Leiden: Brill.
Lightfoot, C. (1988) 'Facts and Fiction: the Third Siege of Nisibis (A.D. 350)', *Historia* 37: 105–25.
Marino, E. (1990), 'Il teatro nel romanzo: Eliodoro e il codice spettacolore', *Materiali e Discussioni per l'Analisi dei Testi Classici* 25: 203–18.
Merkelbach, R. (1962) *Roman und Mysterium in der Antike*, Munich: Beck.

Momigliano, A. (1974) *Alien Wisdom: the Limits of Hellenization*, Cambridge: Cambridge University Press.

Moreau, A. (1992) *'Odyssée* XXI, 101–39: l'examen de passage de Télémaque', in Moreau (ed.) (1992).

—— (ed.) (1992) *L'Initiation: l'acquisition d'un savoir ou d'un pouvoir; le lieu initiatique; parodies et perspectives*, Montpellier: Université Paul-Valery.

—— (1994) *Le Mythe de Jason et Médée: le va-nu-pied et la sorcière*, Paris: Les Belles Lettres.

Morgan, J. (1993) 'Make-Believe and Make Believe', in C. Gill and T.P. Wiseman (eds) *Lies and Fiction in the Ancient World*, Exeter: Exeter University Press.

—— (1996) 'Heliodoros', in Schmeling (ed.) (1996).

Nicolet, C. (1988) *L'Inventaire du monde: géographie et politique aux origines de l'empire romaine*, Paris: Fayard.

Pavel, T. (1986) *Fictional Worlds*, Cambridge, Mass.: Harvard University Press.

Rattenbury, R. and Lumb, T. (eds) (1960) *Héliodore, Les Éthiopiques*[2], Paris: Les Belles Lettres.

Reardon, B. (1969) 'The Greek Novel', *Phoenix* 23: 291–309; repr. in Gärtner (ed.) (1984).

—— (1991) *The Form of Greek Romance*, Princeton: Princeton University Press.

Rehm, R. (1994) *Marriage to Death: the Conflation of Wedding and Funeral Rituals in Greek Tragedy*, Princeton: Princeton University Press.

Rohde, E. (1914) *Der griechische Roman und seine Vorläufer*[3], Leipzig: Breitkopf; repr. (1960), Hildesheim: Olms.

Romm, J.S. (1992) *The Edges of the World in Ancient Thought*, Princeton: Princeton University Press.

Rougemont, G. (1992) 'Delphes chez Héliodore', in Baslez *et al.* (eds) (1992).

Sandy, G. (1982) 'Characterization and Philosophical Decor in Heliodorus' *Aethiopica*', *Transactions of the American Philological Society* 112: 141–67.

Schmeling, G. (ed.) (1996) *The Novel in the Ancient World*, Leiden: Brill.

Segal, C.P. (1962) 'The Phaeacians and the Symbolism of Odysseus' Return', *Arion* 1: 17–64; revised and repr. in Segal (1994).

—— (1967) 'Transition and Ritual in Odysseus' Return', *La Parola del Passato* 116: 321–42; revised and repr. in Segal (1994).

—— (1986) *Pindar's Mythmaking: the Fourth Pythian Ode*, Princeton: Princeton University Press.

—— (1994) *Singers, Heroes and Gods in the Odyssey*, Ithaca, NY: Cornell University Press.

Stephens, S. (1994) 'Who Read Ancient Novels?', in Tatum (ed.) (1994).

Stephens, S.A. and Winkler, J.J. (1995) *Ancient Greek Novels, the Fragments: Introduction, Text, Translation, and Commentary*, Cambridge, Mass.: Harvard University Press.

Swain, S. (1996) *Hellenism and Empire: Language, Classicism, and Power in the Greek World, A.D. 50–250*, Oxford: Oxford University Press.

Szepessy, T. (1957) 'Die *Aithiopika* des Heliodoros und der griechische sophistische Liebesroman', *Acta Antiqua Academiae Hungaricae* 5: 241–59; repr. in Gärtner (ed.) (1984).

—— (1972) 'The Story of the Little Girl who Died on her Wedding Night', *Acta Antiqua Academiae Hungaricae* 20: 341–57.

Tatum, J. (ed.) (1994) *The Search for the Ancient Novel*, Baltimore: Johns Hopkins University Press.

Tierney, M. (1937) 'The Mysteries and the *Oresteia*', *Journal of Hellenic Studies* 57: 11–21.

Turner, V. (1967) *The Forest of Symbols: Aspects of Ndembu Ritual*, Ithaca, NY: Cornell University Press.

—— (1969) *The Ritual Process: Structure and Anti-Structure*, London: Routledge & Kegan Paul.

Vasaly, A. (1993) *Representations: Images of the World in Ciceronian Oratory*, Berkeley: University of California Press.

Versnel, H.S. (1990) 'What's Sauce for the Goose is Sauce for the Gander: Myth and Ritual, Old and New', in L. Edmunds (ed.) *Approaches to Greek Myth*, Baltimore: Johns Hopkins University Press.

Veyne, P. (1988) *Did the Greeks Believe in their Myths? An Essay on the Constitutive Imagination*, Chicago: University of Chicago Press.

Vidal-Naquet, P. (1986a) *The Black Hunter: Forms of Thought and Forms of Society in the Greek World*, Baltimore: Johns Hopkins University Press.

—— (1986b) 'The Black Hunter Revisited', *Proceedings of the Cambridge Philological Society* 32: 126–44.

Vizedom, M. (1976) *Rites and Relationships: Rites of Passage and Contemporary Anthropology*, Sage Research Papers in the Social Sciences 4.

Walden, J. (1894) 'Stage Terms in Heliodorus' *Aethiopica*', *Harvard Studies in Classical Philology* 5: 1–43.

Whitmarsh, T. (1998) 'The Birth of a Prodigy: Heliodorus and the Genealogy of Hellenism', in R.L. Hunter (ed.) *Studies in Heliodorus*, Cambridge: Proceedings of the Cambridge Philological Society [supplement].

Williams, F. (1978) *Callimachus, Hymn to Apollo*, Oxford: Oxford University Press.

Winkler, J.J. (1980) 'Lollianus and the Desperadoes', *Journal of Hellenic Studies* 100: 155–81.

—— (1982) 'The Mendacity of Kalasiris and the Narrative Strategy of Heliodoros' *Aithiopika*', *Yale Classical Studies* 27: 93–158.

Zeitlin, F.I. (1978) 'The Dynamics of Misogyny in the *Oresteia*', *Arethusa* 11: 149–84; repr. in *id.* (1996) *Playing the Other: Gender and Society in Classical Greek Literature*, Chicago: Chicago University Press.

3

GENDER AND IDENTITY IN MUSAEUS' *HERO AND LEANDER*

Helen Morales

It is an infelicitous irony that *Hero and Leander*, a poem which, as this chapter aims to demonstrate, engages centrally with issues of identity, was afforded pride of place in the Western European literary imagination during the Renaissance, because of the complete misidentification of its author.[1] With seeming blithe indifference to points of style and literary allusion which place the text after Nonnus' *Dionysiaca* and thus firmly in *late* antiquity, Renaissance writers and teachers identified Musaeus, its author, with Musaeus of Eleusis, the archaic poet and legendary colleague of Orpheus, which places the work in *early* antiquity. It is possible that this misidentification was courted by the author, who purposefully assumed a pseudonym (although, as Neil Hopkinson notes, Musaeus was a common Late Antique name, at least in Egypt; Hopkinson 1994: 137). However that may be, the misidentification afforded the poet originary status and *Hero and Leander* was used in schools as an introduction to Greek literature. It was either the first or the second book to be published by the Aldine Press in 1494, in which Musaeus is acclaimed in the preface as 'the most ancient poet' (Braden 1978: 81). There were numerous versions of the story, perhaps the most renowned of which is Christopher Marlowe's archly comic *Hero and Leander* (1593), supplemented after his death by George Chapman, which has given us the immortal line, 'Whoever loved that loved not at first sight?' (On Marlowe, see Braden 1978: 57–81; Snare 1989; Heaney 1994; more generally on the reception of the poem see Malcovati 1962; Farber 1961: 96–7; Blakeney 1934: 8–9). However, after scholars reassessed the dating of the poem in the early seventeenth century, with irrefutable arguments for a later date, Musaeus was relegated to relative obscurity. Elements of the poem's style and content which appealed to readers when they thought Musaeus pre-Homeric were singled out for criticism once he was repositioned as Late Antique. Seldom are the speciousness of periodisation and the caprice of the canon revealed with such clarity. There appears to be a circularity of argument in the treatment of *Hero and Leander*. The changing fluctuations in the reception of the poem suggest an attitude that the poem is poor because it is Late Antique. Yet it is also contended that Late Antiquity is neglected because its literature is poor. Thus Michael Grant writes:

> [i]t is partly because of the second-rate character of so many of the writers – despite the excellence of certain other arts . . . that the fifth century has been so gravely neglected. The Classics departments at schools and universities do not care for a period in which good Latin literature was restricted to two men (both Christian) [i.e. Augustine and Jerome] and there was no good Greek literature whatever.
>
> (Grant 1998: 80)

None *whatever?*! So much for 'the divine poem of Musaeus', as Marlowe called it, 'the most beautiful love poem in the world.'

The love poem tells the story of two young people bound by desire, but separated by duty and the Hellespont. Leander of Abydos falls in love with Hero of Sestos, a priestess of Aphrodite, when he meets her at a festival to the goddess. He pursues her and finds his love reciprocated (two-thirds of the poem concern their first meeting and seduction). Leander swims nightly across the water, guided by Hero's lamp, to be with his lover. One night a storm extinguishes the lamp, Leander drowns and Hero kills herself by leaping from her tower to fall beside his corpse. Although in the later tradition the story was purloined for parody (in Shakespeare's *As You Like It*, Leander 'being taken with the cramp was drowned' and in Thomas Nashe's burlesque *Praise of the Red Herring* (1599) both lovers are metamorphosed into fish), Musaeus' poem, with veins of humour, is tragic in tone. It is a 343-line hexameter epyllion (narrative poem). The language is highly stylised, rich in assonance, alliteration, hyperbaton and chiasmus, and the sentence structure is elaborate, with long sentences often employing antithesis and parenthesis. The writing is richly allusive to a range of works, most strikingly to Nonnus' *Dionysiaca* and *Paraphrase of St John*, Achilles Tatius' novel *Leucippe and Clitophon*, Homer's *Odyssey*, the Homeric *Hymn to Aphrodite* and

Plato's *Phaedrus* (cf. Schwabe 1876, Gelzer 1968, Kost 1971, Schoenberger 1978). We have scant secure knowledge about the author. Some manuscripts refer to him as 'grammaticus' and he might be the Musaeus who was a friend and correspondent to Procopius of Gaza.[2] The assertion that Musaeus was a Christian is highly speculative, based as it is on the (slight) resemblance of line 138 of his poem to Luke 1.42. His nationality and when and where he wrote are uncertain. The strength of Musaeus' allusion to Nonnus and Colluthus' probable use of Musaeus suggest that the poem was written some time in the late fifth or early sixth century.

The story of Hero and Leander features in the earlier works of Ovid's eighteenth and nineteenth *Heroides* and is mentioned in Statius' *Thebaid* (6.542–7) and *Silvae* (1.2.87), Ovid's *Amores* (2.16.31), and Virgil's *Georgics* (3.258–63). In the praeceptor's advice in Ovid's *Ars Amatoria*, Leander is a self-sacrificing paradigm for the dedicated lover:

> The simple straightforward way in may be denied you,
> Doors bolted shut in your face –
> So be ready to slip down from the roof through a lightwell,
> Or sneak in by an upper-floor window. She'll be glad
> To know you're risking your neck, and for her sake: that will offer
> Any mistress sure proof of your love.
> Leander might, often enough, have endured Hero's absence –
> But he swam over to show her how he felt.[3]
>
> (2.243–50)

(*All because the lady loves . . .*) Two papyrus fragments appear to feature the myth (*P. Oxy.* 6.864.6–26, a iambic trimeter poem probably of the third century CE and *P. Ryl.* 3.486, a hexameter fragment *c.* first century CE) and it would not be surprising – though no evidence for it survives – if there had been a Callimachean model. According to Martial, the myth was enacted as part of the celebrations for the opening of the Colosseum in 80 CE (*Lib. Spect.* 25).

Despite Karlheinz Kost's assiduous commentary and the publication of recent editions by Enrico Livrea and Neil Hopkinson,[4] there remains much work to be done on the poem's language and literary texture. However, my project here is to consider the discursive constructions of identity in *Hero and Leander*, with gender as the operative category. The first section examines representations of vocality; how vocal expression is perceived and socialised. It observes how the vocal order in *Hero and Leander* is explicitly and strikingly gendered. It argues that, in a more emphatic and elaborate way, the poem conforms to an established literary tradition in which the female voice is marked as different from the male voice and speech is signalled as indicative of sexual status. It contends that the narrative displays a discourse of distorted dissent which we might want to recognise as having a wider significance for gender ideology and the politics of the auditory. The second section focuses more closely on the figure of Hero. It discusses the contradictory terms in which she is portrayed, how these expose the performativity of sexual identity and what kind of fantasy they comprise. This section argues for a reconsideration of certain favoured textual emendations. The third and final section reassesses the dominant ideological interpretation directed by the poem. The impossibility of establishing a precise date and context for *Hero and Leander* precludes a focused functionalist interpretation of the epyllion. However, I argue that the overt concern with marriage and civic identity, which is underplayed in the treatment of the myth in Ovid's *Heroides*, serves to validate socially sanctioned relations and stigmatise the indulgence of individual desire outside of the institution of marriage. It thus proffers a similar 'cautionary tale' to the Greek novels. This reading suggests a very different understanding of the design of the poem and its tragic ending from the critical approaches currently circulating, namely that *Hero and Leander* is best comprehended as a neoplatonic, Christian allegory or as a psychological allegory.

Vocalising identities: dissent of a woman

Identity determines how a person speaks, and how a person speaks plays a part in determining his or her identity. Social identity and vocal order operate in dialectical relation; each informs the other. Concomitantly, identity determines how a person hears. As Kaja Silverman has shown, the acoustical mirror distorts, or as Dunn and Jones put it, 'Listening is always a cultural act, and it is always mediated by a mode of representation' (Dunn and Jones 1997: 8). Ways of speaking are not just indicative of social roles but actively define them; influencing and systematising cultural constructions of self and other. By 'ways of speaking' I mean the full range implied by the term vocality: the pitch and tone of the voice as well as the words which are spoken. Suffice it to mention a few – very different and more complex than I allow for here – examples from antiquity: the 'barbarian' was so named, according to popular understanding, because he or she spoke unintelligibly ('bar, bar, bar'); the kinaedos was expected to be betrayed by his high-pitched whine; Athenian *parrhêsia* and rhetorical skill was in pointed contrast to laconic Sparta and the Roman orator policed his voice with a rigorous regimen (cf. Gleason 1995, esp. 82–130). Women's social roles appear to have been characterised by their lack of speech. From the Classical world to that of Late Antiquity, writers follow Aristotle, quoting Sophocles' *Ajax*, urging that 'Silence is a woman's glory (*kosmos*)' (*Politics* 1.1260a). As Giulia Sissa comments, 'In an anthropology that accords all privilege to articulate, rational language, this is nothing but pure misogyny' (Sissa 1990: 55). An anecdote from Plutarch shows the tenacity of society's fear of women speaking in public. Pythagoras' wife, Theano, unwittingly exposed her arm while in public. When someone commented 'Good-looking arm', she retorted 'Not public property!' 'The arm of a virtuous woman should not be public property,' moralises Plutarch,

> nor her speech, and she should as modestly guard against exposing her voice to outsiders as she would guard against stripping off her clothes. For in her voice as she's gabbing can be read her emotions, her character, and her physical condition (ἐνορᾶται γὰρ αὐτῇ καὶ πάθος καὶ ἦθος καὶ διάθεσις λαλούσης).
>
> (Plutarch, *Mor.* 142D)[5]

As Maud Gleason comments, 'Physiognomical exposure through the voice . . . is especially threatening to women, who must not be heard unless they are seen' (Gleason 1995: 98) and her excellent book discusses the subject at length. When women do speak, their speech is often, as we shall see in *Hero and Leander*, marked. Speech which contains features which mark it as stereotypical refers to expected as well as (or rather than) observed behaviour. With regard to gender, the voice is, to extend Teresa de Lauretis's formulation, a 'technology of gender', an organising principle of gender (de Lauretis 1987). Speech which contains features which mark it as stereotypically masculine or feminine (which has been termed 'genderlect'; cf. Hoar 1992, Spender 1980 and Baron 1986) is a means of regulating and perpetuating gender differences.[6]

Speech and silence have powerful presences in *Hero and Leander* and Musaeus' use of the vocabulary of speaking out (*angel-*) and silence (*siôpê*) is 'obsessive and unexplained . . . throughout the poem'

(Braden 1978: 64). However, it is put to particular use in one major scene: Leander's seduction of Hero (ll. 99–220). Seduction is a lesson in identity. Jane Miller explains how this might work for women:

> seductions . . . [are] all those ways in which women learn who they are in cultures which simultaneously include and exclude them, take their presence for granted while denying it, and entice them finally into narratives which may reduce them by exalting them.
>
> (Miller 1990: 2)

Miller's focus is seduction scenes in modern romance literature where the typical scenario involves the male seducer as an active subject and the female seducee as passive, or less active, object of his desire. There are many differences between this model and ancient concepts of *peithô*, but sufficient points of similarity to make Miller's formulation useful nonetheless. Is it a fair description of what happens to Hero? I want now to consider Hero's seduction; how, in Miller's terms, she learns who she is. In a typically novelistic scene, she first captivates him – love at first sight – at a festival in honour of her deity, Aphrodite. This is less Hero's doing than her beauty's, which, like a heroine from an ancient novel, she wears like a fetish. Smitten, Leander 'had no will to live without having lovely Hero' (l. 89) (a phrase heavy with ironic prescience) and takes action, 'boldly at love's command embracing shamelessness' (l. 99). There follows a complex choreography of gestures:

> Quietly he stepped forward and stood facing the girl;
> And peering sidelong, he darted quivering, conspiring glances,
> With voiceless gestures turning astray the heart of the girl;
> But she, when she recognised Leander's ensnaring desire,
> Rejoiced in his splendid charms; and quietly she also
> Once and again bent on him her own love-quickening gaze,
> With furtive gestures sending her message to Leander,
> And turned away again.

> ἠρέμα ποσσὶν ἔβαινε, καὶ ἀντίος ἵστατο κούρης·
> λοξὰ δ' ὀπιπεύων δολερὰς ἐλέλιζεν ὀπωπάς
> νεύμασιν ἀφθόγγοισι παραπλάζων φρένα κούρης.
> αὐτὴ δ', ὡς ξυνέηκε πόθον δολόεντα Λεάνδρου,
> χαῖρεν ἐπ' ἀγλαΐῃ σιν · ἐν ἡσυχίῃ δὲ καί αὐτὴ

MUSAEUS' *HERO AND LEANDER*

πολλάκις ἱμερόεσσαν ἑὴν ἐπέκυψεν ὀπωπὴν
νεύμασι λαθριδίοισιν ἐπαγγέλλουσα Λεάνδρσ,
καὶ πάλιν ἀντέκλινεν.

(ll. 100–7)

It is Leander who initiates this gestural dance (his experience and
sexual status are not made clear, but earlier we are explicitly told
that Hero is 'unschooled in sexual union' γάμων δ' ἀδίδακτος
l. 31). His desire is described as scheming, sly (πόθον δολόεντα),
a phrase which indicates his active and knowing role. It is also one
of the many allusions which serve to construct Leander as an Odyssean figure and the seduction scene as a whole as written through
and against the Nausicaa episode in the *Odyssey* (a point to which I
shall return in the next section), which further suggests the inequality between Leander and Hero.[7] However, their attraction is then
portrayed in terms which evince mutuality. We are told that Hero
'rejoiced in his splendid charms' (χαῖρεν ἐπ' ἀγλαΐῃσιν, an ambiguous phrase which could mean that she 'rejoiced in her own charms',
i.e. in her power to attract) and repeatedly sent him looks which are
'full of desire' (ἱμερόεσσαν... ὀπωπήν). The phrase used of Hero's
actions, 'furtive gestures' (νεύμασι λαθριδίοισιν), echoes that used
of Leander's four lines previously, also at the beginning of a line,
'voiceless gestures' (νεύμασι ἀφθόγγοισι), a repetition which
underscores the mutuality of their communication. It is quite
emphatic that this first stage of seduction is performed in silence
(ἠρέμα (l. 100), ἀφθόγγοισι (l. 102), ἐν ἡσυχίῃ (l. 104)). Neither
character speaks and all we are told is focalised through the
omniscient narrator.

An allegorical interpretation might understand the silence in
which the proceedings are conducted as having a religious significance, but it also appears, on a more mundane level, that Leander
is following the sound strategic advice given to Clitophon, the sexually experienced, but socially inept hero of Achilles Tatius' novel. At
Leucippe and Clitophon 1.10.2, Clitophon's friend, Clinias, counsels
him on 'how to be a man', *andrizesthai* (here seduction is marked
as a lesson in identity for men too). He proffers the following
wisdom on the role of speech in seduction:

> Now, as far as general principles are concerned and without
> requiring favourable circumstances, listen to this: never
> mention anything Aphrodisiac in her presence, but try to
> reach the real thing without mentioning it. Boys and girls

47

have the same sense of modesty: when it comes to gratifying
their Aphrodisiac instincts, even those who feel ready would
rather not have their feelings named aloud. The shame of it
they think consists in mentioning the words. Now experienced women like the words as well as the deeds.[8]

(1.10.2–4)

Clinias lays down the law about language, gender and sexual
status. According to these cultural codes, a person's sexual status
determines his or her relationship to language. The *pais* and the
parthenos take affront rather than pleasure at verbal references to
sex; they are compromised merely by listening to accounts of 'the
pleasures of Aphrodite'. Women – *gunaikes* – on the other hand,
take pleasure in the words, εὐφραίνει . . . τὰ ῥήματα. Clinias
posits a direct correlation between sexual activity and speech. The
axis of differentiation here is that of age or experience rather than
gender; both boys and girls feel disconcerted by sex talk. In an earlier
Greek novel, neither of the young lovers is sexually experienced, but
the boy can articulate his desire, whereas the girl cannot. Written in
the early first century CE but surviving only in fragments, the Ninus
romance is one of the earliest Greek novels and it tells of the love
between the young man Ninus and the girl Semiramis.[9] They
both feel more confident broaching the subject of marriage with
their beloved's mother (their aunt; the two are cousins) rather than
their own mother. Although the text is very fragmented at this
point, it seems that 'the accustomed modesty for women'
(ἡ συνήθης ταῖς γυναιξὶν αἰδώς, A.1.9–10) contributes to
Semiramis' reluctance to discuss marriage. Ninus petitions Derkeia
with 'an elaborate display of rhetorical style and compositional
finesse',[10] anticipating and countering all possible objections to
the union (A.2.1–38, A.3.1–38, A.4.1–13). He concludes this
virtuoso performance by pre-empting the criticism that he is shameless in bringing up the subject of marriage:

'You may call me shameless for speaking of these matters,
but truly I would have been shameless if in secret
I had tried her virtue and stolen
my enjoyment undercover,
sharing my passion with the night, the wine-cup,
the trusted servant or nurse.
I am not shameless in discussing

with her mother a daughter's
longed-for marriage . . .'

ἀναιδῆ τάχα με ἐρεῖς περὶ τούτων διαλεγόμενον· ἐγὼ δὲ
ἀναιδὴς ἂν ἤμην λάθραι πειρῶν καὶ κλεπτομένην
ἀπόλαυσιν ἁρπάζων καὶ νυκτὶ μέθῃ καὶ θεράποντι καὶ
τιθηνῷ κοινούμενος τὸ πάθος. οὐκ ἀναιδὴς δὲ μητρὶ περὶ
γάμων θυγατρὸς εὐκταίων διαλεγόμενος . . .
(A.3.36–8, A.4.1–7)

The emphatic repetition ἀναιδῆ . . . ἐγὼ δὲ ἀναιδὴς . . . οὐκ
ἀναιδὴς underlines his point.

Ninus' skilful argumentation is in
marked contrast to Semiramis' appeal to Thambe: 'The maiden, however, though her feelings were similar, had no eloquence comparable
to his as he stood before Thambe' (τῇ κόρῃ δ᾽ ἐν ὁμοίοις πάθεσιν
οὐχ ὁμοία παρρησία τῶν λόγων ἦν πρὸς τὴν Θάμβην, A.4.20–
3). Her lack of parrhêsia is explained as follows: 'For as a virgin living
within the women's quarters she was unable to fashion her arguments
with such finesse' (ἡ γὰρ παρθένος ἐντὸς τῆς γυναικωνίτιδος
ζῶσα οὐκ εὐπρεπεῖς ἐποίει τοὺς λόγους αὐτῆς, A.4.23–5).
Semiramis' inability to speak freely is due to her status as a parthenos
and her seclusion in the women's quarters where she is 'unable to
fashion her arguments with such finesse'. The gendering of space
which 'women's quarters' involve and the distance which it imposes
upon Semiramis reflects and gives visual constitution to the gendering of speech which is revealed in this scene and the difference which
it marks between her and Ninus. The maiden's difficulty in speaking
is given lengthy illustration. Semiramis bursts into tears, tries to
articulate but cuts herself short, mimes speaking but does not
manage the words, cries again, blushes, cringes, tries again but grows
pale with fear and is torn between epithumia and aidôs. When she
continues in this distress Thambe speaks for her and comments:
'Your silence communicates better in my opinion than any speech'
(ἄπαντος . . . μοι λόγου κάλλιον ἡ σιωπὴ διαλέγεται, A.5.12–
14). This passage is a wonderfully overt example of language functioning as a technology of gender; boys can articulate desire, girls
cannot.

In Apollonius of Rhodes' Hellenistic epic Argonautica, Medea only
manages to tell her sister of her desire for Jason after battling shame
which thrice holds her back (3.648–55) and prevents her from speaking (3.681–86). Repeated mention of her shame is made during this
episode and, as in the Ninus romance, it is marked as gender- and

HELEN MORALES

status-specific: αἰδὼς παρθενίη (681–2). As Richard Hunter puts it, 'In the battle between αἰδώς and ἵμερος, speech is a function of the latter, silence of the former' (Hunter 1989: 172 on lines 685–6).

The view that a female's speech was influenced by and in turn indicative of her sexual experience is enshrined in the linguistic double meaning of the Greek word *stoma*, meaning both oral and genital mouth or lips. Giulia Sissa documents medical writings which chart the interaction between the two orifices (Sissa 1990: 52–67, 166–7). Galen, for example, compared the clitoris to the uvula, for the clitoris protects the uterus from the cold in the same way that the uvula protects the trachea; the logic runs that a female who opens one of her mouths is thought to open the other. Loose talk suggests sexual promiscuity (Hanson and Armstrong 1986; Nemesianus, *Eclogue* 4.11 and Soranus, *Gynaecology* 3.1.7–10); cf. Brown 1988: 101–2, n. 81 and Gleason 1995: 82–102). Conversely, sexual activity will affect a woman's speech.[11] For a *parthenos*, as Clinias states, taking pleasure in sexual words is almost to perform a physical consummation; it is collusion, complicity. The suggestion of sex is an approximation of the act itself.

Having returned at dusk, Leander's next move is not to speak, but to touch Hero's hand. This is her reaction:

> She in silence
> Like one who is angry, drew away her rosy hand.
> But when he saw in the lovely girl the signs of yielding,
> With bold hand he pulled at her richly broidered gown
> Leading her into the farthest coverts of the lordly temple.
> And on shy tremulous feet the maiden Hero followed,
> Like one who is unwilling, and she lifted her voice so,
> Threatening with words of the kind that women use:
> 'Stranger, what madness is that? Why, wretch, do
> you drag me, a maiden?
> Come, seek another way, and release my gown.
> Shun the wrath of my parents, rich in many possessions.
> It is unfit that you touch the priestess of the goddess Cypris,
> It is beyond contrivance to come to the bed of a virgin.'
>
> (ll. 115–27)

Her speech is forcefully framed and marked as female and virginal. Before her words are quoted, we are told that she threatens Leander 'with words of the kind that women use' (θηλυτέροις ἐπέεσσιν,

50

l. 122). After her speech, the narrator comments: 'Such were the threats she uttered after the way of maidens' (*Τοῖα μὲν ἠπείλησεν ἐοικότα παρθενικῇσι*, l. 128) and in the next line, her threat is again qualified as female (*θηλείης . . . ἀπειλῆς*, l. 129). When Leander speaks, there is no such framing of his words. His speech is fashioned as deceptive and Odyssean, but it is not branded as *male*. It appears, through this omission, as default, neutral, normal. Moreover, the gendered vocality displayed here is ideologically freighted. Hero's words are distinguished as female for a particular purpose, to position and bias what she says. Leander interprets Hero's rejection of him ('the sting of her female threat') as meaning the opposite:

He recognised the tokens of maidens as they surrender.

ἔγνω πειθομένων σημήια παρθενικάων.

(l. 130)

Hero's reaction to Leander touching her hand is reported to us in direct speech. I can detect nothing in that speech as being either syntactically or semantically different and 'female', or in and of itself suggestive of compliance. Rather, there is a discrepancy between what Hero is reported as saying and how her speech is heard and understood. This misrepresentation is then repeated and strengthened in the narrator's explanatory gloss:

For so it is that whenever women threaten youths
Threatening its very self is herald of Love's converse.

*καὶ γὰρ ὅτ᾽ ἠιθέοισιν ἀπειλήσωσι γυναῖκες,
Κυπριδίων ὄαρων αὐτάγγελοί εἰσιν ἀπειλαί.*

(ll. 131–2)

Contrary to their function as threats, women's words act as 'messengers of desire'. Their illocutionary function is one of dissent; their perlocutionary function is that of consent. In other words, when a woman says 'No' to a man, she means 'Yes'. This is anticipated in the narrator's sceptical construal of Hero's gestures, earlier in the scene. She is said to withdraw her hand, 'like one who is angry' (*οἷά τε χωομένη*, l. 116) and to follow Leander, 'like one who is unwilling' (*οἷά περ οὐκ ἐθέλουσα*, l. 121). The repetition of *hoia*,

HELEN MORALES

'like', at the beginning of the lines is a knowing, collusive, indication that her feelings may well be different to those she is expressing.

The authorial comment in lines 131–2 is significant in that it not only directs the audition of Hero's words, but extends this to pronounce on women in general. The sentiments are couched as a *sententia*, or *gnômê*; a generalising statement; the present tense conferring on it a free floating authority, independent of its diegetical context. Sententious statements, as I have discussed at length elsewhere (Morales 1996 and forthcoming), are overtly prescriptive. As Geoffrey Bennington has argued in his study of sententiousness in eighteenth-century French fiction, 'Sententious statements imply a value-judgement grounded in social norms; they transmit a cultural heritage and are inherently conservative' (Bennington 1985: 9). In doing so they 'lay down the law' (Bennington 1985: xi). I can discern five clear *gnômai* in *Hero and Leander*. Four are interjected by the narrator and concern women's behaviour and the fifth by Hero and concerns people's behaviour. Three concern speech (ll. 131–2, ll. 164–5 and ll. 183–4) and the other two women's beauty ('For always at the sight of beauty women are envious', καὶ γὰρ ἐπ' ἀγλΐῃ ζηλήμονές εἰσι γυναῖκες, l. 37 and 'For the far-renowned beauty of woman without flaw / Comes to mortal men keener than a winged arrow,/ And its pathway is the eye; out of the eye's glances / Beauty glides, and journeys into the hearts of men', ll. 92–5; clearly inspired by Achilles Tatius *Leucippe and Clitophon* 1.4.4 and 1.9.4, in turn drawing on *Phaedrus* 250D ff and 255C). Tellingly, this poem chooses to lay down the law about speech and appearance; it is prescriptive on social (and sexual) interaction, privileging visuality and vocality. Hero generalises about man's love of gossip and the importance of discretion:

For the tongue of men is loving of jibes; and that same deed
That a man does in silence, he hears of it in the cross-ways

γλῶσσα γὰρ ἀνθρώπων φιλοκέρτομος, ἐν δὲ σιωπῇ
ἔργον ὅ περ τελέει τις ἐνὶ τριόδοισιν ἀκούει.

Reminiscent of similar sentiments expressed by Nausicaa at *Odyssey* 6.276–84, Hero's sententious statement is not gender-specific. The two *sententiae* on speech interjected by the narrator, however, pronounce on women. The second of these comes after Leander has responded to Hero's rebuff with a long speech which wins her round:

So he spoke and persuaded the girl's heart, though denying,
Leading her spirit astray with love-engendering words.

ll. 158–9

Hero's reaction is to avert her gaze and cover herself with her gown;
her sense of shame and attendant silence are stressed (ἄφθογγος . . .
αἰδοῖ . . . αἰδομένη, ll. 160–2). 'For these are all harbingers of compliance' (πειθοῦς γὰρ τάδε πάντα προάγγελα) comments the
narrator, who adds the sententious flourish:

'. . . a girl's
Silence, when she is won, is her promise to the couch of love'

. . . παρθενικῆς δὲ
πειθομένης ποτὶ λέκτρον ὑπόσχεσίς ἐστι σιωπή

(ll. 164–5)

Woman is in a Catch 22 here: if she vocalises dissent it is interpreted
as consent and if she remains silent, it is interpreted as consent. The
alliteration *parthenikês . . . peithomenês* also echoes *peithomenôn . . .
parthenikaôn* at line 130, further linking the two *sententiae* on
female speech. Both generalisations distort female expression in a
sexual scenario to be read as compliance. Both police the vocal,
laying down the law about speech and gender *in general*.

This can be read as a development of the ideology espoused by
Clinias in *Leucippe and Clitophon*. After his pronouncements on the
differing pleasures on erotic speech enjoyed by adolescents and
adults, Clinias continues with the following statement on a maiden's
behaviour:

Now when there is some sort of agreement to go all the way,
even then women complaisant to the deed prefer to appear
compelled, that they may avert shame of consent by the
sham of constraint.

Κἂν μὲν προσῇ τις συνθήκη τῆς πράξεως, πολλάκις
δὲ καὶ ἑκοῦσαι πρὸς τὸ ἔργον ἐρχόμεναι θέλουσι
βιάζεσθαι δοκεῖν, ἵνα τῇ δόξῃ τῆς ἀνάγκης
ἀποτρέπωνται τῆς αἰσχύνης τὸ ἑκούσιον.

(1.10.6)

The belief that girls dissemble, pretending not to want sexual attentions when in reality they do, has a long history in Graeco-Roman literature. In [Theocritus] Idyll 27, which is almost certainly post-Theocritean, an unnamed maiden is seduced by the cowherd Daphnis. At the beginning of the idyll she declares her commitment to the chaste Artemis, eschewing Aphrodite. She vigorously rejects Daphnis' advances (μὴ ʾπιβάλῃς τὴν χεῖρα, καὶ εἴ γ᾽ ἔτι –, χεῖλος ἀμύξω) (l. 18), states her unwillingness to listen to him (οὐκ ἐθέλω) (l. 11), and declares her fear of marriage and of childbirth. There are signs that she is being won round, when she praises his noble birth and asks for details of his property. However, when he begins to undress her, her language expresses shock (τί ῥέζεις Σατυρίσκε; τί δ᾽ ἔνδοθεν ἄψαο μαζῶν; l. 48) and she punctuates his stripping of her with exclamations of affront: τὠμπέχονον ποίησας ἐμὸν ῥάκος· εἰμὶ δὲ γυμνά (l. 58), as if passive and unwilling. He deflowers her (παρθένος ἔνθα βέβηκα, γυνὴ δ᾽ εἰς οἶκον ἀφέρπω, l. 64) and it is then that we are invited to reassess the girl's resistance and the possibility that it may have been feigned. That she was only pretending to fight him off is implied by her willingness to wander off with him, and the narrator's comment that she returned to tend her flocks, 'with shame in her eyes but joy in her heart', ὄμμασιν αἰδομένοις, κραδίη δέ οἱ ἔνδον ἰάνθη (l. 69). The idyll represents the maiden as dissembling, conveying the message, to put it bluntly, that a girl may say 'no', but that she wants it really.[12]

It is in the sex manual that this becomes an explicit philosophy. The praeceptor in Ovid's *Ars Amatoria* suggests that the lover should mix kisses with his wheedling words, whether or not the woman wishes to give them. If she fights and admonishes the lover:

> uim licet appelles: grata est uis ista puellis;
> quod iuuat, inuitae saepe dedisse uolunt.
> quaecumque est Veneris subita uiolata rapina,
> gaudet, et improbitas muneris instar habet.
> at quae, cum posset cogi, non tacta recessit,
> ut simulet uultu gaudia, tristis erit.

It's all right to use force: that sort of force goes down well with the girls: what in fact they love to yield they'd often rather have stolen. Rough seduction delights them, the audacity of near rape is a compliment – so the girl who

could have been forced yet somehow got away unscathed
may feign delight but in fact feels sadly let down.

(1.673–8; cf. also *Amores* 1.5)

Woman's unwillingness to have sex has no place in the rapist's
charter, which appropriates her expressions of dissent to signify the
contrary: consent. Conversely, a woman's ostensible gladness at not
having been forced is inverted to evince her disappointment. As
Richlin writes,

> The pupil here is led to believe that women do have
> emotions with which to enjoy the experience, but there is
> apparently no way to tell for sure . . . The deletion of
> women's voice here is even more thorough than in the tale
> of Philomela.

(Richlin 1992: 169)

Clinias does not go to the same extremes as Ovid; he advises
Clitophon not to use force if the maiden remains obstinate, as she
is not yet sufficiently softened. However, Ovid, Clinias and Musaeus
theorise that maidens typically express consent as dissent. If consent,
intrinsic to the act of seduction, is fashioned as dissent, then it is
impossible to draw with any certainty the boundary between seduction and rape, between *peithô* and *bia*.

I have three concluding points to make. First, I hope I have shown
that these texts collectively articulate a gendered discourse of distorted dissent. Women's speech is paradoxically both dismissed;
socially disavowed, and overdetermined; marked and projected. In
Hero and Leander and *Leucippe and Clitophon* the mastery over and con-
tainment of the female voice is enacted thematically, through the distorted representations of women's speech, and discursively, through
the prescriptive form of the *sententiae*. That distorted dissent is turned
into a literary convention is part of the violence, as it both enshrines
the travesty more deeply in discourse and affords the possibility for
disavowal (it's only a trope . . .).

Second, the constructions of gender and vocality in *Hero and
Leander* are symptomatic of an ideology which has a long tradition
in Greek and Roman literature. As Richard Miles has discussed in
the introduction to this volume, all too often late antique texts are
'ring-fenced' and read as detached from earlier literature. I hope I
have shown one of the ways in which Musaeus' poem conforms to
and follows precedents.

HELEN MORALES

My third and final point is a political one. It is not only the case that antiquity had a long tradition of hijacking women's speech; modern times evince similar distortions. When that latter-day Leander, Lord Byron, wrote, 'A little while she strove, and much repented;/And whispering "I will ne'er consent" – consented' (*Don Juan* 1.117), he showed himself to be a true fan of Musaeus. When Marilyn Monroe purrs 'When I say "No, No, No" – Do it again', she steps straight out of an Ovidian fantasy. It may well be that it is impossible ever simply or transparently to express desire. Thus Simon Goldhill asks 'to what degree [can] desire . . . be spoken (of) outside the (over)determining framework of language, replete with its proprieties and normative constructions[?]' (Goldhill 1991: 271). But my point is that the framework of language is (over)determined very differently for men than for women. Amy Richlin is right to remind us of the importance of stressing continuities between ancient and modern sexual systems. The imperative to historicise should not – must not – occlude the tenacity of certain constructions of identity. The importance of this is paramount, despite the obvious dangers of tracing a discourse *and more*, and of reifying and possibly perpetuating these constructions: 'misogyny can be conceived of in terms of a *longue durée*' (Richlin 1997: 27), and the discourse of distorted dissent which I have attempted to trace is part of that misogyny and part of that *longue durée*. It continues to manifest itself in the attitudes of judges and jurors and in the thinking of every modern-day Marilyn and Don Juan.

Imbricating identities: Hero(ine) chic

This next section takes as its focus the description of Hero in line 287 as 'a virgin by day, a woman by night' (παρθένος ἠματίη, νυχίη γυνή). This refers to the clandestine nature of Hero's relationship with Leander; by night she enjoys sexual passion with him, but by day she dissembles and lives as if still a virgin, 'in secrecy from her parents' (l. 29). As phrased, with striking chiastic conciseness, the description is a remarkable paradox. Maidenhood and womanhood are two mutually exclusive states; once a *gunê*, a woman can never again be a *parthenos*. However, as Giulia Sissa (who does not discuss Musaeus) has shown, *parthenia* was defined in a multitude of ways, sometimes, but not usually, dependent on having an intact hymen. The debate about the conceptualisation of *parthenia* continued to exercise the pagan and Christian writers of late antiquity.[13] Musaeus'

56

MUSAEUS' HERO AND LEANDER

representation of *parthenia* suggests that no longer to exist it needs witnesses, it needs to be to be spied out: 'the sexuality of a *parthenos* encountered one unbreachable limit: the discovery of its existence. . . . Although it was in fact possible for a *parthenos* to have a sexual life, it was nevertheless forbidden. Dissimulation, clandestinity, and secrecy were necessary conditions' (Sissa 1990: 88 and 90).

Line 287 of *Hero and Leander* evinces the performativity of sexual status, not in the sophisticated theorisation of the word by Judith Butler, but in the more literal sense of it being defined by having or not having an audience. Far from having any absolute referent in physical states, sexual identity, confirms Musaeus, is conferred or denied by the viewer.

Moreover, the phrase *parthenos . . . gunê* represents in metonym how Hero is portrayed throughout the poem. She is represented as having both of these contradictory sexual statuses. These facets of her character's identity coexist and overlap – imbricate – one another. This is manifest on more than one level. I want to turn first to the construction of Hero as a Homeric heroine. There are very many allusions to the *Iliad* and *Odyssey* which cast Hero and Leander as protagonists in a Homeric epic. Leander is addressed in epic apostrophe: 'you, dread-suffering Leander' (αἰνοπαθὲς Λείανδρε, σὺ δ', l. 87) and later proves himself 'stout-hearted' (καρτερόθυμε), an epithet used of Achilles (καρτερόθυμον, *Iliad* 13.350) and 'much-suffering' (πολυτλήτοιο, l. 330), ringingly similar to πολύτλας, an adjective often used of Odysseus. The narrative's relation to the *Odyssey* is especially foregrounded in the seduction scene and in the descriptions of Leander swimming. Like Odysseus, Leander comforts 'his own heart' (*phrena*, l. 244; *Odyssey* 5.355 ff, 376 ff) and ties his clothing above his head before swimming (l. 254; *Odyssey* 14.349 ff). Initially, the association with Odysseus, the phenomenal swimmer, constructs Leander as manly and masculine. As Edith Hall has shown, the ability to swim was viewed as an essential skill for a Greek man. In ethnocentric ideology, barbarians (those effeminates) were likely to drown. '[Swimming] played a small but significant part in the Greek sense of ethnic identity and superiority' (Hall 1994: 49). As the narrative progresses, however, the parallels with Odysseus serve to highlight with pathos the heroes' differing fates. As in the *Odyssey*, the four winds fight with each other and both heroes' legs grow weak and strengths fade. However, in pointed contrast to Odysseus, Leander's prayer to the god is not answered and he is allowed to drown.

HELEN MORALES

Hero plays Nausicaa to Leander's Odysseus. Leander's address to her (ll. 135–9) is a strong evocation of Odysseus' supplication of Nausicaa (*Odyssey* 6.150–75):

'Dear Cypris next after Cypris, Athena next after Athena –
For I will not call you equal of women who walk the earth,
But liken you to the daughters of Zeus, Cronus' son –
Happy is he who fathered you, happy the mother who bore you,
Most blessed the womb that brought you to birth!'

Hero is concerned to avoid *mômos*, censure: μῶμον ἀλευομένη (l. 36), like Nausicaa (*Odyssey* 6.273 ff). The writing of Hero through and as Nausicaa heightens her innocence and virginity. However, whereas Nausicaa is compared with Artemis and addressed like Artemis (*Odyssey* 6.102 ff, 149 ff), Hero is compared with Aphrodite and addressed as Aphrodite (ll. 33, 67). The cumulation of allusions to and similarities between Nausicaa and Hero throw this crucial difference into stark relief. Nausicaa is an Artemis, a virgin goddess, but Hero is allotted Aphrodite as her simile, a contrast which pointedly suggests Hero's womanly sexuality. Moreover, following the assignation of Hero as a 'new Cypris', is an assertion of her desirability:

And she entered the tender hearts of the youths, nor was there any
Man who was not in a rage to possess Hero as a bed-mate.

δύσατο δ' ἠιθέων ἀπαλὰς φρένας, οὐδέ τις ἀνδρῶν
ἦεν, ὃς οὐ μενέαινεν ἔχειν ὁμοδέμνιον Ἡρώ.

(ll. 69–70)

This is a purposive allusion to and elaboration on the suitors' reaction to the appearance of Penelope in the *Odyssey*: πάντες δ' ἠρήσαντο παραὶ λεχέεσσι κλιθῆναι (*Odyssey* 1.366, 18.213; cf. also lines 79–81; Hopkinson 1994: 152), a connection which further sexualises Hero and anticipates her role as 'wife' to Leander. In tracing these nuances in the presentation of Hero, I am not just saying that her characterisation is complex and makes use of several intertexts. The complexity and literary allusions serve to create a particular tension in her portrayal between chastity and sexual experience. As both Nausicaa and Penelope, she is both *parthenos* and *gunê*.

This contradictory, imbricatory dual aspect of Hero has already been established through her social position as priestess of Aphrodite whose duty it is to remain chaste. Leander points out that the two things are irreconcilable, exploiting the anomaly for his own amorous ends:

'It is not fitting a virgin attend on Aphrodite.
Cypris takes no pleasure in virgins; if you are willing
To learn the amorous laws of the goddess, and her goodly rites,
Here is our couch, our wedding.'

παρθένον οὐκ ἐπέοικεν ὑποδρήσσειν Ἀφροδίτῃ,
παρθενικαῖς οὐ Κύπρις ἰαίνεται. ἢν δ' ἐθελήσῃς
θεσμὰ θεῆς ἐρόεντα καὶ ὄργια κεδνὰ δαῆναι,
ἔστι γάμος καὶ λέκτρα.
(ll. 143–6)

He backs up this logic with exempla from myth of Heracles and Atalanta, figures who have strived not to succumb to Aphrodite and have suffered the consequences. 'Do not wake wrath in Cypris', he warns (l. 157). Commenting on Hero's position as chaste priestess of Aphrodite, Hopkinson writes:

Since no full study exists of the evidence for conditions of tenure of Greek priesthoods, it is impossible to say whether or not Hero's chastity is intended to seem unusual or unnatural. Certainly it is not unique: Pausanias speaks of a temple of Aphrodite in Sicyon which could only be entered by a γυνὴ νεωκόρος, ἧι μηκέτι θέμις παρ' ἄνδρα φοιτῆσαι and a παρθένος ἱερωσύνην ἐπέτειον ἔχουσα (2.10.4).

(Hopkinson 1994: 145–6)

In Pausanias' account, the woman may not have intercourse *after* she has been appointed, implying that it is not a prerequisite, nor even likely, that she is a virgin at the time of her appointment. The virgin attendant holds office for one year alone. Neither of these posts seems very akin to that held by Hero. However that may be, it is surely a mistake to approach Hero's status as a realistic representation with a historical referent.[14] It is a fantasy, a deliberate and titillating paradox. Insensitivity to this leads Hopkinson and most modern editors to emend at line 33. The manuscripts have, and

HELEN MORALES

Gelzer retains: ἄλλη Κύπρις ἄνασσα, σαοφροσύνῃ τε καὶ αἰδοῖ.
Hopkinson, Livrea, Kost and Orsini emend the text, following the
tradition of the Renaissance editors Aldus Manutius and Janus
Lascaris, in replacing the τε with δε. Hopkinson explains: '[This
links] the second half of the line with what precedes: "she was a
second Aphrodite in prudence and modesty". But Aphrodite, though
occasionally referred to as αἰδοίη is hardly famed for those qualities'
(Hopkinson 1994: 146–7). The same reasoning influences him to
adopt a further emendation at line 38, substituting μετ᾽ Ἀθήνην
for Ἀφροδίτην, which is deemed more suitable because Athene is
'goddess of the σαοφροσύνη and αἰδώς which govern her modest
actions and maintain her precarious virginity' (Hopkinson 1994:
147).

However, these editors miss the point that it is quite consistent
with the representation of Hero as oxymoronically chaste and
sexually active to describe her as a contradiction. 'Another Cyprian
goddess in sôphrosunê and aidôs' continues the paradox of her being
'a priestess of Aphrodite, and unschooled in love's ways' as she is
described two lines above. It is also slyly salacious, a knowing
wink to the reader that the untenability of Hero's position promises
some action. Hero is trapped not so much by 'desire and fate' (l. 307),
but by the irreconcilability of the demands imposed on her. Hero's
'lesson in identity', then, does bear out Jane Miller's proposition;
the narrative 'reduces' by 'exalting' her. It is a situation which
continues to be exploited for humour. As Braden writes: 'In some
dark joke, Hero's sexual fulfilment is accomplished only through
breaking the rules of her public role as priestess of Aphrodite'
(Braden 1978: 80). In his version of the story, Marlowe calls Hero
a 'Venus Nun', a phrase which conveys her paradoxical identity,
but which is also an Elizabethan term for whore, which relocates
the myth into the context of Elizabethan prostitution and thus
directs a different but by no means unconnected reading to that of
its source. Hero's being both virgin and love-goddess puts her in
that class of fantasy to which, with some variation, the Greek
novel heroines Callirhoe,[15] Leucippe and Chariclea belong, as does
the 'Prostitute Priestess' of Seneca's practice exercise in declamation,
Controversia 1.2 (on which see Richlin 1992: 16–18). Aphrodite's
virgin, Nausicaa Penelope, *parthenos gunê*: the fantasy on offer in
the imbricatory aspects of Hero's identity is titillatory Hero(ine)
Chic.

Socialising identities: a deranged marriage

The question which has most exercised scholars of Musaeus is that of allegory. One interpretation, promoted zealously by Thomas Gelzer, suggests that '*Hero and Leander* seems designed to demonstrate the ethical claims of a Christian Neoplatonist' (Toohey 1992: 215; Gelzer 1975: 316–22). Gelzer summarises his approach:

> [T]he three sections of the poem represent the life of a philosophical soul – Leander – according to the pattern which the Neoplatonists found in the *Phaedrus*. The first part (28–231) represents the soul's life in heaven before birth, in which it is by its original vision of its own god chosen and called to follow him in the heavenly procession; the second part (232–288) is its life on earth, where recollection effected through love leads it to exaltation and mystic union with its god; the third part (289–343) is its release from the chains of the body and the foreshadowing of its reward in the afterlife in the highest and culminating union with God.
>
> (Gelzer 1975: 319)

This would put Musaeus in the company of, among others, Proclus, Hermias of Alexandria and Prudentius. Not all have been convinced (see the review of Nachtergale 1976), least of all by the contention that it is a Christian poem, which is tenuous, given the lack of sustained Christian content, and reliant on equally contentious biographical arguments (cf. p. 43 above). It is not my project here to debate Gelzer's analysis in any detail. I remain sceptical that there is sufficient 'signposting' for the poem to have been designed as a deliberate allegory, in contrast with a work like the *Psychomachia*. However, as Robert Lamberton points out in his sensitive discussion of the issue, this by no means precludes it having been *read* as an allegory, as Procopius of Gaza appears to have done and as Philip Philagathos in the twelfth century and Ioannes Eugenikos in the fifteenth century did with Heliodorus' *Aethiopica* (cf. Dyck 1986, MacAlister 1996: 108–12, Agapitos 1998):

> Whether or not Musaeus' poem was an allegory may have been up to Musaeus' audience, not Musaeus. There are precedents in late antiquity for a popular literature playing with and hinting at secondary meanings of a theological

or theosophical nature. . . . It may not be unreasonable to view an allegorical *Hero and Leander* as a logical development, in this sense, from the later romances.

(Lamberton 1986: 160)

Gordon Braden suggests that the poem be read as a psychological allegory:

We do not need psychoanalysis to tell us what the outburst of the anonymous young man (74–83) makes explicit, that the restless activity of the *pandêmios heortê* is primarily that of frustrated, itchy sexuality. And the storm that blows out the λύχνος makes sense as a psychological allegory: a revenge upon the private vision by the very energy required to maintain its secrecy. The lovers' privacy, we would now say, becomes psychotic. Or, more simply, they just panic.

(Braden 1978: 81)

Both of these interpretations have their merits, but neither gives sufficient weight to the almost obtrusive emphasis throughout the poem on the social. In exploring the poem's concern with civic identity, I do not wish to exclude the allegorical interpretations from the polyvalent possibilities offered by this text. Indeed, if one were to follow Origen's schema for allegorical composition, that every text must be interpreted on three levels of comprehension: the superficial story level, the moral level and the elevated theological level, then this reading would correspond to his second level.

The emphasis on the social starts even from the inception of desire. Eros shoots his arrow 'into both cities together, / Kindling a youth and a maiden' (l. 19). We are introduced to Sestos and Abydos before we are told the names of Hero and Leander. They are referred to as 'Of each of their two cities each the fairest star' (l. 22), a common enough formulation (cf. Callimachus fr. 67.5 about Acontius and Cydippe) but one given extra resonance in this context. Hero, we are told, in pointed contrast to Nausicaa, lives in her ancestral tower with only a maid for company and is excluded from society:

Never did she mingle among the gatherings of women,
Nor enter the graceful dance of young girls of her years

(ll. 34–5; cf. ll. 191–2)

However, she is forced to mix with people when the time comes for the public festival (πανδήμιος ἑορτή) of Aphrodite (πανδήμιος seems to me preferable to the textual variant πασσυδίῃ, 'with all speed' or 'all together', because of the elaboration on the festival's far-reaching audience (ll. 44–50) and because of the adjective's allusion to Aphrodite's cult title, Pandemos). This is where, like a heroine from a Greek novel, she is desired by all and falls in love with Leander. Like Leucippe, it is her parents who thwart Hero's relationship with Leander:

'. . . for how could you, a vagabond,
A stranger and not to be trusted, mingle in love with me?
We cannot openly come into a righteous marriage,
For it was not my parents' will.'

(ll. 177–80)

This is reiterated a few lines later:

'I have for my neighbour the sea, by my parents' hateful will.
Neither are near me girls of my age, nor any dances
Of youths at hand.'

(ll. 190–2)

However, unlike Leucippe's parents, Hero's parents have forbidden her ever to be married. When a heroine in a Greek novel eventually marries, she does so with the support of her family and community. Hero, however, marries covertly, 'in secret union' (l. 221), with night as their bridal attendant (l. 232). They marry 'in secrecy from her parents' (l. 381) in a ceremony that is an inversion of the normal marriage ceremony:

Wedding it was, but without a dance; bedding, but hymnless.
None glorified in song Hera the union-maker,
Nor did the attendant gleam of torches flash on the bed
Nor was there any who gambolled and sprang in leaping
    dance,
Nor father nor lady-mother intoned the hymenaeal;
But laying ready the couch in the hour of consummation
Silence made fast the bed; Gloom was the bride's attendant,
And it was a marriage afar from the singing of hymenaeals.

(ll. 274–81)

HELEN MORALES

The repeated negatives at the beginnings of lines 275–8 stress that this is a wedding in negative; every detail happens contrary to established practice. Instead of the expected bridal chamber attendants or, as is common in Hellenistic literature, overseeing deities, Silence (Σιγή) and Gloom ('Ομίχλη) attend, a poignant, almost sinister substitution.

It could hardly be made more explicit that the union of Hero and Leander is not sanctioned by society. It is because of this, the narrative logic suggests; because of the couple's privileging of individual desires over family duty and social responsibility, that the couple perish, not because of any tempest. In their recent and challenging analyses of the ancient Greek novels, Kate Cooper and Judith Perkins have argued that their narratives of personal relationships are designed to be read metonymically, as social commentaries on civic relations. Perkins writes that in the Roman empire 'social identity began to be perceived or imagined through the language of personal attachment and marriage' (Perkins 1995: 66). Cooper explains:

> At a symbolic level, the craving for marriage served as a vehicle to propel a suspension and reassertion of established identity for both microcosm – the individual – and macrocosm – the city, or even the empire. At a literal level, what was also under discussion was marriage as a social institution. The peculiar power of romance to create complicity meant that an author could rely on readers to see in a tale of young lovers an allegory of the condition of the social order – and be influenced by his views of how that order should be perpetuated.
>
> (Cooper 1996: 31)

The approach of Cooper and Perkins can usefully be applied to Musaeus. The dominant reading offered by *Hero and Leander* is not a Neoplatonic Christian allegory, nor a psychological allegory, but an 'allegory of the social order'. Whereas the Greek novels (arguably, though with various and nuanced complications, especially in the case of Achilles Tatius, which Cooper's reading oversimplifies) validate marriage and social order through celebration of them, I suggest that *Hero and Leander* also validates marriage and social order by showing – and lamenting – what happens when society's rules and institutions are denied. It thus constitutes a negative paradigm to the ancient novel, but with a similar ideological stance. This neces-

64

sitates a readjustment of the position I stated earlier, namely that this approach would not exclude a Christian allegorical reading. More scrupulously, it could actively affirm such an interpretation; the polyphony of the narrative might not be so varied after all. A more phenomenological approach might argue that the auratic impact of the suicide blonde's zappy ending exceeds the moral censure in the cautionary tale. Like *Romeo and Juliet*, the sheer sentimentality of the story of Hero and Leander and its unashamed 'You and Me Versus the World' romanticism is what fascinates, and continues to fascinate, long after the moral is forgotten. Towards the beginning of the poem, the narrator addresses the reader directly and jolts the temporal setting into the present day:

> . . . but you, if you ever journey thither,
> Seek me a tower out, where once Hero of Sestos
> Stood, holding the lamp, and pointed the way for Leander;
> And seek the sea-resounding strait of ancient Abydos,
> Which still laments, I fancy, Leander's fate and love.
>
> (ll. 23–7)

The invitation to be a tourist of tragedy, to retrace the landmarks and there muse upon the events of the story (paying homage like the impassioned followers of Kurt Cobain and Michael Hutchence) evokes a nostalgia and milks it for pathos. The story's emotional impact might transcend the poem's dominant ideological imperative, but remains in tension with its conservative logic. As with its representation of Hero and with its distorted configuration of female dissent, the epyllion ultimately upholds rather than challenges traditional mores. It is no surprise that in the sixteenth and seventeenth centuries it was fashionable to publish versions of *Hero and Leander* at Italian weddings. It is the perfect narrative for that most privileged site for affirming identity, the marriage ceremony. The bride and bridegroom will, during the wedding at any rate, subordinate their individual identities to those of the society and state; unlike Hero and Leander, we rarely swim against the tide.

Notes

1 Part of this chapter was delivered as a lecture entitled 'Gendered V(o)ices in Later Greek Literature' to the Society for the Promotion of Hellenic Studies in May 1998. Thanks to Russell Shone, Pat Easterling for gracious chairing, and Nick Lowe, Richard Janko and Pat Easterling for helpful

suggestions. The written version has benefited considerably from the generous criticisms of Simon Goldhill, Richard Hunter and Helen Ward. Heartfelt thanks to them, to Richard Miles for being a patient and encouraging editor, to Rob Bown for sharing his expertise in German, to Lucy Cresswell and Helen Ward for many discussions about gender and identity (always with wit and intellectual rigour) and to Simon and Shoshana Goldhill for much support during the summer in which this chapter was written, the very least of which was teaching me how to swim.

2 Two of Procopius' letters address Musaeus (147 and 165), one of which thanks him for a book which Procopius has read and adapted (165. Text ed. by Garzya and Loenertz 1963).

3 Translation by Peter Green in the Penguin *Ovid: The Erotic Poems*.

4 Kost 1971, Livrea 1982, Hopkinson 1994 in addition to Orsini 1968 and Gelzer 1975. I have used Gelzer's edition with Whitman's translation (with a few alterations) throughout. The lexicon of Bo (1966) has also proved useful.

5 The translation is Maud Gleason's (Gleason 1995: 98). The same story is told in Clement, *Stromata* 4.522C. The Babylonian Talmud is more succinct: 'A woman's voice is nakedness' (Berachot 24A). On this and the eroticisation of the female mouth in Rabbinic Judaism (200–600 CE), see Eilberg-Schwartz (1995).

6 As Richard Hunter points out to me, this is all the more significant and pervasive in inflected languages, such as Greek. Of course, ignoring or denying that there are differences between male and female speech can also be a way of denying gender inequality. Few, however, do this as dogmatically as Neil Lyndon. In his best-selling diatribe *No More Sex War*, he discusses a review of Deborah Tannen's book on gender and speech called *You Just Don't Understand: Men and Women in Conversation* by Mary Beard in the *London Review of Books*, 15 August 1991. Beard summarises Tannen's argument as follows:

> Men, she argues, use conversation as a means of establishing status; they use it to exhibit their own knowledge and skill – holding stage through verbal performance such as storytelling, joking, or imparting information. Women, by contrast, use talk as a means of establishing intimacy, connection and rapport; they use it not as a mechanism for domination, but as part of a 'negotiation for closeness', in which people try to seek and give confirmation and to reach consensus. If this is right, it can be no surprise that women working in male institutions feel a sense of not belonging: they can never quite be one of the lads, because in the last resort they do not speak the lads' language.

This is an argument that Lyndon refutes, insisting that language is un-gendered and neutral. He dismisses the idea as 'one of the most pustulant lines of piss in the crock of cant that is modern feminism' (Lyndon 1992: 46 and 55). No lads' language, here, then.

7 This whole scene bears comparison with Theocritus *Idyll* 2 and its relation to Homer, on which see Goldhill 1991: 261–72.

8 The translation is Jack Winkler's in Reardon 1989.

9 On the plot, historical background, authorship and discussion of the four papyrus fragments see Stephens and Winkler 1995: 23–31; Rattenbury 1933: 212–19; Perry 1967: 153. I use Stephens and Winkler's text and translation.

10 Stephens and Winkler 1995: 23.

11 These ideas were so pernicious that the sexologist Havelock Ellis argues that voice pitch and the size of the larynx are directly related to sexual activity. He writes:

> while a bass [singer] need not fear any kind of sexual or other excess so far as his voice is concerned, a tenor must be extremely careful and temperate. Among prostitutes, it may be added, the voice and the larynx often tend to take a masculine direction. This has been investigated at Genoa by Masini, who finds that among 50 prostitutes 29 showed in a high degree the deep masculine voice, while the larynx was large and the vocal cords represented that of a man; only 6 out of the 50 showed a normal larynx; while of 20 honest women only 2 showed the ample masculine larynx.
>
> (Ellis 1934: 97; cf. Baron 1986: 73)

Harvey 1992: 95 discusses a 1635 tract on midwifery in which it is stated that the length of the umbilical remaining attached to the child after the cord had been severed was thought to be related to the size both of sexual organs and of the tongue, and it was therefore deemed necessary to cut a girl's umbilical cord much shorter than a boy's.

12 The 'Cologne fragment' of Archilochus (fr. 196W2) is a good illustration of the ambiguity of male discourse. In the fragment, the girl who has stimulated the desire of the narrator attempts to divert his interest away from herself and towards another, more experienced and actively desirous woman, Neoboule. He, however, rejects the suggestion with scathing remarks about Neoboule's promiscuity. Despite the girl's professed reluctance, the couple end up indulging in what we would call 'heavy petting' (Archilochus 478.9–53 in Page 1974).

13 The bibliography for this subject is huge. Brown (1988) and Clark (1996) are both stimulating and have further bibliography.

14 There is scant evidence in Fehrle (1966) who does not mention Musaeus. A fragment of an Orphic hymn (frag. 101 Abel) appears to refer to Aphrodite as παρθένος αἰδοίη, which Fehrle wonders might be brought about by 'syncretism' (Fehrle 1966: 205–6).

15 A similar textual crux occurs at *Chaereas and Callirhoe* 1.2 when Callirhoe is described as a *parthenos* who has 'the beauty of Aphrodite *parthenos*', τὸ κάλλος . . . Ἀφροδίτης παρθένου, but some editors delete παρθένου, presumably on similar grounds, e.g. Hercher 1859.

Bibliography

Agapitos, P.A. (1998) 'Narrative, rhetoric, and "drama" rediscovered: scholars and poets in Byzantium interpret Heliodorus' in R.L. Hunter (ed.) *Studies in Heliodorus*. Cambridge Philological Society Supplementary volume no. 21: 125–56.

Baron, D. (1986) *Grammar and Gender*. New Haven and London.
Bennington, G. (1985) *Sententiousness and the Novel. Laying down the Law in Eighteenth-Century French Fiction*. Cambridge.
Blakeney, E.H. (1934) *Musaeus, Hero and Leander*. Oxford.
Bo, D. (1966) *Musaei Lexicon*. Hildesheim.
Braden, G. (1978) *The Classics and English Renaissance Poetry*. New Haven, esp. 55–153.
Brown, P. (1988) *The Body and Society: Men, Women, and Sexual Renunciation in Early Christianity*. New York.
Clark, G. (1996) '"The Bright Frontier of Friendship": Augustine and the Christian Body as Frontier' in R.W. Mathisen and H.S. Sivan (eds) *Shifting Frontiers in Late Antiquity*. Aldershot: 217–41.
Cooper, K. (1996) *The Virgin and the Bride. Idealized Womanhood in Late Antiquity*. Cambridge, Mass.
Dunn, L.C. and Nancy A. Jones (1997) *Embodied Voices*.
Dyck, A.R. (1986) Michael Psellus. *The Essays on Euripides and George of Pisidia and on Heliodorus and Achilles Tatius*. Vienna.
Eilberg-Schwartz, H. (1995) 'The Nakedness of a Woman's Voice, the Pleasure in a Man's Mouth. An Oral History of Ancient Judaism' in H. Eilberg-Schwartz and W. Doniger (eds) *Off With Her Head! The Denial of Women's Identity in Myth, Religion, and Culture*. Berkeley and Los Angeles.
Ellis, H. (1934) *Man and Woman: a Study in Secondary and Tertiary Sexual Characteristics*. London.
Farber, H. (1961) *Hero und Leander*. Munich.
Fehrle, E. (1966) *Die kultische Keuschheit im Altertum*. Giessen.
Garzya, A. and R.-L. Loenertz (eds) (1963) *Procopii Gazaei Epistolae et Declamationes* (Studia Patristica et Byzantina). Buch-Kunsterlag Ettal.
Geanakoplos, J. (1978) *Greek Scholars in Venice*. Cambridge, Mass.
Gelzer, T. (1967 and 1968) 'Bermerkungen zur Sprache und Stil des Epikers Musaios', *Museum Helveticum* 24: 129–48 and 25: 11–47.
—— (1975) *Musaeus. Hero and Leander*. Trans. C.H. Whitman, with C.A. Trypanis (ed.) *Callimachus* in the Loeb Classical Library, Cambridge, Mass.
Gleason, M.W. (1995) *Making Men. Sophists and their Self-Representation in Ancient Rome*. Princeton.
Goldhill, S. (1991) *The Poet's Voice. Essays on Poetics and Greek Literature*. Cambridge.
Grant, M. (1998) *From Rome to Byzantium. The Fifth Century AD*. Routledge.
Hall, E. (1993) 'Drowning by Nomes: the Greeks, Swimming and Timotheus' "Persians"' in H.A. Khan (ed.) Nottingham Classical Literature Series 2: 44–80.
Hanson, A. and D. Armstrong (1986) 'The Virgin's Neck: Aeschylus' Agamemnon 245 and Other Texts', *British Institute of Classical Studies* 33: 97–100.
Harvey, E.D. (1992) *Ventriloquised Voices. Feminist Theory and English Renaissance Texts*. London.
Heaney, S. (1994) *Extending the Alphabet: On Christopher Marlowe's 'Hero and Leander'*. The Pratt Lecture, 1993. Department of English, Memorial University of Newfoundland.
Hercher, R. (1859) *Erotici Scriptores Graeci*. Vol. 2. Teubner, Leipzig.

Hoar, N. (1992) 'Genderlect, Powerlect and Politeness' in L.A.M. Perry, L.H. Turner and H.M. Sterk (eds) *Constructing and Reconstructing Gender: the Links among Communication, Language and Gender*. New York: 69–77.

Hopkinson, N. (1994) *Greek Poetry of the Imperial Period. An Anthology*. Cambridge.

Hunter, R.L. (1989) *Apollonius of Rhodes. Argonautica* Book Three. Cambridge.

Kost, K. (1971) *Musaios. Hero und Leander*. Bonn.

Lamberton, R. (1986) *Homer the Theologian. Neoplatonist Allegorical Reading and the Growth of the Epic Tradition*. Berkeley.

Lauretis, T. de (1987) *Technologies of Gender*. Basingstoke.

Livrea, E. with P. Eleuteri (1982) *Musaeus. Hero et Leander* Teubner, Leipzig.

Lyndon, N. (1992) *No More Sex War: the Failures of Feminism*. London.

MacAlister, S. (1996) *Dreams and Suicides. The Greek Novel from Antiquity to the Byzantine Empire*. Routledge.

Malcovati, E. (1962) 'Rileggendo Museo', *Athenaeum* 40: 368–72.

Miller, J. (1990) *Seductions: Studies in Reading and Culture*. London.

Morales, H.L. (1997) A Scopophilai's Paradise: Vision and Narrative in Achilles. PhD thesis. Cambridge.

Nachtergale, G. (1976) Review of Gelzer's edition in *L'Antiquité Classique* 45: 252–4.

Orsini, P. (1968) *Musée. Héro et Léandre*. Budé, Paris.

Page, D.L. (ed.) (1974) *Supplementum Lyricis Graecis*. Oxford.

Perkins, J. (1995) *The Suffering Self. Pain and Narrative Representation in the Early Christian Era*. London.

Perry, B.E. (1967) *The Ancient Romances: A Literary-Historical Account of their Origins*. Berkeley.

Rattenbury, R.M. (1933) 'Romance: Traces of Lost Greek Novels' in J.U. Powell (ed.) *New Chapters in the History of Greek Literature*. Vol. 3. Oxford.

Reardon, B.P. (ed.) (1989) *Collected Ancient Greek Novels*. Berkeley and Los Angeles.

Richlin, A. (1992) *The Garden of Priapus: Sexuality and Aggression in Roman Humor*. New York.

—— (1997) 'Towards a History of Body History' in M. Golden and P. Toohey (eds) *Inventing Ancient Culture: Historicism, Periodization and the Ancient World*. London: 16–35.

Schoenberger, O. (1978) 'Zum Aufbau von Musaios' Her und Leander', *Rheinisches Museum* 121: 255–9.

Schwabe, L. (1876) *De Musaeo Nonni Imitatore Liber*. Tübingen.

Sissa, G. (1990) *Greek Virginity*. Trans. A. Goldhammer. Cambridge, Mass.

Snare, G. (1989) *The Mystification of George Chapman*. Durham, NC and London.

Spender, D. (1980) *Man-made Language*. London.

Stephens, S.A. and Winkler, J.J. (eds) (1995) *Ancient Greek Novels: The Fragments*. Princeton.

Toohey, P. (1992) *Reading Epic. An Introduction to Ancient Narratives*. London.

4

PRUDENTIUS' *PSYCHOMACHIA*

The Christian arena and the politics of display

Paula James

Introduction

Prudentius' *Psychomachia* is part of an important corpus of Christian writings produced by an author well versed in classical literature. The poet who straddles the fourth and fifth centuries CE is generally recognised as a polemical proselytiser for the 'official religion' and one who broke new ground in appropriating classical genres for Christian subject-matter. His *Peristephanon* is a case in point: 'Prudentius reclaimed classical poetic discourse for the martyrs' crowns.'[1] The following contribution to the debate on the *Psychomachia* has a similar underlying premise, but rather than travelling on the well trodden paths of Prudentius' literary precedents, the emphasis will be upon his success in reconstructing the pagan locale of spectacle, in particular the arena as a place of public punishment.

Prudentius is no longer the widely read poet of the medieval and Renaissance periods. As for the *Psychomachia*, this became a poem critics loved to hate; it enjoyed a focus of attention as early allegory, mainly due to C.S. Lewis's allusion to it in *The Allegory of Love* (1936), but this influential scholar did not view it as satisfying or successful, on ethical or aesthetical grounds. Although the poem's preface is a celebration of biblical heroes, heroines and significant Old Testament battles, the main body of the text, about 900 lines of dactylic hexameter, depicts the struggle, in graphic combat to the death, between Christian Virtues and pagan Vices. It is this bloodthirsty centre piece that has caused discomfort; the personifications of good qualities as violent female warriors delivering a series of

70

body blows to the Vices, also portrayed in Amazonian mould. The ecstatic energy of the Christian 'soldiers' produces powerful effects but the conception itself has puzzled the critics and commentators on the poem.

Prudentius' motives and literary techniques continue to tease the commentators, who have suggested a number of both simple and sophisticated explanations for the choice of an anonymous arena as a place of inner religious struggle. Calling upon Christ as his 'muse' of inspiration, to tell it to the poet as it really is, Prudentius proceeds to bring the constant attack upon the Soul out in the open:

> prima petit campum dubia sub sorte duelli
> pugnatura Fides, agresti turbida cultu,
> nuda umeros, intonsa comas exerta lacertos;
> namque repentinus laudis calor ad nova fervens
> proelia nec telis meminit nec tegmine cingi,
> pectore sed fidens valido membrisque retectis
> provocat insani frangenda pericula belli.
> ecce lacessentem conlatis viribus audet
> prima ferire Fidem Veterum Cultura Deorum.
>
> *Psychomachia* (21–9)

Faith first takes the field to face the doubtful chances of battle, her rough dress disordered, her shoulders bare, her hair untrimmed, her arms exposed; for the sudden glow of ambition, burning to enter fresh contests, takes no thought to gird on arms or armour, but trusting to a stout heart and unprotected limbs challenges the hazards of furious warfare, meaning to break them down. Lo, first the Worship-of-the-Old-Gods ventures to match her strength against Faith's challenge and strike at her.[2]

It seems that Faith is entering a battle arena, woefully ill-equipped to face the enemy. The logic is clear as she is by her nature unassailable, but in Prudentius she is actively seeking confrontation, an unexpected move. She initiates the fight in the familiar guise of a Christian martyr with no chance against a properly armoured opponent. This is the first indication that the Virtues are going to fight back and turn the tables in a locality traditionally associated with their physical defeat and spiritual victory. This is precisely the problem Prudentius presents to later readers. The Christian Virtues viciously defeat the pagan Vices but where do they stand on the moral high ground?

The Christian conundrum

The ambivalences of pagan 'places' appropriated by Christian congregations will emerge during the discussion. I shall be arguing that Prudentius presents his Soul Battle poem as a public display, an entertaining spectacle for those of the faith who were regularly urged to abstain from the Colosseum in Rome and from the arenas in the provinces. In this study of the *Psychomachia* the intention is to redraw the boundaries of the discussion and enhance appreciation of the poem as a barometer of a broader cultural discourse. The phrase *homo spectator*[3] has taken its place alongside *homo necans* and *homo ludens*. The importance of spectacle and the theatricalisation of real life or at least the perception of actual events as performance forms an essential background to this subject. Prudentius' poem will be viewed as a theatre of punishment produced for the delight and edification of a Christian audience.

The first question to explore is the correspondence between the pagan and Christian *mentalité* as far as punishment and performance are concerned. Love of enemies is not absent from the agenda of early Christianity; it had already made an appearance in Stoic philosophy.[4] However, demonic assailants of the true religion were in a different category and Christianity was no stranger to concepts of righteous vengeance. This point is relevant to my approach to Prudentius because the richly allusive literary texture of the poem enhances the energetic visualisation of public punishment meted out to the criminal Vices. A more controversial concept of cross-fertilisation relates to the pleasure and leisure of diverse social strata. Was Prudentius satisfying a general need for spectacle which crossed over social, intellectual and religious boundaries? No matter that the language of the *Psychomachia* is pitched at the level of the sophisticated reader, it is simultaneously appealing to the enjoyment of blood, guts and gore, to the thrill of viewing the dissection of vile bodies. It is even possible to detect elements of the 'fatal charade' in the literary dressing up of Luxuria, a crucial moment in the battle, when a dangerous and deceptive opponent is revealed and repulsed by the doubly personified Sobrietas.[5]

The *Psychomachia* creates a 'generic' arena in which Prudentius produces a display worthy of the Colosseum with his battles between the Vices and Virtues. The ambience of the *munera* has not escaped the attention of Prudentius' commentators but few have pursued this line of enquiry. Resonances of the arena have been noted and some interesting anomalies have been pointed out by Malamud in regard to martyrdom imagery incongruously evoked for evil personalities both in Claudian and Prudentius.[6] However, the idea of the *Psychomachia* as an ideological reconstruction of the amphitheatre has not been fully exploited. The exuberant depiction of bloodthirsty battles in a confined space conjures up the visual experience of the arena. In providing a graphic literary spectacle for his readers, Prudentius resignifies the nature and function of the shows within the Christian context.

This approach inevitably raises the 'message' of the *munera* in social, emotional and political terms. It is clearly necessary to construct a cultural framework for the phenomenon of the games and there is certainly a consensus amongst the experts that the central function of the arena was to serve as a designated time and space for judicial punishment. Those who wish to bend the stick in this direction argue that for the viewing public this was a formal occasion when *Romanitas* was reaffirmed.[7] Consequently, they may play down the aspects of enjoyment and entertainment which the more judgemental earlier scholars have tended to emphasise with appropriate protestations of horror and revulsion. However, the ancient commentators are by no means a united voice in this respect. As Gunderson notes, 'the disgust expressed in literature for partisans of the games is especially strong when a self-consciously refined member of the elite, like Messala, sees members of his own class betraying his idealized conception of nobility' (1996, p. 114).

Locating the cultural space

The *Psychomachia* is tapping into the shared space of the spectacle. The poem creates a safe intellectual locality in which a hierarchy of reception mimics the hierarchy of seating at the amphitheatre; at the same time social cohesion is confirmed by the communal viewing of evil threats overthrown.[8] In her discussion of where the elite might meet the masses in a *naïveté commune*, Palmer cites the popularity of the shows (animal shows in particular) and the glaringly pictorial realism which invaded the elevated style in literature.[9] For instance, in Ammianus Marcellinus there is a preoccupation with lurid and realistic detail depicting death and violence – with an eye on the theatricality of the event. The evidence is, however, that the language of spectacle permeated literary genres far earlier and that it became highly explicit in the reign of Nero. Hence, Bartsch makes the point that

> from his [Nero's] time on, interest in the confusion of frames inherent in the linking of fabula (myth) and poena (punishment) not only found expression in the production and popularity of fatal charades in the amphitheatre, but also resurfaced as literary descriptions of real deaths during theatrical performances and deaths somehow theatricalised in the offstage world of the Empire.[10]

She goes on to cite passages from Tacitus, the deaths of Otho and Vitellius as episodes of *les morts mises en scene* in 69 CE, a year of living dangerously and dying theatrically.

The power of spectacle permeates the cultural output of the Roman world. Ovid in his *Metamorphoses* portrays the terrible punishments of Actaeon and Orpheus in this way, and explicitly and comically, in his mini epic of Book 4, turns Perseus' tussle with the sea monster into a piece of theatre. People enjoyed displays of fighting and dying. Our post-classical rationalisation of the games as fulfilling an important function 'in the moralization and maintenance of Roman social roles and hierarchical relations' (Gunderson 1996, p. 115) is undoubtedly valid, but it is not a conclusion explicitly articulated in the ancient writers. Rather, it is our way of negotiating the contradictory perspectives of the contemporary literature, which alternates between anxiety at the highly charged emotional atmosphere of the arena, and admiration and approbation of gladiatorial display which demonstrated exemplary courage and fighting skills, in other words, Roman military *virtus* in full view of the Roman citizens.[11]

Traditionally, the amphitheatre had been a place where authority, law and order, and therefore Roman rule and the unassailability of the empire, was constantly restated. The arena acted as a place of empowerment for its onlookers; it stirred its spectators in a variety of ways and not least to feel confident in the community's violent and unequivocal overthrow of any perceived threats. If we are right to suppose that the programme of the arena with its public punishment, encompassing appropriate retribution, was a major means of sustaining community identity, then playing out the battle for the Christian soul publicly and on a grand scale, as spectacle, was much more than compensating the faithful for 'missing the fun' of the games.

Ambivalent associations

It has to be remembered that for the Christian polemicist the most unpalatable aspect of the shows was the constant presence of pagan rituals and ceremonies, the religious context in which all this suffering and death took place. The corruption of the soul was compounded by the idolatrous ceremony of the displays. Both Tertullian and Prudentius point out that this was a time of celebration of pagan deities, that the arena resonated with the rites and rituals of pagan worship and the spiritual as well as the emotional atmosphere was utterly unwholesome.[12] Prudentius attacks the implicit sacrifices to the king of the dead as the most dangerous aspect of the 'games', for the chthonic deities took real shape as demons in the Christian psyche. This was heathen worship with a sacral base. The corpses were removed by a figure representing the god Mercury who, as psychopompus waiting in the wings, took the dead on a symbolic journey to Hades. For the Christian writers this touch of awe and religiosity in the proceedings accentuated their Satanic flavour.[13] In summary, the arena was to be avoided because of its libidinous levels of excitement and its dangerous religious ambiences.

Even though the cultured and educated Christian thinker might share the worries of the pagan philosophers about the emotional 'high' of the amphitheatre, Tertullian, writing in the second century CE, was quite capable of celebrating the punishment of pagan persecutors using the model of the arena and the metaphor of spectacle. Tertullian's vision of Judgement Day (at the close of his *De Spectaculis*) as retribution and revenge in performance is succinctly summed up by Wiedemann as 'the Second Coming in terms of a spectacle: the mass execution of traitors, i.e. pagans, in a cosmic arena under the presidency of Christ'.[14] It is quite possible that this brief vision inspired Prudentius to create the powerful imagery of the soul as both a beleaguered battleground and a triumphal location where ultimately the Virtues would conquer and dispatch the Vices in the style of the arena executions. At face value, Tertullian's idea of vengeance as an 'entertainment' in the style of the very pagan *munera* he has so roundly condemned reads rather strangely.[15] However, pagans and Christians alike tended to accept the salutory dimension to public punishment. Nor was there anything wrong with the open manifestation of political coercion, provided the spectators and perpetrators were united 'on the side of the angels' in their exercise of power.

Prudentius, then, as the-fourth century literary heir to Tertullian's metaphor of Judgement Day as an arena, gives a comprehensive and creative realisation to the legitimate destruction of the dissenting demons of the soul, and all under the presidency of Christ. Christianity is *editor* and demonstrates its status and power with an entertaining show. This is the cultural framework I am suggesting for the poem, one which confronts the problem of bloodthirsty Virtues reaffirming the Christian victory in an unequivocal triumphalism. It is this aspect of Prudentius' *Psychomachia* that has given rise to discomfort among Christian critics.[16] More sympathetic and sophisticated treatments of his bizarre cast of Virtues and Vices have emanated from Smith, Haworth, Nugent and Malamud in recent years,[17] but every commentator feels that there are tensions to be addressed in the poet's realisation of the spiritual personnel.[18]

The bad and the beautiful

The poem's influential legacy to the medieval allegory is not the concern of this discussion but it is worth noting that the challenge of Prudentius' 'personifications' continues to tease a range of finely tuned minds.[19] Smith's explanation of Christian Virtues who borrow titles from pagan deities and cult *numina*, who crow over defeated enemies in terms purloined from pagan epic, is that Prudentius is experimenting in a parodic undercutting of Virgil, debunking by allusion rather than reprising with incense. Smith argues that Virgil's status as a literary icon is hardly being celebrated by the technique of literary *sparagmos*. In Prudentius' poem, pagan culture is being excised or perhaps exorcised along with the pagan Vices who appear in the narrative.[20] Smith's contention that, in the hands of Prudentius, the Virgilian clusters or centos lose all the original thematic unity they possessed in the *Aeneid*, that the allusions are frequently inverted or incongruous, leads him to conclude that the content of the pagan epic is being undermined by the dismantling of its form.

Nugent prefers to talk in terms of the appropriation of Virgil and the survival of the pagan poet's conceptual power, even when the means of its expression have been fragmented and integrated into the text of a Christian polemic;[21] Nugent and Malamud concentrate on aspects of interchangeability within the literary texture of the *Psychomachia*. Although sworn enemies, the Virtues and the Vices cross boundaries even through their war of words; linguistic as well as imagistic fluidity pervades the work. They suggest that Prudentius himself was aware of the dangers of 'becoming one's enemy', conveying the message, albeit subliminally, that the Christian soul has to be vigilant against pernicious interaction and infection in its close confrontation with the demons of the Soul. These approaches illustrate underlying ambivalences within Prudentius' poetic structure and within the methodology he has chosen for an uplifting ethical exegesis.[22]

The unequivocal and merciless killing of the Vices by the vengeful Virtues can be negotiated by modern readers if they are prepared to engage with the uncompromising response to deviants and criminals (real and perceived) that characterised the judicial process of the Roman arena. The battles described by Prudentius are in part reruns of epic scenes. They start out as paired combats typical of gladiator contests but they turn out to be largely ill-matched fighters. The Vices are initially so summarily dispatched that one thinks of the gratuitous maiming and executions that so disappointed and disturbed Seneca at the matinee performance.[23] However, just as the parade and disposal of the enemies of Rome reassured the citizens at the games and proved the unassailable position of the emperor and the empire, the Christian could take comfort in the spectacle of the hostile Vices thoroughly defeated and danger removed.

The cachet of suffering

For Christian hegemony to ring true, for a real sense of empowerment to be conveyed to the reader/spectator, there is another vital way in which the Roman amphitheatre would need radical resignifying in the Christian context. By Prudentius' time the history of the martyrs was bound up with the status of suffering rather than the solidarity of spectating. The persecutions and showy punishments constituted a public record of Christian faith, resilience and resurrection, so the discourse of Christianity had already capitalised upon the arena as a place where the condemned could show strength as victims and expose Roman hegemony as fragile, even superficial, at a time when it was celebrating its total control. Whatever qualms Tertullian had about witnessing the punishment of the innocent, Christian and non-Christian, the arena was subsequently portrayed as the place for the display of Christian virtues in the period of persecution. The figures of the faithful fill the pages of such works as *The Acts of the Martyrs* and they are the subject of Prudentius' *Peristephanon*. It is the victims' almost ecstatic delight in pain, the ability to withstand, even be strengthened spiritually by, the breaking of their bodies that graphically characterises the descriptions of the tortures inflicted upon them.[24]

It is significant that the provincial governors began to feel distinctly uneasy about putting on public torments for these 'superhumanly' constructed sufferers – or so the evidence suggests.[25] It is also important to remember that this era of extreme suffering borne by confessed Christians was represented by later writers as an affirmation of the power of the Almighty and a celebration of the strength of his followers. Clearly the spectacle of suffering, even that which at the time had taken place with a minimum number of witnesses, is being legitimised after the event. Christian readers are encouraged to marvel at the limits of endurance the heroes and heroines of their religion were able constantly to extend. Famous deaths, i.e. punishments, which were traditionally enacted in public view are in Christian literature combined with the scenes of suffering which had been private trials of faith. All such spectacles of suffering are joyous to behold, not because deviants are dispatched but because the children of God empower the congregation who witness their courageous transition to immortality.[26]

I am labouring these points because the *Psychomachia* also displays Christian virtues, not just in an apparently abstract form, but also in the guise of well-known biblical figures who were seen as embodying these virtues. However, Prudentius presents the reader/spectator with punitive viragos who oppose pagan Vices in a far more active way. Only Patientia deliberately frustrates and destroys her potential and proclaimed persecutor by doing nothing. Generally in the *Psychomachia* the Christian fight is won by winning, not by losing! These Virtues are liberated from the location of the Christian body and then given the corporeal form of fighters. Suddenly the arena and its death-dealing displays are acceptable spectator sport. If the Vices confusingly come across as martyrs because they are the ones hacked and mutilated, then the pathetic ease with which most of them are annihilated rapidly removes any temporary martyrs' crowns they might seem to be claiming by reason of the role reversal.

The challenge of the arena was not only the religious connotations of the location, its pagan ritualistic resonances, but the fact that the empowerment of the place for Christians emanated from their persecution as spectacle, rather than the sight of themselves as persecutors. For Malamud and Nugent the blurred distinctions between Virtues and Vices come with the territory, a shifting moral high ground.

Haworth suggests that the Virtues parody cult deities in the enemy pantheon and that all the identities are thrown into the melting pot as a consequence. Malamud believes that the Vices can be portrayed as martyrs if Virtues take on the *personae* of persecutors and disturb their personal equilibrium by displaying an unattractive triumphalism.[27] However, Prudentius would surely not have seen his rerouting of the arena spectacle as a risk-taking venture. The message was intended to be unequivocal. The Vices were condemned criminals and really did deserve to die.[28]

On with the show

Prudentius' preface and finale are crucial to his resignification of the spectacle which occupies the main body of the work. The introduction deals with an external battle and heralds Abraham as the faithful patriarch able to pursue and destroy the capturers of Lot. The importance of keeping inner faith is illustrated by the miracle of Sarah's fertility and the promise of an heir. This retelling of a famous story from Genesis provides an explicitly Christian border to the single-combat scenes which are to follow. The grand finale, after the fighting, is the construction of a temple to Sapientia. The discredited pagan rituals give way to the proper Christian ceremony of celebration. These are the fighting heroes of the prevailing religion. Prudentius' Christian audience were, in the context of his poem, converted into legitimate spectators of right and proper punishments, so it seems only fair that the champion Virtues know how to entertain.

Compare the condemnation by Prudentius of the sacrifices to Dis in the arena with the legitimate spectator sport offered by the sacrifice of the guilty Vices; first, the *Contra Symmachum*:

> respice terrifici scelerata sacraria Ditis
> cui cadit infausta fusus gladiator harena,
> heu, male lustratae Phlegethontia victima Romae!
> nam quid vesani sibi vult ars inpia ludi?
> quid mortes iuvenum? quid sanguine pasta voluptas?
> quid pulvis caveae semper funebris, et illa
> amphitheatralis spectacula tristia pompae?
> *Con. Symm.* 1.379–85

Reflect upon the criminal sacrifices to terrifying Dis. The luckless gladiator is dispatched and falls on the sand for the god's sake. Piteous, he is the ill-judged offering to Phlegethon so that Rome may be cleansed! For what is the justification for this irreligious skill being displayed in a senseless entertainment? What's the point of young men dying, of pleasure feasting on blood, of the dust of death ever enveloping the arena, and those fearful spectacles, the procession put on in the amphitheatre?

However, the spectacle of Faith triumphing over the worship of the pagan gods is a different matter:

illa hostile caput phalerataque tempora vittis
altior insurgens labefactat, et ora cruore
de pecudum satiata solo adplicat et pede calcat
elisos in morte oculos, animamque malignam
fracta intercepti commercia gutturis artant.
difficilemque obitum suspiria longa fatigant
exultat victrix legio, quam mille coactam
martyribus regina Fides animarat in hostem.

Psychomachia (30–7)

But she, rising higher, smites her foe's head down, with its fillet-decked brows, lays in the dust that mouth that was sated with the blood of beasts, and tramples the eyes under foot, squeezing them out in death. The throat is choked and the scant breath confined by the stopping of its passage, and long gasps make a hard and agonising death. Leaps for joy the conquering host which Faith, their queen, had assembled from a thousand martyrs and emboldened to face the foe.

The reduction of the Vices to the status of sufferers is all part of the process, once the table-turning commences. Prudentius' Christian viragos realise the fantasies of female martyrs, such as St Perpetua, who dreamed they were victorious gladiators defeating demons, even Satan himself, in public view of the emperor and people. The excitement of watching females fight is a separate psychological issue,[29] but there is a strong element of novelty in the display produced by Prudentius simply because the Virtues, as Nugent has pointed out, become viragos. Vices and Virtues are paired and have stylised entries, arriving on the 'battlefield' as if signalled to do so. All the elements of gladiator combats are here, especially when

victorious Virtues utter the jubilant cry *'hoc habet'*, the battle between
Lust and Chastity: line 54:

> tunc exarmatae iugulum meretricis adacto
> transfigit gladio; calidos vomit illa vapores
> sanguine concretos caenoso; spiritus inde
> sordidus exhalans vicinas polluit auras.
> 'hoc habet', exclamat victrix regina, 'supremus
> hic tibi finis erit. semper prostrata iacebis,
> nec iam mortiferas audebis spargere flammas
> in famulos famulasve Dei, quibus intima casti
> vena animi sola fervet de lampade Christi.'
>   The death of Sodomita Libido l. (49–57)

> Then with a sword thrust she [Chastity] pierces the dis-
> armed harlot's throat, and she spews out hot fumes with
> clots of foul blood, and the unclean breath defiles the air
> nearby. 'A hit!' cries the triumphant princess. 'This shall
> be thy last end; forever, shall thou lie prostrate, no longer
> shalt thou dare to cast thy deadly flames against God's man-
> servants or his maidservants; the inmost fibre of their pure
> hearts is kindled only from the torch of Christ.'

The manner of the defeat of the Vices becomes increasingly bizarre.
The Virtues, like the martyrs, are capable of provoking the
uncontrollable rage of their previous persecutors. Roberts in his
critique of Prudentius' *Peristephanon* conducts a survey of suffering
to illustrate the coherence of the programme Prudentius' poetry presents. The poet of the *Peristephanon* emphasises the spiritual strengths
brought into play by the martyrs in the face of Saevitia, Ira and even
Blanditiae, for the torturers' techniques did not exclude flattery and
temptation; there was a regular mix of savagery and cajoling deception in the effort to conquer the Christian soul. The mythologisation
of martyrdom paints a picture of resilient faith continuing to speak
in spite of all the torturers' efforts to silence their victims, to
constrain and physically dismember the martyrs. It is ironically
the torturer who is depicted as contorted with anger and frustration
while the tortured remain serene and spiritually whole.[30] To a certain
extent these exchanges, which are the stuff of the martyrdom narratives, are reprised on the battlefield of the Soul.

In the *Psychomachia* Ira self-destructs once she realises that none of
her weapons can move or damage Patientia. Ira has addressed

Patientia in the words of a persecutor and taunted the Virtue with the
fact that she must suffer her wounds in silence, but it is her own low
frustration tolerance that is her downfall. The scene relives the tradition of martyr narrative, but this time the virtues in their bodily
form survive intact:

> quam super adsistens Patientia, 'vicimus,' inquit,
> 'exultans Vitium solita virtute, sine ullo
> sanguinis ac vitae discrimine; lex habet istud
> nostra genus belli, furias omnemque malorum
> militiam et rabidas tolerando extinguere vires
> ipsa sibi est hostis vesania seque furendo
> interimit moriturque suis Ira ignea telis.'

Psychomachia (154–61)

Standing over her, Long Suffering cries: 'We have overcome
a proud Vice with our wonted virtue, with no danger to
blood or life. This is the kind of warfare that is our rule,
to wipe out the fiends of passion and all their armies of
evils and their savage strength by bearing their attack.
Fury is its own enemy; fiery Wrath in her frenzy slays herself
and dies by her own weapons.'

Luxuria: spicing up the spectacle

Clearly Prudentius believes that the Christian 'spectator' deserves a
programme as varied and miraculous as his pagan counterpart.
After the short sharp shock treatment meted out to Ira, Libido and
Superbia, Luxuria arrives armed with a novel fighting strategy and
representing the first real threat from the opposing side. Superbia's
speech was a rhetorical *tour de force* but she was dispatched without
difficulty. The power of words is undermined by her destruction,
for she falls headlong into a ditch dug by deceit. The comical anti-
climax of Superbia's descent vindicates the proverb; in Prudentius'
field of conflict, Pride really does come before a fall. The Virtues
are hardly being threatened at this stage and rather a repetitive formula is setting in. The entry of Luxuria, tipsy, bedecked and apparently harmless, disarms the Virtues. Luxuria does not speak but her
looks are deadly to the resolve of the opposing troops (lines 310–30).
Luxuria is a seductively effete character and the Virtues are ready to
fall at her feet. The appropriate adversary to deal with this enfeebler
of the fighting spirit is Sobrietas who grimly rallies the troops.
The Ovidian reminiscences of this speech will be explored below.

Keeping 'in text' for the moment, the following scene is one of unequivocal victory for the Virtues after an extremely awkward moment.

In contrast to Pride's empty and impotent blustering at 206ff, Sobrietas' rallying speech, which matches the rhetorical techniques employed by Superbia, is a prelude to the fearsome rout of Luxuria. It takes a Virtue with considerable moral clout to pull the entranced and deluded troupe of Virtues together with sharp reminders of their noble ancestry and proven fighting mettle. She calls upon successes of the past, all concrete battles which are now being reactualised on the metaphorical plane. Nugent suggests that Prudentius' technique of personification concretises or puts into action abstract generalisations from both epic and the Bible.[31] Prudentius also introduces heroes and heroines of the faith (taken from the Old and New Testament) alongside the very virtues they have exhibited and the vices they have grappled with as embodied in their opponents and persecutors. It is tempting to treat this strategy as a knowing cultural cross-fertilisation, a way of varying the edifying spectacle of the liberated soul with the miraculous validation of biblical figures, their testing, their suffering and their combats of epic dimension. Of course all this takes place in a literary medium, but it is visually striking poetry and extravagantly phrased to maximise the impact of the allusions.

> addit Sobrietas vulnus letale iacenti,
> coniciens silicem rupis de parte molarem.
> hunc vexilliferae quoniam fors obtulit ictum
> spicula nulla manu sed belli insigne gerenti,
> casus agit saxum, medii spiramen ut oris
> frangeret, et recavo misceret labra palato
> dentibus introrsum resolutis lingua resectam
> dilaniata gulam frustis cum sanguinis inplet.
> insolitis dapibus crudescit guttur, et ossa
> conliquefacta vorans revomit quas hauserit offas
> *Psychomachia* (417–26)

Soberness gives her the death-blow as she lies, hurling at her a great stone from the rock. As chance put this weapon in the standard-bearer's way (for she carries no javelins in her hand, but only the emblem of her warfare), chance drives the stone to smash the breath-passage in the midst of the face and beat the lips into the arched mouth. The teeth within are loosened, the gullet cut, and the mangled tongue fills it with bloody fragments. Her gorge rises at the strange meal; gulping down the pulped bones she spews up again the lumps that are swallowed.

The manner of Luxuria's destruction is the ultimate humiliation, fitting nicely with concepts of punishment in the arena, where part of the appropriateness of the punishment might be the mockery of the aspirations and self-advertisement of the victims.[32] The garotting and physical implosion inflicted upon Luxuria by Sobrietas is graphic even amongst all this hacking of the Soul's enemies to death. The killing of this seductive figure is particularly savage and is the culmination of the stopping-up imagery identified by Nugent. She itemises the orifices, both verbal and erogenous, which are closed off and hideously mutilated by the Virtues, whose own points of access are presumably permanently barred. Nugent suggests that there is a strong sexual undertone to all this activity, as if the Vices are endless open mouths of corruption and obscenity, crying out for closure by the chaste and the just.[33] Unlike the famous Christian martyrs who are portrayed as spirited and unconquerable under sexual torture and dismemberment, the Vices show little resilience in the face of similar physical attacks. They are easily silenced and it is only Discordia, at the very end, who makes a brave attempt to have the last word. Sobrietas disposes of Luxuria after her body has been mangled in the chariot wheels in a way which makes her a mass of revulsion, a total disfigurement.

The sacrificial model

The appearance of Luxuria in the *Psychomachia* is one of the most telling pieces of scene-stealing which Prudentius achieves. It involves not Virgil, who provides a number of his hemistichs and who has attracted most scholarly attention as Prudentius' poetic store, but Ovid. I would like to propose a reading of this particular example of *imitatio*, and to argue that this has a deeper significance than Prudentius knowing where to go for his rhetorical models in order to match his dramatic requirements.[34] Any reader well versed in Ovid's *Metamorphoses* will recognise the reprise of Book 3, the Theban tragedy. For Luxuria read Bacchus, a seductive and effete presence from the East, and Sobrietas falls into place as Pentheus, the fatally earnest king who attempts to rally his city against the disruptive and corrupting influence of a false god. The fact that Ovid actually describes Pentheus as *contemptor superum,* despiser of the gods above, is grist to the Christian poet's mill, for this is precisely the Christian message in regard to the pagan gods.[35]

> 'quis furor, anguigenae, proles Mavortia, vestras
> attonuit mentes?' Pentheus ait, 'aerane tantum
> aere repulsa valent et adunco tibia cornu
> et magicae fraudes, ut, quos non bellicus ensis,
> non tuba terruerit, non strictis agmina telis,
> femineae voces et mota insania vino
> obscenique greges et inania tympana vincant?'
> Ovid, *Metamorphoses* (3.531–7)

'What madness, snake sons, progeny of Mars, has addled your brains?' Thus spoke Pentheus. 'Is bronze struck on bronze, and a flute with hooked horns and charlatan magic, so potent that men like yourselves, fearless in the face of the sword of war, the clarion call of battle, the ranks of weapons at the ready, should crumple before girlish voices, madness induced by wine, lecherous hordes and hollow drum beats?'

Pentheus continues in disbelief and horror trying to lift the blindness from his people and reveal that they are being defeated and humiliated by a Dionysiac flower power:

> 'o iuvenes, propiorque meae, quos arma tenere,
> non thyrsos, galeaque tegi, non fronde, decebat.'
> *Met.* 3.540–2

'O young warriors, my generation, it is the brandishing of weapons which becomes you, not the sporting of the thyrsus; your heads should be hidden by the helmet, not bedecked with garlands.'

> 'at nunc a puero Thebae capientur inermi
> quem neque bella iuvant nec tela nec usus equorum,
> sed madidus murra crinis mollesque coronae
> purpuraque et pictis intextum vestibus aurum.'
> *Met.* 3.554–6

'And now Thebes is to be captured by an unarmed boy, who takes no pleasure in war nor weapons nor horsemanship but

85

who revels in having his hair moistened with myrrh oil, in soft garlands and in the wearing of brightly coloured garments with gold weave.'

The exotic but apparently equally ineffectual Luxuria also destroys the warlike spirit of the Virtues, who are rallied as follows by Sobrietas:

> 'quis furor insanas agitat caligine mentes?
> quo ruitis? cui colla datis? quae vincula tandem,
> pro pudor, armigeris amor est perferre lacertis,
> lilia luteolis interlucentia sertis
> et ferrugineo vernantes flore coronas?
> his placet adsuetas bello iam tradere palmas
> nexibus, his rigidas nodis innectior ulnas,
> ut mitra caesariem cohibens aurata virilem
> conbibat infusum croceo religamine nardum.'
>
> *Psychomachia* (351–9)

'What blinding madness is vexing your disordered minds? To what fate are you rushing? To whom are you bowing the neck? What bonds are these (for shame!) you long to bear on arms that were meant for weapons, these yellow garlands interspersed with bright lilies, these wreaths blooming with red-hued flowers? Is it to chains like these you will give up hands trained to war, with these bind your stout arms, to have your manly hair confined by a gilded turban with its yellow band to soak up the spikenard you pour on.'

The unmistakable allusion to Ovid's interpretation of the Theban myth functions on several levels. In every version of the legend Pentheus receives the ultimate punishment for opposing what turns out to be, against the odds, a true god. Ovid, however, does not allow his Pentheus to be directly manipulated and transformed by the god but sends him out in full battle dress to meet his bizarre fate at the hands of his mother.[36] This cannot alter the fact that Prudentius allies his Sobrietas to a defeated king and Luxuria to the triumphant Bacchus.

The story of Pentheus was an attractive legend for Christian writers, lending itself to lessons in faith and suffering. Clement of Alexandria wishes that Pentheus had been armed with the Christian faith in his fight against decadence.[37] Prudentius re-enacts the myth, dressing it up as Virtue versus Vice and reversing the ending, which it is in his power to do. Where Christ holds sway Luxuria, whatever form she takes, could never defeat a representative of Sobrietas. This is a fatal charade in a literary medium. Coleman discusses the popularity of mythological 'plays' in the arena and how the reconstruction of the myths demonstrated to the onlookers the ingenuity, inventiveness and remarkable resources of their rulers. The poet Martial described and no doubt embellished the 'miraculous' sights in his panegyrics to the emperor Titus. Whatever form these reconstructions of legendary deaths took, Martial is exuberantly complimenting the emperor not only on the novelty of the spectacle but also on the ruler's near-godlike capacity for bringing unbelievable fables alive. He has validated the mythological past, a gift normally granted to and by the gods. In the arena accurate representation of mythical events was not *de rigeur* as long as the main characters were recognisable. Prudentius as controller and master of ceremonies is glorifying the omnipotence of Christ who is the ultimate *editor* of this spectacle. The introduction of Luxuria as a Vice sporting *nova pugnandi species,* a new form of fighting – and Prudentius apostrophises this phenomenon in a way reminiscent of Martial's *De Spectaculis* – suggests a new excitement for the reader! *Species* carries connotations of the showy and dangerously deceptive. Prudentius is surely also implying that the Roman pagan arena cannot boast a monopoly of miraculous sights.

The final curtain

After the graphic execution of Luxuria her band of followers are scattered and fly in confusion. Avaritia makes an opportunistic entry to pick up the scattered spoils of Luxuria and Prudentius exploits her presence to give a diatribe on human weaknesses generally and human acquisitiveness in particular. Foiled by Ratio (Reason), Avaritia tries a different strategy, one involving a brief metamorphosis into Frugality, but this is counteracted by Ratio expanding herself into Operatio (Good Works).[38] Avaritia's technique of *maskarova* is another theatrical move, a novel way of fighting, and it is subsequently echoed by Discordia's cunning disguise as a rank-and-file Virtue, a parting shot of the Vices when it seems that the enemy has been routed. Discordia is able to make one ineffectual hit at the victorious army, when the performance appears to be at an end, a true *coup de théâtre*. Discordia is a dangerous latecomer who has hidden herself among the victorious Virtues. Her flight of eloquence on discovery is cut short by Faith, who had been first into battle, naked and unprotected, at lines 21–7, and who now appears to have acquired a weapon:

non tulit ulterius capti blasphemia monstri
Virtutum regina Fides, sed verba loquentis
inpedit et vocis claudit spiramina pilo,
pollutam rigida transfigens cuspide linguam.
carpitur innumeris feralis bestia dextris;
frustratim sibi quisque rapit quod spargat in auras,
quod canibus donet, corvis quod edacibus ultro
offerat, inmundis caeno exhalante cloacis
quod trudat, monstris quod mandet habere marinis.
discissum foedis animalibus omne cadaver
dividitur, ruptis Heresis perit horrida membris.

Psychomachia (715–25)

No further did Faith, the Virtues' queen, bear with the outrageous prisoner's blasphemies, but stopped her speech and blocked the passage of her voice with a javelin, driving its hard point through the foul tongue. Countless hands tear the deadly beast in pieces, each seizing bits to scatter to the breezes, and give to the dogs or throw to the carrion crows, or thrust into the foul, stinking sewers, or entrust to the possession of the sea monsters. The whole corpse is torn asunder and parcelled out to unclean creatures; so perishes frightful Heresy, rent limb from limb.

Discordia not only suffers the fate of a Pentheus but she goes down in the manner of an arena spectacle in a messy approximation of the myth. Malamud compares the scene with the ripping apart of Rufinus in Claudian's roughly contemporaneous poem and suggests that both figures reprise a martyr's fate. *In Rufinum* depicts the Eastern regent as the demon of discord and political dismemberment who is capable of dividing the closest of friendships and the most harmonious of alliances. In Prudentius the demon herself, Discordia, is aptly described as suffering the fate of her mortal embodiment.

Malamud suggests a subtext of uneasiness at this point. The Virtues rejoice in an action of *discordia*.[39] For Malamud the final battle of the *Psychomachia* ends in a Pyrrhic victory for the Virtues, with Discordia spreading violence and disruption through the army of the Virtues. On the other hand, they are finally disposing of Heresy itself by leaving no room for reconstitution. We may be witnessing here just the sort of uncompromising response to the deviants and criminals that characterised the judicial process of the arena. The Vices are justly condemned criminals – there are no wrongful convictions here – and they suffer appropriate retribution at the hands of the warrior Virtues. Just as the parade and disposal of Roman enemies reassured the citizens at the games and proved the unassailable position of their emperor, the Christian could take comfort in the spectacle of the hostile Vices thoroughly defeated and danger removed. However, the Soul has to be ready to face future onslaught, just as the shows need to go on in the arena. Both the Christian psyche and the Roman state required regular cleansing.[40]

By concentrating upon what we understand as the arena's ideological functions, we can begin to elaborate upon areas of correspondence between pagan and Christian consciousness, to speculate upon what common needs might be answered by the set menu of the programme with all its sense of occasion and its open agenda of Roman imperial power and cohesion. I have argued that the arena serves equally well as a literary metaphor for the Christian victory and by portraying it in these terms Prudentius provides not only the safe spectacle for his audience but a morally regenerating sight reaffirming the unity, the unassailability and the constant regeneration of the city of God in the Soul.

The amphitheatre and its spectacle emerge as a shared cultural space but also as a disputed territory, as the inner struggle of the Soul takes on an overtly public dimension. Bearing in mind Witke's comment that when men became Christians they did not stop being Romans (1971, p. 110), the dual consciousness of the ancient audience then stands out in sharper relief. The *Psychomachia* demonstrates Prudentius' ability to reconstruct the Roman arena as spectacle through a literary medium and to express the unequivocal victory of Christian virtues and the establishment of a city of God through the highly accessible imagery of pagan *munera*, execution by combat and the manifestation of myth through miraculous display.

Notes

1 Clark (forthcoming).
2 The translations are taken from J.H. Thomas's Loeb edition, Harvard University Press, 1949, reprinted 1993.

3 See Habinek, 1990, pp. 49–50.
4 See Theissen, 1992, p. 117: 'The motives for loving one's enemies and for non violence . . . Love of enemies is sovereign behavior, behavior that makes human beings godlike', and p. 119:

> Love of enemies is not what Nietzsche thought: it is an act of sovereignty, not the reaction of people who are ground down; it is the generalization of a sovereign attitude which even someone who is outwardly inferior can adopt.

5 The phrase 'fatal charades', coined by Coleman, 1990, refers to the replay of high points from legendary stories.
6 For Discordia equalling Claudian's Rufinus and paradoxically facing a martyr-like death in the 'arena' of the *Psychomachia*, see Malamud, 1989, pp. 57ff and the further discussion at the end of this chapter.
7

> Executions carried out within the framework of a Greek myth were certainly spectacular, grotesque and sometimes titillating, like Roman comedy or mimes; but that does not mean that they did not have, or were not perceived by the audience as having, a moral or an educative purpose.
>
> Wiedemann, 1992, p. 85

8 Gunderson, p. 116, following Foucault, proposes 'no radical outside' to the arena. When a Roman took up a position in the sand, in the seats, or outside the building like a Juvenal or a Messala, the apparatus of the arena served to structure the truths of these positions. Easterling and Miles (chapter 5, this volume), examine the aspect of civic identity and cultural congruity in places of public performance.
9 Palmer, 1989, p. 34, criticises the positing of 'a form of Christian double think by means of which men of culture could accept for the sake of its spiritual value what they would normally reject in a secular context'. Palmer's emphasis is upon credulity as a key point of correspondence, whatever the cultural or intellectual background. She warns against discovering or assuming an 'anachronistic rationalism'. Both Palmer (pp. 44–9) and Gunderson, p. 114, transfer this way of looking to a broader cultural milieu and identify a common passion for performance, display and deadly sports.
10 Bartsch, 1994, p. 55. Bartsch discusses the move from representation to replication in the arena (51–2), the violation of the theatrical by the actual which complicates and distorts the relationship between image and referent in the process of watching. The realism of 'fatal charades' will be addressed towards the end of this chapter.
11 Cicero *Tusculans* 2.17.41, Pliny *Panegyric* 33.1ff.
12 Tertullian *De Spectaculis* 12, 16, Prudentius *Contra Symmachum*, 2, *passim*.
13 For rituals of the arena perpetuating ancient Roman customs of funeral rites, and the inference that this was human sacrifice with victims devoted to *di inferi*, and therefore to the devil, see the discussion in Solmsen, 1965, pp. 242–3.

14 Wiedemann, p. 150 re Tertullian, *De Spectaculis* 29. Other sources for Prudentius' inspiration have been cited by Hanna, 1977: e.g. Cyprian's *De Mortalitate* 4, Ambrose's *De Cain et Abel* 1413ff and *Genesis* 14.

15   vis et pugilatus et luctatus? praesto sunt, non parva et multa. aspice impudicitiam deiectam a castitate, perfidiam caesam a fide, saevitiam a misericordia contusam, petulantiam a modestia adumbratam, et tales sunt apud nos agones in quibus ipsi coronamur. vis autem et sanguinis aliquid. habes Christi.

                                          de Spectaculis, 19–30

Would you have fightings and wrestlings? Here they are – things of no small account and plenty of them. See impurity overthrown by chastity, perfidy slain by faith, cruelty crushed by pity, impudence thrown into the shade by modesty; and such are the contests among us, and in them we are crowned. Have you a mind for blood? You have the blood of Christ.'

16 As noted in the introduction to this discussion, the most critical and the most influential of the detractors is Lewis, 1936, pp. 68–9. No writer on the *Psychomachia* can ignore his indictment, which has become a creative spur to scholars who vigorously defend Prudentius' structure and symbolism.

17 See Smith, 1976, Haworth, 1980, Nugent, 1985 and Malamud, 1989.

18 'that fighting is an activity that is not proper to most of the Virtues' (Lewis, 1936, p. 69).

19 Haworth, in his opening chapter, questions assumptions about the process of personification which includes a critique of Lewis's position. Nugent points out that the Virtues are embodiments and not personalities, concluding that 'Lewis' squeamishness arises from clinging to the notion of the particular individual which is irrelevant at Prudentius' level of abstraction' (p. 20).

20 I agree wholeheartedly with Smith's critique of those who perceive merely meaningless pastiche or formulaic decoration in the process of *imitatio*. (See p. 235.) In chapter IV, 'The Assault upon Vergil', he argues that Prudentius 'puts forth Vergil in *cento*-like fragmentation in order to summon up an image of the City of Man disordered by sinful strife: if Vergil is the architect of this city, so much the worse for him' (p. 296).

21 'I would prefer to talk in terms of the appropriation of Vergil, for I believe Prudentius is less concerned with undermining the Classical master than with transferring Roman excellences to Christian contexts' Nugent, pp. 39–40).

22 The claim to *virtus* is a case in point where its linguistic duality challenges 'the myth that *virtus* and *vitium* are neat polarities' (p. 83). Malamud continues the concept of words doing battle, the struggle that takes place on the field of semiotics (p. 56), and focuses on the laceration of the tongue and language as the combined instrument of deception and ambiguity, particularly in the mouth of Discordia (p. 65).

23 Letter 7.

24 Clark (forthcoming) describes the triumph of the body through the act of suffering and the ecstatic embracing of pain by the martyrs.
25 This is Potter's contention (pp. 61–5).
26

> The tortured showed more bravery than the torturers. The blood which flowed might have sufficed to put out the fire of persecution, even to put out the flames of Gehenna with its glorious gore – What a spectacle this was for the Lord – how sublime, how magnificent, how acceptable to God's eyes is the allegiance and devotion of his soldiers.
>
> Cyprian *Letter* 7/10, quoted by Wiedemann, 158–9

27

> On literary grounds, the *Psychomachia* is, as Macklin Smith has claimed, an 'assault upon Vergil', a mock heroic poem intended for an audience which had been rigorously schooled in Homer and Vergil. But, historically considered, it is a satire on pagan cult worship, a worship devoted to the service of so many preposterous gods, such as the deified Virtues.
>
> Howarth, p. 104

In contrast, Nugent, p. 24:

> Whether wearing the purple be taken to signify senatorial or triumphal prerogatives, these specifically Roman features are now clearly appropriated by Fides and her army of Christian martyrs. It is a particularly fitting conclusion to this first episode of the poem, in which Prudentius himself has been shown to employ a poetic strategy which appropriates the old epic technique yet dismantles it and creates of its fragments a new, allegorical one.

28 For arguments against Christian compassion and humanitarian approaches to pain in the ancient world, see Wiedemann, pp. 150–3.
29 See Gunderson, pp. 142ff.
30 For the supernatural strength of *passio*, see Roberts, pp. 63–5.
31 Nugent (pp. 36–40) cites Quilligan on the 'narrative that often simply enacts statements made by the Bible'. However, Nugent's study draws in the Virgilian narrative and identifies the visual realisations of such general ideological positions as *parcere subiectis, debellare superbos*, 'sparing the subdued and waging uncompromising war on the arrogant', with the result that 'both because the Virtues triumph over opponents who show unmistakable Roman affinities and because, in winning victories, the Virtues appropriate to themselves as well the Roman associations with victory' (p. 40).
32 See Coleman's comments on punishments devised for the parodic re-enactment of unacceptable behaviour (pp. 46–7). A comic and anticlimactic end has just been engineered for Superbia.
33 Paul Allen Miller (pp. 267–8) explores orgasmic fluidity as a feminine attribute and the throat as the oral/anal zone of erotic pleasure and sexual innuendo.

34 This is the main thrust of Ferdinand Alexander's (1936) perceptive comparison with the Ovidian passages.
35 Another Ovidian figure accused as *contemptor* is Orpheus, *Metamorphoses* 11.7. Ovid portrays the killing of Orpheus as spectacle with consistent imagery from the arena. (See G.M.H. Murphy's commentary in the Bristol Classical Press series, 1979.) Orpheus' death at the hands of the Bacchantes, whom Ovid transforms into beasts even though the wild animals themselves are entranced and disarmed by his song, was re-enacted in the Colosseum (Martial *De Spectaculis* 25 (21b)). Paradoxically, the unfortunate victim who played Orpheus' part was mauled by a bear, thus losing the whole point of the original myth. As Coleman observes (p. 67):

> In a society where myth was the cultural currency, the ritual event of ordinary life might naturally be set in a mythological context; to put it more broadly, Greco-Roman mythology provided an all-encompassing frame of reference for everyday Roman experience. A superficial appropriateness was quite adequate; points of detail did not have to correspond.

36 For the suggestion that Ovid reheroises Pentheus after possible innovations to the myth by Euripides, see James, 1991–3.
37 Clement of Alexandria (*Protrepticus* 7) also discussed in this volume by Easterling and Miles (chapter 5).
38 The double metamorphoses are the subject of a stimulating discussion in Nugent, pp. 80–2.
39 Malamud subjects this passage to an appropriate dissection: she argues (pp. 53–4) that Claudian allows Rufinus to lose his savagery and become a human victim of the soldiers' bestiality, so Prudentius, in reprising this passage for the destruction of Discordia, reiterates a Roman theme of violence becoming infectious, that an enemy is only defeated by the victor acquiring his adversary's characteristics.
40 Nugent notes (pp. 60–1) that victory has paved the way for the foundation of the city's temple; the land is reclaimed for the shrine to Sapientia and this is appropriate to both pagan and Christian teleological concepts of history. The Colosseum, the model for many subsequent arenas, was itself the result of clearing away the building and the image of Nero. Martial (*De Spectaculis* 1 and 2) emphasizes the new age it heralds when the benefits of empire will be shared and the glory of Rome extended to the citizens of Rome.

Bibliography

Alexander, F. (1936) 'Beziehungen des Prudentius auf Ovid', *Wiener Studien* 54, 166–73.
Bartsch, S. (1994) *Actors in the Audience: Theatricality and Double Speak from Nero to Hadrian*. Cambridge, Mass.
Clark, G. (forthcoming) 'Bodies and Blood: Late Antique Debate on Martyrdom, Virginity and Resurrection', in D. Montserrat (ed.) *Changing Bodies, Changing Meanings: Studies in the Human Body in Antiquity*. London.

PAULA JAMES

Coleman, K. (1990) 'Fatal Charades: Roman Executions Staged as Mythological Enactments', *J.R.S.* 80, 44–73.
Gunderson, E. (1996) 'The Ideology of the Arena', *Classical Antiquity* 15, 113–49.
Habinek, T. (1990) 'Lucius' Rite of Passage', *M.D.* 25, 49–66.
Hanna, R. (1977) 'The Sources and Art of Prudentius' *Psychomachia*', *C. Ph.* 72, 108–15.
Haworth, K.R. (1980) *Deified Virtues, Demonic Vices and Descriptive Allegory in Prudentius' Psychomachia.* Amsterdam.
James, P. (1991–3) 'Pentheus Anguigena: the Sins of the Father', *B.I.C.S.* 38, 81–93.
Lewis, C.S. (1936) *The Allegory of Love.* Oxford.
Malamud, M. (1989) *Prudentius and the Poetics of Transformation.* Ithaca, NY and London.
Miller, P.A. (1998) 'The Bodily Grotesque in Roman Satire: Images of Sterility' in B. Gold and S. Morton-Braund, eds. *Vile Bodies. Arethusa* 31.3, 257–84.
Nugent, S.G. (1985) *Allegory and Poetics: the Structure and Imagery of Prudentius' Psychomachia.* Frankfurt.
Palmer, P. (1989) *Prudentius and the Martyrs.* Oxford.
Plass, P. (1985) *The Game of Death in Ancient Rome: Arena Sport and Political Suicide.* Madison.
Potter, D. (1993) 'Martyrdom as Spectacle' in R. Scodel (ed.) *Theatre and Society in the Classical World.* Ann Arbor.
Roberts, M. (1993) *Poetry and the Cult of the Martyrs: the Liber Peristephanon of Prudentius.* Ann Arbor.
Smith, M. (1976) *Prudentius' Psychomachia: A Re-examination.* Princeton.
Solmsen, F. (1965) 'The Powers of Darkness in Prudentius' *Contra Symmachum*: A Study of his Poetic Image', *Vigiliae Christianae* 19, 237–57.
Theissen, G. (1992) *Social Reality and the Early Christians*, tr. M. Kohl. Minneapolis.
Wiedemann, T. (1992) *Emperors and Gladiators.* London.
Witke, C. (1971) 'Prudentius and the Tradition of Latin Poetry', in *Numen Litterarum: The Old and the New in Latin Poetry from Constantine to Gregory the Great.* Leiden.

5

DRAMATIC IDENTITIES

Tragedy in late antiquity

Pat Easterling and Richard Miles

The question of whether tragedy was performed in late antiquity and, if so, in what form, has provoked considerable scholarly debate. Much of this work has been influenced by the Gibbonesque model of decline and fall. Culture as an articulation of society mirrors the political decline of the empire. Even scholars who attempt to distance themselves from such a model find it hard not to portray theatre in the middle and late empire as a pale reflection of the dramatic glories of the past.[1] Tragedy becomes a stagnant elite literary exercise which even the educated classes approached in a half-hearted manner, whilst the rest of the populace indulged in the intellectually vacuous pleasures of the pantomime and mime.[2] Scholarship has made a careful distinction between the activities of the tragic pantomimes and tragedy, between late antiquity and the 'Classical world', and ultimately between text and performance. This chapter will argue that these suppositions are essentially unhelpful in understanding the role that tragedy played in the cultural milieu of late antiquity. The argument will centre on two main considerations:

(a) Tragedy should not be categorised simply as a medium that reached perfection in fifth-century Athens and was in decline from then onwards. By creating a rigid definition of what can and cannot be considered a tragedy we create distinctions that simply did not exist in late antiquity. Both pagan and Christian writers of the fourth, fifth and sixth centuries evidently still perceived it to be within their remit to discuss tragedy both as a text and *as a performance medium*. We are impressed by the overwhelming frequency of references in pagan and Christian authors to tragedy in some form or other, sometimes to particular playwrights, plays, or characters ('as Euripides makes Medea say . . .'), sometimes just to 'tragic stories' or the idea of the tragic. The sheer range and extent of the evidence force us to the conclusion that tragedy continued to have strong symbolic value, as something of much wider cultural resonance than an exclusively 'high-brow' art form, and that whether or not it was actually performed it was still *imagined* as a performance medium. If this approach is justified it means that one can sidestep factual questions about whether anything that could be defined as 'tragedy' was actually being staged in the fourth and fifth centuries and later, and concentrate instead on how tragedy in the broadest sense was used by people of the time in their construction of identity.

(b) Tragedy is an appropriate tool with which to think about ideas of culture and identity in late antiquity. As an art form strongly associated with the Classical past, tragedy had strong cultural associations for the people of late antiquity whether pagan or Christian. As such, it was a useful vector for individuals to think not only about the past but also the present and future and to stake a claim to their own roles within these time-scales. Discussion about tragedy in late antique texts helps illuminate the cultural congruity of both pagan and Christian elites whilst also offering the scholar insight into the self-representation of Greek, Roman and Christian in late antiquity.

Tragedy and performance in late antiquity

There is no indication that tragedy, as represented by a whole play with three actors and chorus, survived as a performance piece much after the early third century in the Greek East, and it had probably disappeared at an earlier date in the Latin West (Jones 1993: 48, Barnes 1996: 170–3, Weismann 1972: 34). In terms of actual performance, tragedy seems to have metamorphosed into a succession of excerpts recited or sung by a *tragicus cantor* or *tragôidos,* who might be accompanied or accompany himself on the cithara. The *tragôidos* wore a distinctive costume of a gaping mask and long-sleeved garment, and he performed in high-heeled boots, sometimes on stilts (Friedländer 1928: 98–100, Weismann 1972: 41–2, Pasquarto 1976: 161–2, Baumeister 1987: 118).

The themes associated with tragedy were also transmitted through another form of the theatre, the pantomime, which we know was very popular in late antiquity. Pantomime first appears on the stages of Latin-speaking areas of the Roman empire from the end of the first century BC, yet it was only accepted into Greek sacred festivals in the late second century AD. Pantomime drew its themes and stories from tragedy; all the scenes were dance solos performed by a virtuoso masked actor, backed by musicians, whilst another actor or a chorus might be used to provide narrative continuity. During the performance the pantomime impersonated all the characters both male and female. As Beacham has noted, 'The task was to give an impression of the whole ensemble and the relationship of one character to another while preserving the sense of the plot and creating graceful and expressive movements and gestures' (Beacham 1991: 142).[3]

It was on pantomime and mime, rather than tragedy or comedy, that the Church fathers concentrated their attack (Vandenberghe 1955: 35, Pasquarto 1976: 97–157). This, scholars have argued, shows that tragedy was no longer thought of as a performance medium but had come instead to be seen as an essentially text-based literary genre like any other. On this view fourth- and fifth-century references to tragedy were derived from literary references in earlier authors and through the limited performances of the *tragôidoi*, pantomimes and mimes (Barnes 1996: 170–3, Weismann 1972: 34). The conclusion to which these arguments lead is that in late antiquity some kind of cleavage takes place between theatre as text (as represented by tragedy and comedy) and theatre as performance (pantomime and mime).

If, however, one looks at the discourses of the later sophists such as Libanius and Choricius and the polemics of the Church fathers against the theatre, it soon becomes apparent that neither of these two elite groups recognised such a polarity. Both speak about all forms of drama, including tragedy, in terms of *performance*. Schouler in his study of the attitudes of the Greek sophists to the theatre has shown conclusively that later writers such as Libanius and Choricius of Gaza, although their information concerning tragedy was derived from the literary texts of the grammarians, frame their arguments around performance (Schouler 1987: 273–5). Late antique Christian writers make the same assumptions. Augustine, for example, is concerned with the reaction of the spectator who is actually watching the play rather than the reader of a text:

> I was much attracted by the theatre, because the plays reflected my own unhappy plight and were tinder to my fire. Why is it that men enjoy feeling sad at the sight of tragedy and suffering on the stage, although they would be most unhappy if they had to endure the same fate themselves? Yet they watch the plays because they hope to be made to feel sad, and the feeling of sorrow is what they

enjoy. What miserable delirium is this! The more a man is subject to such suffering himself, the more easily he is moved by it in the theatre. Yet when he suffers himself we call it misery, when he suffers out of sympathy with others we call it pity. But what sort of pity can we really feel for an imaginary scene on the stage?

(Augustine, *Conf.* 3.2, trans. H. Chadwick)

His eastern contemporary, John Chrysostom, bishop of Antioch and then Patriarch of Constantinople, expresses the same anxieties. It is with tragedy as a performance piece that his concerns lie. In one sermon he talks about the impossibility of remaining chaste when one's soul would have been filled up with base desires after watching spectacles and songs on tragic themes such as women hanging themselves when rejected in love and men falling for their stepmothers (John Chrysostom, *In 1 Thess. hom.* 5).

Although the Christian Church roundly condemned the theatre as a vestige of paganism, many of its other objections mirror the more qualified rhetorical and even playful disapproval of the pagan sophists. These centre around the effects that drama had on the spectator viewing at the theatre. Tragedy is particularly picked out for its excess: its ability to churn up the emotions of the audience.[4] As with other forms of drama, tragedy is also accused of deceit, with men dressing up and pretending to be women.[5] What is striking here is that both groups articulate their views on a dramatic genre, which is supposedly no longer performed on the stage, in relation to performance.

In essence tragedy as a dramatic form had changed, but in the cultural imagination of late antiquity it did not simply exist on the pages of a book. As Jones has succinctly pointed out in relation to modern evidence,

A social historian of the year 4000 would be unwise to infer that *Kiss Me Kate* had driven the *Taming of the Shrew* from the stage; that Verdi's *Otello* and *Falstaff* represented an unmistakable decline in taste; or that only the 'small circle of the educated' watched Shakespeare in the Park.

(Jones 1993: 48)

It must also be remembered that theatrical performance as such was as important a facet of civic and cultural life in the later Roman empire as at any time in antiquity. The cessation of original dramatic composition and the appearance of the first Christian emperors made little impact on the theatre, despite often draconian legislation against it. The theatres at Corinth, Argos, Athens, Phlious and Epidaurus were in use to at least the end of the fourth century; at Hierapolis and Aphrodisias usage seems to carry on until the the sixth and seventh centuries respectively (Green 1994: 161–2). Theatres were also built in the new Christian city of Constantinople (Dagron 1974: 316).

Treatises, sermons, correspondence and council records reveal that the theatre was an important symbol of the battle for cultural hegemony being waged by the Christian Church in the urban centres of late antiquity. Theatre is constructed as a direct rival to the Christian church not just as a physical space but also as an alternative and well-established interpretation of the past, present and future.

The theatre's role as a facet of civic identity is explicitly recognised in Christian polemics. The sites of theatrical performance were one of the few truly public spaces in the antique city. It was in the theatre that all sections of the citizenry gathered together to watch and be watched (Bartsch 1994: 63–97, Gebhard 1996). Christian polemicists explicitly recognise the link between civic identity as represented by the theatre and personal morality. Novatian, writing in third-century Africa, makes the following observation:

> No man – regardless of his background or profession – is spared by the despicable tongue of these rogues. Yet everyone still frequents the theatre. Indecorum, commonly encountered, evidently delights to know and to learn of vice. There is a general rush to that despicable brothel of public shame, to the teaching of obscenity. Nothing is done in private that is not learned in public.
> (Novatian, *De Spect.* 6.2; cf. Tertullian, *De Spect.* 17.99)

Again and again, Christian writers proclaim the total incongruity between Christian teaching and the communality of the theatre.[6] Christian emperors often found themselves caught up in this struggle, needing to fulfil their civic role as provider of public entertainment whilst not seeming to be supporting paganism.[7]

The reaction of John Chrysostom to the emperor Theodosius' punitive measure of shutting down the theatre in Antioch reflects this position. In a sermon given a few days after the imperial edict, John argues that by closing the theatre, the emperor has not taken away Antioch's civic dignity but has enhanced it. The reputation of a city is built not on its large and beautiful stuctures but on the piety and virtue of its inhabitants. Here we see the formulation of a Christian civic identity in direct opposition to the classical model, with church representing the former and theatre, the latter (John Chrysostom, *Ad pop. Antioch. hom.* 17.9–10).

Both Church writers and pagan sophists are fundamentally interested in drama as performance because both recognise the centrality of performance to their respective institutions. Both consider it their role to provide cultural leadership of the late antique city through text and performance.[8] With the sophists this leads to an empathy with the activities of the theatre, as it provides a focus for civic identity (Schouler 1987: 284–7). In contrast, the Christian Church perceived the theatre as a dangerous rival. This rivalry revolves around performance. John Chrysostom complains that on theatre days in Antioch his church is empty and that: 'their vehement shouts, borne in the air from that place, resounded against the psalms which we were singing here' (John Chrysostom, *Ad pop. Antioch. hom.* 15.1). The performances in the church are in direct confrontation with those going on in the theatre. In another sermon, John again reverts to this theme when unfavourably comparing the chorus of the theatre with his own monastic choir (John Chrysostom, *In Matt. hom.* 68.4–5).

It is therefore possible to conclude that tragedy as a theatrical medium was still an important construct in late antiquity for both Christian and pagan elites because of its strong associations with performance and civic identity. It would be wrong to assume that these were concepts that the early Church appropriated from the pagan classical past. As with their pagan contemporaries such as Libanius and Choricius[9] in their different generations, who are also primarily interested in the idea of tragedy as a performance medium, the leaders of the Christian Church were primarily products of the classical tradition. However much Christian polemicists attempted rhetorically to slough off that tradition and distance themselves from it, the filter through which they saw the world about them was primarily a classical one.

Tragedy, identity and the reception of the past

Tragedy, more than other forms of theatre, epitomised 'high' classical culture. The writers of the Second Sophistic often mock tragedy for its pretensions. It was a common currency through which the sophists could display their *paideia* and Hellenism.

To begin with an example from the performance tradition. The sophist Eunapius of Sardis (fourth century) tells the story of an unnamed *tragôidos* in the time of Nero, who decided to leave Rome and go on tour because at Rome he was the object of the emperor's professional jealousy. He went 'to display his vocal powers' to half-barbarian audiences, to a city which had a theatre but evidently had not had visits from tragic performers before. For a start the spectators were terrified at the sight of him, but he took aside some of the local elite and explained the nature of the mask and the platform-soled boots that increased his height, and then tried another performance. The role he was acting was that of Euripides' Andromeda. This time he gradually accustomed the audience to his vocal range, but the weather was extremely hot, and he suggested they should wait till the cool of the evening. By now, however, they were wildly enthusiastic for him to carry on, and he let himself go in a passionate rendering of his part.

> This untrained audience was unable to respond to most of the features of tragedy: the majesty and grandeur of the language and style, the charm of the metre, the clarity of the character-drawing, most finely and compellingly designed to move the hearer, and in addition they were unfamiliar with the plot, but even stripped of all these advantages he enthralled them with the beauty of his enunciation and his singing.

The story ends with a grotesque scene: a week later the city was hit by an epidemic, and the whole population lay in the streets suffering from violent diarrhoea, 'singing [or "crying out"] as best each one could the melody [presumably that of Andromeda's famous monody] without managing a very clear rendering of the words: Andromeda had had a dire effect on them' (*Historici graeci minores*, fr. 54, Blockley 1981–3).

Some obvious points at once suggest themselves. First, the passage is set not in the author's own time but three centuries earlier, so as a piece of hard evidence for performance it is problematic, but it does tell us something about how a writer of the fourth century might imagine the effects of tragic performance. Clearly the suffering Andromeda, chained to a rock and singing a passionate aria, was thought to be a theatrical and musical – one might say operatic – subject capable of arousing thrilling emotion. The emphasis here is on performance and the empathetic response it might evoke, not on moral or political argument or on social comment. Perhaps it is not accidental that *Andromeda* was a play with strongly erotic subject-matter, and what is described here may help to explain why theatrical shows were so vehemently denounced by many of the early Christian writers for their dangerously emotive power.

The second point is of course the use of tragedy as a cultural marker. A 'half-barbarian' audience like this one lives in a city that has a theatre, but never before has it had visits from tragic actors on tour, and the effect on the spectators is complex: first terror at the sight of the *tragôidos* in high boots and gaping mask, then rapture at his extraordinary skills as a performer. For the knowing reader with true Hellenic *paideia* the model of reception is different: the cultivated spectator is prey neither to superstitious fear nor to the excesses of enthusiasm and can appreciate the performance with a discriminating sense of its refinements of form and content – its language, metre, character portrayal and so on. Tragedy on this model is the embodiment of high style and high seriousness as well as of emotions on a grand scale.

A tradition had developed which persisted until the sixth century with Choricius of Gaza, whereby the supremacy of tragedy in the dramatic canon of literature was acknowledged whilst at the same time its antiquity and esoteric nature were gently ridiculed (Beacham 1994: 185). Lucian, and later writers such as Libanius and Choricius, attempt to appropriate the cultural authority of tragedy to strengthen their defence of less exalted forms of theatre. Their arguments revolve around the premise that tragedy is more excessive than mime and pantomime and that the latter actually are derived from tragedy (Lucian, *De Sal.* 26–2; Libanius, *Or.* 64.75; Choricius, *Or.* 8.118 and 141–2).

Both Libanius and Choricius make the argument that if you ban either pantomime or mime then you must put a stop to all tragic performances too. Both authors raise the rhetorical stakes by emphasising the importance of tragedy to Hellenism. Libanius challeges the reader to:

> Come forward and say 'Previous generations were corrupted by tragedy and they were destroyed by comedy. Homer destroyed Greece and before Greece he destroyed himself, as he imitated Briseis lamenting and Penelope and the wounded Aphrodite.[9] Say that it is also now necessary for the theatre to be closed to the actors and for the schools (*didaskaleia*) to be closed to the poets, so that a *tragôidos*

> will not come on stage and imitate Pasiphae drifting into a
> monstrous passion, nor again a comic actor imitate women
> in Menander giving birth, and many other things (of the
> sort).
>
> (Libanius, *Or.* 64.73. Cf. Choricius, *Or.* 8.141–2)

Christian use of tragedy is of a more complex nature. Many of the
Christian references to tragedy in late antiquity reflect the ongoing
debate within the Church about what it was actually to be a
Christian. One is confronted with the struggle between *simplicitas*
and the common classical heritage of those who made up the ranks
of the Christian elite. The inconsistency in approach is startling.
A common theme in the homilies of John Chrysostom, a man
whose work is deeply dependent on classical *paideia*, is the cultural
supremacy of Christian *simplicitas* over classical learning. We witness
him favourably comparing illiterate country priests to the pagan
philosophers.

> And were you to question any one of these, who live a
> country life at the spade and plough, as to the dogmas
> respecting which the pagan philosophers have talked over
> an infinite amount, and have expended a multitude of
> words, without having been able to say anything sound,
> one of these would give you an accurate reply from his
> store of wisdom.
>
> (John Chrysostom, *Ad pop. Antioch. hom.* 19.3)

While engaged in forging or maintaining ties of *amicitia* with one
another, the Church fathers oscillate between relying on the bond
of Christian fellowship and using their classical *paideia*. It is these
two conflicting allegiances that made up the self-representation of
the Christian elite in late antiquity. This is clearly illustrated in a
letter written by Gregory of Nazianzus, part of that well-educated
Cappadocian Christian clique, to Basil of Caesarea's younger brother,
Gregory of Nyssa, in an attempt to try and persuade him to return to
his position in the Church after he had taken up a position as a
professor of rhetoric. Gregory of Nazianzus quickly resorts to their
common bond of *paideia* to win his friend over. A reference to
Euripides' *Phoenician Women* is used as an illustration of the dangers
of ambition.[10]

Whilst condemning all forms of theatre, Christian writers highlight their cultural congruity with their pagan peers by privileging

tragedy over pantomime and mime.[11] Tragedy represents the classical past and is mined for examples to back up the Christian polemicist's teaching.[12] The actions represented in the tragedies are mirrored in contemporary society and are therefore useful for instruction. Using examples from tragedies is justified by the argument advanced by Clement of Alexandria that even the ancient Greeks could not have been completely impervious to God's word.[13]

It is not surprising that tragedy was used by late antique Christian writers. Their anti-pagan polemics were aimed at both Christian and pagan audiences, the aim being to consolidate the one and bring about the conversion of the other. The past that was portrayed in these tragedies was a common one. This was a shared language. Clement in the second century demonstrates the subtlety with which this shared language could be used, offering the educated pagan reader a chance to reinterpret his cherished classics rather than abandon them. In the final chapter of the *Protrepticus* there is an extended evocation of the *Bacchae* and its Dionysiac language which depends on close familiarity with the play and proposes a way of reading the Bacchic mysteries as the revelation of Christianity. The passage begins (12.91) with a quotation of *Bacchae* 918–19, where Pentheus says he sees 'twin suns, twin Thebes', and Clement describes this as raving under the influence of mere images (*eidôla*), being intoxicated with ignorance. 'Come', he says to Pentheus,

> not with the thyrsus or the ivy; throw off your headband and fawnskin, and I will show you the *logos* and the mysteries of the *logos* according to your own way of seeing the world (*eikôn*). This is a mountain loved by God, not Cithaeron as in tragedies; it is wineless, shaded by holy groves, the haunt, not of the sisters of Semele, *maenades* initiated into the distribution of raw flesh, but of daughters of God, the beautiful *amnades* (lambs). Their rites (*orgia*) are those of the *logos*, their *choros* is sober, their *thiasos* is one that longs to receive the Father.

These images of maenadic activity (and of the dramatic performance of a chorus in the theatre) are followed by another direct address to a character in the play, Teiresias, referred to simply as 'old man'. He is to let himself be led (*cheiragôgou*, recalling *Ba.* 193, 363–4), leaving behind Thebes, his prophetic art and the Bacchic rites, and leaning instead on the wood of the Cross. The climax for the blind prophet (as for the reader) will be to *see* the Christian mysteries. The way Clement engages directly with the *dramatis personae* and offers them new action, new costumes or props and new self-definition, suggests a close imaginative engagement with the pagan text, engagement of a more complex kind than a rhetorician's typical deployment of quotation. No doubt the choice of play is not accidental, and the metaphorical use of the language of mystic initiation had precedents in pagan philosophy (there is plenty of it in Plato and Plutarch), but there is nothing of the cliché in Clement's handling of it.[14]

John Chrysostom in both letters and treatises contextualises biblical stories by alluding to themes gleaned from tragedy. In a letter to the Christian heiress, Olympias, he describes the story of Abraham in Egypt being like a tragedy (John Chrysostom, *Ep. ad Olympias* 8.10.29). In a treatise the story of Isaac and Jacob is likened to the tragic tales of the young men from Thebes (John Chrysostom, *Ad Stagirium a Daemone Vexatum* 2.10).

In the long run the fact that tragedy kept its place in the standard curriculum of the elite was to be crucial for its continuing influence, enabling it to be perceived as morally and stylistically 'correct' (with a few necessary adjustments) and suitable for the formation of young Christian minds.[15] What gave tragedy its particular educational power was its richness in memorable sentiment, stylish words of wisdom in the approved dialect, which could be learned and imitated by the student who aspired to correctness of composition in a highly archaising language. When Dio Chrysostom in the second century set out advice on a programme of rapid reading, allegedly for an inquirer who had made his way in the world without getting a fair share of *paideia* to match his present status, the list of essential classic poets could be boiled down to three: Homer, always acknowledged as the fountainhead of everything classic; Euripides among the tragedians; and Menander among the comic poets (Dio Chrysostom, *Or.* 18.7). Leaving aside Homer, we find Euripides and Menander continuing to hold their place as sources of gnomic sayings and memorable expressions for writers of the later empire, and collections like the *Menandrou Monostichoi*,[16] one-liners much used by educators (which included many quotations from Euripides as well as from Menander) or the *Eklogai* and *Anthologion* of John of Stobi (fifth century) show the type of sources from which the quotations might come.[17] The writers of rhetorical handbooks advised using famous sayings to adorn one's own prose;[18] this emphasis on style and imitation gave enormous prestige to the classical models, and because poets were potentially just as useful as prose authors for the aspiring speaker or writer[19] there was always a demand for texts of the most famous plays, or at least of select passages drawn from them and circulated in anthologies.

It would be misleading, however, to see this use of tragedy and its themes purely as an elite exercise. It was not just the educated echelons of late antique society who identified with these stories. The homilies of John Chrysostom, delivered in the churches and martyr shrines of Antioch and Constantinople, are littered with references to tragedy and tragic themes.[20] These are not erudite references, designed simply to illustrate the *paideia* of the preacher, but are often simple and vague allusions. Women are instructed to dress like tragic actors with their arms and hands covered by long sleeves (John Chrysostom, *In 1 Tim. hom.* 8.2). Here is a typical example:

> Then their [the ancients'] dramas were replete with adultery, lewdness and corruption of all kinds . . . One man loved his stepmother, a woman her stepson and in consequence hanged herself . . . Would you see a son married to his mother? This too happened amongst them and what is horrible, though it was done in ignorance, the god whom they worshipped did not prevent it, but permitted this outrage to nature to be committed, even though she was a person of distinction. And if those, who, if for no other reason, yet for the sake of their reputation with the masses might have been expected to keep to virtue rushed headlong into vice, what was likely to be the conduct of the greater part who lived in obscurity?. . .The wife of a certain one fell in love with another man and with the help of the adulterer killed her husband on his return. The majority part of you will know this story. The son of the murdered man killed the adulterer and after him his mother, then he himself became mad and was haunted by furies. After this the madman himself killed another man and took his wife. What can be worse than these disasters?
> (John Chrysostom, *In Tit. hom.* 5.4; cf. *In Phil. hom.* 15.5; *In 2 Thess. hom.* 1.1)

This is an explicit recognition of a shared cultural language and identity, and it brings home an important point, that however much these Christian writers attempt to distance themselves from pagan learning and culture, they are of course products of it themselves. It is therefore not surprising when we find them communicating with their audience through classical symbols and imagery. The classical past was a shared experience and one which involved the collective conciousness of the whole city. It was the most effective medium at the disposal of the Christian preacher. The tragic themes of antiquity would have been well known to the entire populace through the performances of the *tragôidoi* and pantomimes and many other less direct cultural channels. Material evidence from late antiquity confirms the importance of tragedy as a symbol of Hellenism and the classical past. A number of mosaics depicting stage performances of tragedy have been found in private houses (Bieber 1961: 239–40, figs 789–91). Similar scenes have been found on artifacts in both eastern and western parts of the empire right up into the sixth century: sarcophagi, ivory consular diptychs, marble statuettes, gems and bronzes (Bieber 1954: 250–2, Green 1994: 150–3, Webster 1967: 100–2). At the other end of the social spectrum it appears that tragedy was still an important and popular source of images: a large number of tragic terracotta masks and both figurines and lamps depicting scenes from tragedy and dating from the third and fourth centuries have been discovered in the Agora at Athens. These were cheap souvenirs sold at fairs and festivals and beside shrines around the theatres (GrandJouan 1961: 59–60, Webster 1967: 41–3, Green 1994: 150–64).

To conclude: both pagan sophists and Christian writers in late antiquity were interested in tragedy, however defined, as a performance genre. This interest can be directly linked to both groups' aspirations to be perceived as the centre of both civic and cultural identity in the late antique city. For Christian preachers such as John Chrysostom, aware that in general terms both text and performance were essential to their teaching, the theatre, which had traditionally played a central part in the life of the classical city, was perceived and rhetorically constructed as a dangerous rival to the Church and its message. Tragedy, because of its associations with Hellenic high culture, was a useful subject not only for the sophists but also for the Church fathers, but the cultural congruity of the two groups was qualified by Christian belief in the superiority of *simplicitas* over classical learning, which was to have a decisive influence on later cultural developments.

Notes

1 Friedländer 1928: 97,

> Far more than comedy, tragedy found an audience among the educated minority. The nerves of the mass were attuned to the arena, and unaffected even by the most horrid realism. The mimicry of the stage could not affect them and ideal figures were meaningless shadows; how should they care for Hecuba? But even in cultured circles, there were few who did not prefer the merry scenes of Plautus, which all seemed drawn from their own actuality, to the fates of the rulers and heroes of primitive Greece.

Barnes 1996: 170, 'But it is hard, perhaps impossible, to find similar evidence for real drama after the Severan period.'

2 Beacham 1991: 151,

> Later it [the theatre] ceased, certainly, to be a place where elevated dramatic art could flourish, as comedy and tragedy dwindled into rare revivals if they did not vanish altogether. Their place was usurped by the virtuosity and titillation of mime, and the visual grace or splendour of the pantomime. The theatre may have become ever more a medium of sensation than of thought: its achievements dazzling or seductive to the eyes, delightful to listen to, and even profoundly moving, but rarely probing or provocative. The audience may well have been capable of sensitive and critical appreciation: their theatre did not, however, appeal to or stimulate them very profoundly on an intellectual level.

See also Bieber 1961: 235–6, Barnes 1996: 167.
3 For the general development of pantomime in the Roman era see Jory 1996, Nicoll 1931: 132–4. For the popularity of pantomime in Late Antiquity see Baumeister 1987, Vandenberghe 1955: 35–8.
4 Novatian, *De Spect.* 6.2–5; Lactantius, *Div Inst.* 6.21; John Chrysostom, *In 1 Thess. hom.* 5.4; *In Matt. hom.* 68.4–5; *In Act. hom.* 10.3–4. Even Tertullian admits to some congruity in the Christian and Pagan positions:

> For often the censors would destroy the theatres at their very birth: they did it in the interests of morals, for they foresaw that great danger to morals must arise from the theatre's licentiousness. So here the Gentiles have their own opinion coinciding with ours as evidence, and we have the preliminary judgement of human morality to reinforce Christian law.
>
> (*De Spect.* 10)

5 Pagan: Lucian, *Pro Salt.* 29; Libanius *Or.* 64.64, 72–75. Christian: Lactantius, *Div. Inst.* 6.21; Arnobius *Adv. Nat.* 7.33; Tertullian *De Spect.* 10.96 and 23, 101–2; John Chrysostom, *In 1 Thess. hom.* 5.4.
6 Tertullian, *De Spect.* 27.103:

> Do you think that seated where there is nothing of God he will turn his thoughts to God . . . That sharing of emotions, that agreement, or disagreement in backing their favourites, makes an intercourse that fans the sparks of lust. Why, nobody going to the Games thinks of anything else but seeing and being seen. But whilst the tragic actor declaims he will think of the crying aloud of one of the prophets! Amid the strains of some flute player he will think in himself upon a psalm!

7 See Blänsdorf 1990, who argues that Christian emperors attempted to circumvent this problem by entrusting these shows to their magistrates, thereby distancing themselves from potential financial cost, crowd trouble and the disapproval of the Church. This would seem to be backed up by Barnes 1996: 174–5, where he argues that the conflicting attitudes of the imperial edicts concerning the Maiouma in the reign of Arcadius reflect the conflicting views of successive praetorian prefects rather than a change of heart on the part of the emperor.

8 On Christian uses of text and performance in their liturgical practices and martyr festivals see Pasquarto 1976: 251–358, Baumeister 1987: 120–1, Dix 1975. On Christian martyrdom and spectacle see Potter 1993. See Sticca 1970: 7–10 for how the Latin Passion play was the product of the growth of the special ceremonies, processions, hymns and acts of ritual that developed within the general framework of Christian worship rather than from a parallel secular theatrical tradition. For sophistic attitudes to performance see Schouler 1987: 275–6.

9 On Choricius' likely paganism see Barnes 1996: 179.

10 Greg. Nazianzus, *Ep. ad Greg.* Note also the inclusion of biographical details of Greek tragedians in Eusebius' *Chronicon*: Aeschylus (496 and 477), Sophocles (471, 469, 438 and 408) and Euripides (469, 443 and 408). For information on the inclusion of the tragedians in the *Chronicon* see Mosshammer 1977: 303–19.

11

> Of these plays the more tolerable are comedies and tragedies, that is, dramas composed by poets for presentation on the stage, which, though the stories contain many disgraceful items, are not, at least, like many other shows, expressed in obscene language. They are even included in the curriculum of what is termed a select and liberal education, and boys are forced by their elders to read and learn them.
>
> (Augustine, *De Civ. Dei* 2.8)

12 Novatian, *De Spect.* 7:

> Since the evils of the present day do not suffice to glut the sensuality of our times, recourse has to be had to the theatre where the aberrations of a past age are again presented. It is not permissible, I repeat, for faithful Christians to be present. It is absolutely unlawful for these whom – to charm their ears – Greece sends everywhere to all who are instructed in her vain arts [mime, pantomime, musical accompaniment and] . . . senseless ravings of the tragic voice.

13 Clement of Alexandria, *Protrepticus* 7: 'It may be freely granted that the Greeks received some glimmerings of the divine word and gave utterance to a few scraps of truth. Thus they bear witness to its power which has not been hidden'(trans. G.W. Butterworth). Clement then uses quotation from Euripides' *Orestes* (591–2 and 594–6), *Alcestis* (755–60) and *Ion* (442–7) with their unflattering portrayals of Apollo, Heracles and other divine beings.

14 Cf. Basil of Caesarea, *Ad Adul.* 2 for the language of mystic initiation.

15 Basil of Caesarea, *Ad Adulescentes* is the classic statement of this general approach.

16 For discussion and bibliography see Easterling 1995: 153–60.

17 On the long history of anthologies before the time of Stobaeus see Piccione 1994; Euripides is quoted about 870 times in Stobaeus.

18 See e.g. the *progymnasmata* of Hermogenes and Aphthonius in Rabe, *Rhetores Graeci*, Kennedy 1983: 104–8, and *Diaeresis zêtêmaton* in Walz 8 for Sopater.

19 Typically the objective was to write Attic prose, but there were more adventurous authors who imitated the form of tragedy, too, from Artavasdes, the king of Armenia mentioned in Plutarch's famous story of the performance of the *Bacchae* at which Crassus' head was substituted for the head of Pentheus (*Life of Crassus* 32–3) to Synesius, bishop of Cyrene in the fourth century (evidence in Synesius, *Dio* 62) and whoever was the author of the *Christus Patiens*.

20 Chrysostom heavily edited and reworked his homilies before publication. However, this indicates that the sermons can be read as an elite self-representation of what could be communicated to a socially diverse audience. Pasquarto 1976: 165 argues that there is no evidence of tragedy being played in the Antioch of John Chrysostom, but it must be said that this does not nullify the fact that John presupposes that his congregation would have some knowledge of the staging of tragedy and its themes.

Bibliography

Barnes, T.D. (1996) 'Christians and the Theatre', in W.J. Slater (ed.), *Roman Theater and Society: E. Togo Salmon Papers I*, Ann Arbor: University of Michigan Press.

Bartsch, S. (1994) *Actors in the Audience: Theatricality and Double-Speak from Nero to Hadrian*, Cambridge, Mass.: Harvard University Press.

Baumeister, T. (1987) 'Das Theater in der Sicht der alten Kirche', in G. Holtus (ed.), *Theaterwesen und dramatische Literatur*, Tübingen: Francke.

Beacham, R. (1994) *Roman Theatre and its Audience*, London: Routledge.

Bieber, M. (1961) *The History of the Greek and Roman Theatre*, Princeton: Princeton University Press.

Blänsdorf, J. (1990) 'Der spätantike Staat und die Schauspiele im Codex Theodosianus', in J. Blansdorf (ed.), *Theater und Gesellschaft im Imperium Romanum*, Mainzer Forschungen zu Drama und Theater 4, Tübingen: Francke.

Blockley, R.C. (1981–3) *The Fragmentary Classicising Historians of the Later Roman Empire*, Liverpool: Francis Cairns.

Dix, G. (1975) *The Shape of the Liturgy*, reprinted, London: Dacre Press.

Easterling, P.E. (1995) 'Menander: Loss and Survival', in A. Griffiths (ed.), *Stage Directions*, London: BICS Supplement 66.

Friedländer, L. (1928) *Roman Life and Manners under the Early Empire*, trans. J.H. Freese and L.A. Magnus, London: Routledge.

Gebhard, E.R. (1996) 'The Theater and the City', in W.J. Slater (ed.), *Roman Theater and Society: E. Togo Salmon Papers I*, Ann Arbor: University of Michigan Press.

GrandJouan, C. (1961) *The Athenian Agora Vol. VI: Terracottas and Plastic Lamps of the Roman Period*, Princeton: Princeton University Press.

Green, J.R. (1994) *Theatre in Ancient Greek Society*, London: Routledge.

Jones, C.P. (1993) 'Greek Drama in the Roman Empire', in R. Scodel (ed.), *Theater and Society in the Classical World*, Ann Arbor: University of Michigan Press.

Jory, E.J. (1996) 'The Drama of Dance: Prolegomena to an Iconography of Imperial Pantomime', in W.J. Slater (ed.), *Roman Theater and Society: E. Togo Salmon Papers I*, Ann Arbor: University of Michigan Press.

Kennedy, G.A. (1983) *Greek Rhetoric under Christian Emperors*, London:

Mosshammer, A.A. (1977) *The Chronicle of Eusebius and Greek Chronographic Tradition*, Lewisburg: Bucknell University Press.

Nicoll, A. (1931) *Masks, Mime and Miracles: Studies in the Popular Theatre*, London: Harrap.

Pasquarto, O. (1976) *Gli Spettacoli in S. Giovanni Crisostomo: Paganesimo e Cristianesimo ad Antiochia e Costantinopoli nel iv secolo*, Rome: Orientalia Christiana Analecta 201.

Piccione, R.-M. (1994) 'Sulle fonti e le metodologie compilative di Stobeo', *Eikasmos* 5: 281–317.

Potter, D. (1993) 'Martyrdom as Spectacle', in R. Scodel (ed.), *Theater and Society in the Classical World*, Ann Arbor: University of Michigan Press.

Schouler, B. (1987) 'Les Sophistes et le théâtre au temps des empereurs', in P. Ghiron-Bistagne and B. Schouler (eds), *Anthropologie et théâtre antique: Actes du Colloque International Montpellier 6–8 Mars 1986*, Montpellier: Université Paul Valéry.

Sticca, S. (1970) *The Latin Passion Play: Its Origins and Development*, Albany: University of New York Press.

Vandenberghe, B.H. (1955) 'Saint Jean Chrysostome et les Spectacles', *Zeitschrift für Religions- und Geistesgeschichte 7*.

Webster, T.B.L. (1967) *Monuments Illustrating Tragedy and Satyr Play*, London: BICS Supplement 20.

Weismann, W. (1972) *Kirche und Schauspiele: Die Schauspiele im Urteil der lateinischen Kirchenväter unter besonderer Berücksichtigung von Augustin*, Würzburg.

6

TRANSLATE INTO GREEK

Porphyry of Tyre on the new
barbarians

Gillian Clark

> [Amelius] dedicated the book to Basileus, to me. The name
> Basileus belonged to me, Porphyry, because I had been
> called Malkos in my ancestral language (it was my father's
> name too), and Malkos means *basileus*, if you want to trans-
> late it into Greek.
>
> (Porphyry, *Life of Plotinus* 17)[1]

When Porphyry told his readers about these versions of his name, it
was not because he wanted to make a point about cultural identity in
the late third century. He wanted them to know that it was he who
had, years before, been the leading light in the seminar of Plotinus,
and was therefore the best interpreter of his philosophy. His edition
of Plotinus came out in 301, thirty years after Plotinus died, in the
context of Diocletian's efforts to reaffirm Graeco-Roman traditional
religion. There had probably been an earlier edition, but Porphyry
rearranged the various writings of Plotinus into enneads, groups of
nine, arguing that this made it easier to follow Plotinus' thought
(Saffrey 1992: 31–64). To justify this forceful editorial activity, he
gave the *Enneads* a preface, 'On the Life of Plotinus and the Order
of his Writings', which includes an account of the seminar as he
knew it in 263–8, its final years. The seminar of Plotinus raises,
and helps to answer, questions about Roman citizenship and Greek
culture in relation to languages, traditions and religions which
were neither Roman nor Greek.

Porphyry's names trace his personal history (Smith 1987: 719–22).
He was born Malkos of Tyre around 233, a generation after
Septimius Severus gave his city the status of a Roman colony. If

that was when his family became Roman citizens, his name could, when necessary, be L. Septimius Malchus. At Athens, where he went for advanced study, he acquired another name. His teacher Longinus duly translated Malkos into Greek *Basileus*, 'King' (*Life of Plotinus* 21), but also gave him the nickname Porphyrios, 'purple'. This was a clever choice, for purple came from Tyre and was the colour worn by kings, and it stuck when he went on to Italy to work with Plotinus. Perhaps Malkos sounded too much like *malakos*, 'soft'; perhaps L. Septimius Malchus adopted Porphyrius as an *agnomen* (Millar 1997: 249); or perhaps it was just that Plotinus and Amelius liked nicknames (*Life* 7, 17), and either 'Tyrian Purple' or 'The King' seemed an appropriate comment on Porphyry's arrival. He began by reading a paper which aimed to refute Plotinus on a fundamental question of late Platonist philosophy, whether there are objects of thought distinct from acts of thought (or, in Platonist terminology, intelligibles outside the intellect). If there are, Plotinus was wrong to think that the philosopher discovers his true nature by returning into his own acts of thought. It took several attempts (*Life* 18) to convince Porphyry that Plotinus was right.

Thereafter, Malkos/Basileus was Porphyry the philosopher, sometimes called Porphyry the Tyrian or Porphyry the Phoenician. He left Rome in 268 for Sicily, and spent some time there: Christians seized the chance to label their most hated opponent as Porphyry the Sicilian (Augustine, *Retractations* 2.25.1), a name implying backwoods stupidity. He also visited Carthage, the daughter-city of Tyre, but it is not known how long he stayed, when he returned to Rome, or whether he settled in Rome for the rest of his life. Eunapius, writing biographies of philosophers a century later, reported only that he lectured in Rome and was said to have died there (Brisson 1982: 104–8). Porphyry did not deny his ancestral name, and although he allowed it to be displaced by a Greek nickname, the nickname at least invoked his native city. He may have had property, or family, in Tyre throughout his life. But he did not choose either to settle there as a teacher of philosophy and a respected citizen, or to represent himself to his readers as a Phoenician from a glamorous eastern city (Bowersock 1990: 45–8), drawing on the ancient wisdom of his heritage. Do any, or all, of the names that others gave him help us to understand how he might have understood himself? Was he 'always on the move, a pure intellectual with no true fatherland' (Saffrey 1992: 33), a Phoenician, a Hellene, a

Roman, or a philosopher, journeying in search of wisdom wherever it could be found?

I

Plotinus taught in Rome from the 240s to the late 260s (Brisson 1992: 6–9), and brought together philosophers from very different regions of the empire. He had a Latin name and came from Egypt. Amelius, who worked with him for twenty years, was from Etruria. Porphyry mentions, among his students, Eustochius and Serapion from Egypt, Zethus from Arabia and Paulinus from Scythopolis in Palestine. They may not have come, as Porphyry did, specifically to work with Plotinus. Serapion was a rhetor with business interests, the other three were doctors, and Zethus had political concerns from which Plotinus failed to dissuade him. Zethus also had a personal connection in that his wife's father Theodosius had, like Plotinus, been a student of Ammonius, who taught in Alexandria. The seminar met (*Life* 9) in the house of Gemina, who was certainly a Roman lady, possibly even the widow of an emperor (Saffrey 1992: 32; this was, admittedly, a time of many and short-lived emperors). Plotinus himself was on good terms (*Life* 12) with the emperor Gallienus, who reigned from 253 to 268; the murder of Gallienus, combined with the terminal illness of Plotinus, may have caused Plotinus to leave Rome and his students to disperse (Brisson 1982: 75–6). Roman senators also came to the seminar. Most of them combined philosophy with politics, but Rogatianus, who refused either to perform his duties as praetor or to live in his own great house (*Life* 7), was a living proof that asceticism is good for the health (*On Abstinence* 1.53.3). He had been so crippled (perhaps by arthritis) that he had to use a carrying-chair, but was cured by eating only every second day.

This looks like a Roman seminar in every sense of the word, located in the capital city, connected to the urban elite, and exemplifying the famous claim of Aelius Aristides (*To Rome* 61) that Rome had made an empire into a city, politically united and with a common culture. According to Porphyry, anyone who wanted could come to the meetings (though perhaps Gemina's porter would not have admitted strangers who lacked an introduction). But the seminar was inclusive only within limits, for its common culture, like its working language, was Greek. Greek was the *lingua franca* of the eastern Mediterranean and of all cultured people from the West, and Rogatianus and his fellow-senators were probably bilingual. But, as Augustine discovered a century later (*Confessions* 1.14.23), the kind of Greek that less prosperous westerners struggled through at school was just not adequate for dealing with Greek philosophy. The easterners could probably have managed some Latin. Even before they came to work in Rome, they might have learned Latin for political reasons, especially if there were long-established Roman colonies in their homelands (Millar 1997: 245–6). But they saw no reason to do philosophy in Latin. Porphyry grew up in a Roman *colonia* (and near Berytus, which later became a centre for the study of Roman law) and lived in Rome for at least five years, but his writings do not acknowledge any personal knowledge of Latin. Even a passing comment that 'some Latins are called, in their own language, Aper and Scorpus and Ursus and Merulus' (*Abst.* 4.16.5) was derived from his source. Interestingly, he did not include Latin in his examples of languages that Greeks cannot understand (*Abst.* 3.3.4–5), but that might mean either that Latin was not a problem (it was far closer to Greek than the examples he did use, such as Aramaic and 'Indian'), or that Latin was being deliberately ignored (cf. Swain 1996: 41–2). He did not mention any students of Plotinus from the western Mediterranean, or show any awareness of a western philosophical tradition.

The focus of late Platonist philosophy was Greece and the Near East, and its traditions invoked Egypt and Syria, Babylon and India (Festugière 1944: 19–44). Italian philosophers could connect themselves to these traditions through the Pythagorean presence in the Greek cities of the south, which was supposedly (but anachronistically) an influence on the laws and cults ascribed to King Numa (Cicero, *Rep.* 2.289). Poseidonius (Rankin 1987: 221–2) made a valiant attempt to extend the cultural club to Gaul, and Celts, especially Druids, earn an occasional mention in the third century. Diogenes Laertius, unusually, adds the Druids to the roll-call of barbarian wisdom, and links them (but very briefly) with the Indian Gymnosophists (1.1, 1.6); Hippolytus, a Christian contemporary of Porphyry, claims (*Refutation of all Heresies* 1.2.17) that Zalmoxis the Pythagorean taught them; and Iamblichus (*Pythagorean Life* 151) has Pythagoras synthesising wisdom learned not only from Orphics, Egyptians, Chaldaeans and Magi, but from the rituals at Eleusis, Imbros, Samothrace and Lemnos, and of the Celts and Iberians. If these are western Celts and Iberians (rather than those of the Black Sea region), perhaps the Iberians were contributed by the neo-Pythagorean Moderatus, who came from Cadiz. But the rarity of such claims suggests that no one was very interested in making them. The seminar of Plotinus was a Greek-speaking enclave which depended on the presence of Plotinus in Rome. We do not know why he went there, but perhaps no special explanation is needed: several philosophers chose to work in the capital city (Frede 1997: 218). After his death, Platonist philosophy continued to have an effect in Italy. Marius Victorinus, who translated some Platonist texts into Latin, may even, in his youth, have met Porphyry in Rome (Aug. *Conf.* 8.2.3 with O'Donnell 1992: 3.13–15). Augustine was given some of these translations, when he arrived in Milan a century after the death of Plotinus, probably by Manlius Theodorus who led a Platonist study group (Aug. *Conf.* 7.9.13, with O'Donnell 1992: 2.419–20). Ambrose of Milan read Plotinus in Greek (Madec 1974: 61–71). But the group that worked with Plotinus did not outlast his death, and Porphyry, though he may have continued to teach in Rome, had no known successor or students there. Eunapius (456) clearly lacked traditions and memories of Porphyry as a teacher, but located him firmly in the eastern Mediterranean succession of Plotinus, Porphyry, Iamblichus and the students of Iamblichus.

II

The seminar of Plotinus exemplified both ease of movement under the Roman peace and within the common Greek culture, and the continuing divide between Hellenism and the western Mediterranean. It also exemplified a less welcome consequence of 'making the empire into a city', namely the drain of talent away from cities. Philosophers could travel in search of wisdom, but their cosmopolitanism and their philosophical commitment might mean that their native cities lost resources, both human and financial. Philosophy, almost always, required an advanced and therefore expensive education. (Cynic and Epicurean claims that it did not were usually made by people who had previously had the education.) Anyone who could afford to devote his life to philosophy, however simple his needs, probably had enough inherited wealth to incur civic obligations in his home town. Teachers were sometimes (not consistently) exempt from such obligations on the grounds that their work was a contribution to the city (Kaster 1988: 114–21); but the exemption was for teachers of literature and rhetoric who trained young men in the skills they needed for civic life, and who could themselves be used as ambassadors, not for teachers of philosophy who tried to avoid the distractions of civic life and perhaps lived somewhere else.

Platonists had to decide how the traditional obligation of the good man to maintain family, city and cult could be reconciled with Plato's teaching on the philosopher's need to disengage the soul from worldly concerns and desires. Many students of Plotinus continued to have families, property, financial and political concerns. But Plotinus himself had left his obscure Egyptian birthplace to seek a teacher in Alexandria, travelled into Persia with the Roman army, and settled in Rome for reasons not known to us. Porphyry tells us (*Life* 1, 3, 9) that he refused to talk about his family, parents or country, and though he had wards, he had no children. Amelius left Italy to settle in Apamea in Syria, perhaps because it was the home town of the philosopher Numenius whom he greatly admired, and adopted a son there (Brisson 1982: 65–9). Porphyry may have maintained property and family ties in Tyre. He had stepchildren in Italy from his marriage to Marcella, widow of another student of Plotinus, but declared that he had not married her in the hope of children of his own (*To Marcella* 1). In *On Abstinence* (4.20.3), so far from endorsing the usual Platonist opinion that the only proper use of sex is for the procreation of legitimate children, he argued powerfully that all sexual intercourse is contamination because it is a mixing of opposites: male and female, soul and body if conception occurs, living body and dead seed if conception fails.

On Abstinence is exceptional in its portrayal of a philosopher seeking God in solitude, 'alone to the alone' (2.49.1). It is almost obsessively concerned with contamination by what goes into the body, and it rejects both political involvement and traditional civic worship. The *Life of Plotinus* shows a much wider range of lifestyles and varieties of civic involvement among the students of Plotinus, and Porphyry's own student (or fellow-student) and sparring-partner Iamblichus provides a contrast (Clark 1999). After some philosophical travels, he settled on estates in his Syrian homeland (though in a different area from his birthplace Chalcis), and Ariston son of Iamblichus, who married a woman student of Plotinus, was probably his son (Dillon and Hershbell 1991: 17–24). His students (Fowden 1982: 40–3) continued mobile: they did not move so far as the students of Plotinus, but perhaps that was because Iamblichus lived in Syria, not in Rome. They came from Greece and Cappadocia as well as the eastern Mediterranean coast. Aidesius returned to Cappadocia then moved to Pergamum; Chrysanthius went back to Sardis, where he taught Eunapius, and spent some time in Ephesus.

Iamblichus, unlike Porphyry, emphasised community living and shared worship. He imagined a philosophic lifestyle for the disciples of Pythagoras, and used it to inspire his own students. His Pythagoreans live in philosophical communities, with their families, at a peaceful distance from the cities of South Italy. Nevertheless, at least some of them help to administer the cities – but only after lunch (*Pythagorean Life* 97), having spent the morning in philosophy.

III

The diverse Roman citizens who studied with philosophers shared Greek culture and readiness to put philosophy above local ties, and were always willing to journey in search of the right teacher. They did not always return from their journeys, and may not have kept any special commitment to their homelands or to their ancestral traditions. Twentieth-century scholarship on Porphyry, and on other philosophers from the eastern empire, has only recently begun to notice the dangers of orientalism (Millar 1997: 241–2). Numenius, Plotinus, Porphyry and Iamblichus all came from the Near East, and that has too often been taken to show that Neoplatonism is a place of struggle between the darkness of oriental superstition and the light of Greek rationality. The present trend is rather to suggest that Iamblichus, in particular, reconciles Greek philosophical understanding with a deeper religious commitment derived from his ancestral tradition (Athanassiadi 1981, Fowden 1986, Shaw 1995). But Porphyry and Iamblichus came from the one area of the Near East where there is no clear evidence for the survival of a local language and its culture (Millar 1993: 264–309).

Even if tradition survived, Porphyry 'the Phoenician' shows no sign of identifying himself as either Syrian or Phoenician, of understanding local languages (Phoenician if it was still spoken or written, Aramaic, biblical Hebrew), or of knowing local customs and traditions otherwise than in the reports of Greek authors (Millar 1997). His perspective throughout is that of a Greek writer dependent on Greek sources for an account of non-Greek cultures. Did he speak any languages other than Greek and, presumably, some Latin? In the course of an argument that animals have language, even if we cannot speak their languages, he comments that 'not every human being finds it easy to learn or to imitate not just animal languages, but as many as five human languages' (*Abst.* 3.4.6). Speculation is tempting here. Traders, or even scholars, in Phoenicia might well want to use Greek, Latin, Aramaic in its Syriac and Nabatean versions, Palmyrene, perhaps one of the Persian languages. (This is less daunting than it sounds: present-day Anglophone classicists are usually assumed to have at least a reading knowledge of French, German and Italian in addition to their Greek and Latin, and some add Spanish or Russian or Hebrew or other languages from countries where Rome once ruled or where the classics are still studied.) Perhaps Porphyry implies that he did speak five languages, but still could not converse with animals or birds, not even with the partridge which made friends with him at Carthage and responded when he spoke to it (*Abst.* 3.4.7; Sorabji 1993: 80–6). He notes that it never started the conversation, and that it made different sounds when conversing with partridges.

But Porphyry's argument about animal language depends on the experience of hearing a language which you cannot translate, or even hear as language rather than noise, whereas other people can:

> Now since that which is voiced by the tongue is *logos* [discourse] however it is voiced, whether in barbarian or Greek, dog or cattle fashion, animals which have a voice share in *logos*, humans speaking in accordance with human customs and animals according to the customs each has acquired from the gods and nature. And if we do not understand them, so what? Greeks do not understand Indian, nor do those brought up on Attic understand Scythian or Thracian or Syrian: the sound that each makes strikes the others like the calling of cranes. Yet for each their language can be written in letters and articulated, as ours can for us; but for us the language of Syrians, say, or Persians cannot be articulated or written, just as that of animals cannot be for any people. For we are aware only of noise and sound, because we do not understand (say) Scythian speech, and they seem to us to be making noises and articulating nothing: they just make a sound which sometimes lasts a longer time and sometimes a shorter time, but the modification to convey meaning does not strike us at all. Yet to them their speech is easy to understand and very distinct, just as our accustomed speech is to us; and similarly in the case of animals, understanding comes to them in a way which is peculiar to each species, but we can hear only noise deficient in meaning, because no one who had learned our

language has taught us to translate into it what is said by
animals.

$(Abst. 3.3.3–5)^2$

But, Porphyry observes, there are humans who do understand at least
some of what birds and animals say, so their speech is in principle
translatable (even if not by him). He later claims some understanding
on the other side: 'animals do not hear our speech as noise, but they
have an awareness of the difference among [linguistic] signs, and that
comes from rational understanding' (*Abst.* 3.15.2). His argument
here reworks a traditional comparison between the speech of barbarians, such as the half-Egyptian Danaids in Aeschylus, *Suppliants*
(57–62), and the calls of birds. The priestesses at Dodona were
called 'doves', Herodotus suggests, because they originally spoke a
barbarian language:

> I think the Dodonans called the women 'doves' (as they still
> do) because they were barbarians, and seemed to them to
> make sounds like birds. They say that after a time the
> dove spoke with a human voice: that was when the
> woman said things they could understand. But so long as
> she spoke barbarian, she seemed to them to make sounds
> like a bird, for how could a dove speak with a human
> voice? And by saying it was a black dove, they show that
> the woman was Egyptian.
>
> (Hdt. 2.57; Harrison 1998)

Porphyry uses the comparison to argue that birdsong may be a
language, just as the speech of barbarians, unintelligible to us, is
nevertheless a language. 'We' are Greek speakers and explicitly not
Syrians – though it would be unwise to build too much on familiar
examples of foreigners. Indeed, 'we' are speakers of pure Greek.
Porphyry, a true pupil of Longinus, comments (*Life* 13) that Plotinus
sometimes made mistakes in Greek; they were of the kind which, we
learn from Augustine (*Conf.* 1.18.28), were called 'barbarisms', faults
of pronunciation rather than grammar. His argument about animals
suggests an awareness of Atticist snobbery (cf. Swain 1996: 17–64):

> How can it not be ignorant to call only human speech *logos*,
> because we understand it, and dismiss the speech of other
> animals? It is as if ravens claimed that theirs was the only
> language, and we lack *logos*, because we say things which

are not meaningful to them, or the people of Attica said that Attic is the only language, and thought that others who do not share in the Attic way of speaking lack *logos*. Yet an Attic speaker would understand a raven sooner than a Syrian or Persian speaking Syrian or Persian. But surely it is absurd to judge rationality or irrationality by whether speech is or is not easy to understand, or by silence or voice.

(*Abst.* 3.5.2–3)[3]

But, as these two quotations show, the point about *logos* is more important than snobbery or even ethnocentricity. It is puzzling that *logos*, the ability to reason and to make sense of the world, should express itself so differently in human languages and make human communication such a problem. Julian (*Against the Galilaeans* 143a) says that the presiding *daimones* of nations, which give them their distinctive characters, also give them different languages. Augustine remarks (*City of God* 19.7) that 'dumb animals' even of different species can associate more easily than humans who do not speak each other's language: when people cannot communicate, difference of language outweighs similarity of nature, and a man would prefer to be with his own dog than with a foreign human. Porphyry's argument goes further: by refusing to acknowledge that an unfamiliar sequence of sound is a (potentially) intelligible language – something that could, if we found an interpreter, be translated into Greek – we also refuse to acknowledge that those who utter the sounds are engaged in (potentially) intelligible thought.

IV

The 'ancestral language' which gave Porphyry his original name of Malkos, like the 'ancestral language' of Egypt (*Abst.* 4.9.5, 10.4) and the 'local language' of the Magi (4.16.1), could be translated into Greek, but was not part of Greek culture.[4] Porphyry's self-identification with Greek speakers, and with their inability to understand non-Greek language, might seem to relegate Phoenicians (and other Near Easterners) to the status of barbarians, makers of unintelligible noises. But here we meet an ambivalence which has a long history. When Philo of Byblos, in the late first or early second century, wrote what he said was a translation of the ancient Phoenician history of Sanchuniathon, he was prepared to call his ancestors barbarian, but he did it with respect: 'the most ancient of the *barbaroi*, especially the Phoenicians and the Egyptians' (Bowersock 1994: 43). According to

Greek prejudice, Phoenicians not only did not speak Greek, but had effeminate oriental customs, and inherited the role of the Trojans in the great war against Greece. (Nero's tour of Greece was enlivened by the 'discovery' of the pre-Homeric version of the Trojan War, allegedly written in Phoenician letters by Dictys the Cretan (Bowersock 1994: 23).) But it was Phoenician letters, transmitted from Tyre by Cadmus in the distant past, which had allowed the Greeks to record Greek language (Swain 1996: 17–18). Likewise, Egyptians did not speak Greek and their customs were, according to Herodotus, the reverse of Greek. But Herodotus also thought (2.49–50) that Egypt gave Greece its religious traditions and the names of its gods; and Plato (*Timaeus* 21e–22b) imagined Solon the lawgiver being instructed by Egyptian priests, who told him that the Greeks were children in comparison with Egyptian antiquity. The 'ancient barbarians' were the source of the *nomoi*, the laws and religious rules, which structured Greek society, and of the writing which allowed those rules, and other expressions of thought, to be made intelligible to all.

In the early centuries CE, the cultural role of the *barbaroi* was changing. Aelius Aristides continued to use the opposition of Greek and barbarian, but commented (*To Rome* 63) that Romans divided the world into Roman and non-Roman, those who did or did not accept the civilisation which the Romans had inherited from the Greeks. Phoenicians and Egyptians were within the Roman empire and by Porphyry's lifetime were Roman citizens. (So, of course, were Gauls and Germans, but this did not make them any more widely used as a source of barbarian wisdom.) Christianity was a further complication, because Christians (including Greek Christians) used 'Greek' as a label for aliens who were outside the household of faith and unwilling to accept the truth, argued for the superiority of Jewish scripture over anything Greek, and made Egypt a symbol not of ancient wisdom but of enslavement to worldly goods. It is very difficult to document just how much influence Christians had, before Constantine, on the self-awareness of non-Christians; but for those (including Porphyry) who identified themselves as culturally Greek, Christians, whatever their origin and education, had rejected Hellenism for barbarian scriptures.

These cultural shifts may help to explain why, in Graeco-Roman philosophy and religion, the ancient admiration for barbarian wisdom was on the increase. This too has often been interpreted as a falling away from Greek rationality in pursuit of 'le mirage oriental' – a Neoplatonic decline from unity into multiplicity and confusion (Festugière 1944: 1.20–44). But Neoplatonists saw themselves as engaged in the right understanding of Plato, who said (*Laws* 657a) that Greeks were restless and innovative, several times acknowledged a debt to the wisdom of Egypt, and, according to tradition, actually travelled there to participate in its mysteries. Jews and Christians said that this explained his obvious borrowings from Moses, who grew up in Egypt (Frede 1997: 234–5), and the philosopher Numenius (O'Meara 1989: 10–14) famously referred to him as 'Moses talking Attic Greek'. Numenius, and other Neoplatonists, also held Pythagoras in respect (though they had different opinions on his status relative to Plato), and the traditions about Pythagoras showed him travelling the Mediterranean world to absorb wisdom from all possible sources. When Porphyry compiled accounts for the life of Pythagoras included in his *Philosophic History*, he found stories (*Life of Pythagoras* 6, 11) that Pythagoras studied with Egyptians (geometry and theology), Chaldaeans (astronomy), Phoenicians (arithmetic), Magi (ritual and ethics), and even Hebrews (dream interpretation) and the king of Arabia (unexplained): the last two are from Antoninus Diogenes, who had a lively imagination. The mobile philosophers of late antiquity thought it right to continue this tradition, whether by personal travels or by reading. Plotinus, according to Porphyry (*Life* 3), wanted to study the philosophy of the Persians and Indians, and therefore joined the army, which was about to leave on an expedition against the main national enemy. Porphyry may be wrong (Edwards 1994); what is interesting is that he suggests it.

Texts which claimed to record the ancient wisdom of Chaldaeans and Egyptians, Magi and Brahmans, were interpreted as reinforcing the authority, universality and antiquity of Platonist teaching (Festugière 1944, Turcan 1975). This was not difficult, since their authors, even if not themselves Greek, were usually influenced by Greek culture and especially by Platonism. Any 'oriental' inheritance in these texts has been filtered through Greek ethnography and philosophy, and different beliefs about the soul have more to do with philosophical debates about Plato and Aristotle than with Egyptian or Iranian theological tradition (Blumenthal 1996). As Iamblichus said, Hermetic texts often use philosophical language, 'because they were translated from Egyptian by men who were not ignorant of philosophy' (*Mysteries of Egypt* 8.4.265). The texts ascribed to Hermes Trismegistus are probably from the late first to the third centuries CE; but Plato said that Egyptian priests translated sacred texts for Solon, so other Greek translations could claim antiquity (Copenhaver 1992). The 'Chaldaean Oracles', which Porphyry appears to have put on the philosophical agenda with his Neoplatonist commentary, were probably compiled by a Platonist father-and-son team in the second century: they too laid claim to ancient wisdom (Majercik 1989).

The 'pagan oecumenism' (Athanassiadi 1993: 3) of late Platonism may look like the insouciant confidence of the late twentieth-century New Age that Black Elk, Lao Tse, the Zend-Avesta and Celtic priestesses all taught ecologically sound pantheism. It was also an accepted rhetorical strategy for claiming an authoritative voice. Thus, when Porphyry wrote a *Letter to the Priest Anebo* which asked a series of questions about Egyptian metaphysics, Iamblichus recognised that it was directed to him and concerned with the theology and religious practice of philosophical Greeks. He replied in the person of Anebo's spiritual master Abammon, citing (*Myst.* 8.5.267–8) not only the Hermetic Corpus, but the prophet Bitys who interpreted Hermetism to King Ammon, having found it engraved in hieroglyphs in the sanctuary at Sais: the very place where Egyptian priests, according to Plato, had instructed Solon.

This debate on religion included an important question about barbarian language. One of Porphyry's challenges to Anebo was about translation: why do priests engaged in theurgic ritual (that is, the use of sacramental words and objects to convey spiritual help) use barbarian divine names rather than 'ours', that is, Greek? Iamblichus replied that the language of sacred races, such as the Egyptians and Assyrians, is itself sacred and appropriate to the nature of the gods. The divine names are not just a human convention, and some things are not translatable.

> When words are translated, they do not keep entirely the same sense: every people has some particular characteristics which cannot be conveyed in language to another people. And even if it were possible to translate these words, they would not retain the same power. Barbarian words have great impact and conciseness; they lack ambiguity, complexity and multiplicity of expression, and for all these reasons are appropriate to the Greater Ones.
>
> (*Myst.* 7.5.257)

If words and prayers have lost their effectiveness, it is because of Greek liking for novelties and departure from tradition.

The Greeks are natural innovators; they have no ballast, but are carried about in every direction. They do not safeguard what they receive, but quickly lose it and change everything in their restless search for words. But the barbarians are stable in their customs and remain constant to the same words, so they are dear to the gods and offer them words which find favour: no one is allowed to change them in any way. That is my reply to you on the subject of names which are unutterable and of those which are called barbarian but are really religious.

(*Myst.* 7.5.259)

Iamblichus claimed the religious high ground as a barbarian (rhetorically Egyptian, perhaps Syrian by tradition), casting Porphyry as an argumentative Greek, in a neat variant on the well-known tactic of claiming that one's opponent is interested only in debate, not in finding the truth. The theme of Greek inferiority recurs in a text of the Hermetic Corpus which argues – in Greek – that Egyptian mysteries cannot be translated into Greek.

Hermes [. . .] said that those who read my books will find the composition very simple and clear, but on the contrary it is obscure and conceals the meaning of the discourse; and it will be even more obscure when later on the Greeks want to translate our language into theirs. This will be the greatest distortion and obscuring of the text. The discourse, when expressed in our ancestral language, makes clear the meaning of the words, for the quality of the sound [*phônê*] and the ⟨lacuna⟩ of the Egyptian words have in themselves the activity of what is said. Do everything you can, O king (and you can do everything) to prevent these mysteries reaching the Greeks, and to prevent their pretentious, dissipated, over-ornamented idiom from eroding the gravity and solidity and active idiom of these words. The Greeks, O king, have pointless discourses which achieve only demonstrations, and that is what Greek philosophy is, a noise of discourses. We use not discourses, but sounds [*phônai*] full of action.

(*Corpus Hermeticum* 16.2)

This contrast challenged a distinction considered by Porphyry, among others: that non-rational creatures may have *phônê* which expresses a state of feeling, but only rational creatures have articulate discourse, *logos* (Sorabji 1993: 80–6). But another text of the Corpus took the opposite view:

> Father, do not the other animals use *logos*?
> No, my child, only *phônê*, and *logos* is very different from *phônê*. *Logos* is common to all humans, but each species of animal has its own *phônê*.
> But do not humans have different *logos*, father, in different nations?
> Different, yes, my child, but humanity is one, so *logos* is also one, and when translated it is found to be the same in Egypt or Persia or Greece.
>
> (*CH* 12.13)

Porphyry and Iamblichus agreed that ancient barbarian religious traditions can be interpreted as conveying a Platonist message: the soul must be detached from material concerns, and must return to God by moral and intellectual purification. But Iamblichus argued that Greek philosophers must, like Plato and Pythagoras, learn from barbarian wisdom by entering into its mysteries, whereas Porphyry's position was that all non-Greek languages (including, for him, those of non-human animals) express a common *logos* and are potentially translatable into Greek, just as the religious practices of non-Greek cultures express a common understanding and can be interpreted through the reports of Greek authors.

V

Porphyry saw in religion both a common philosophical culture uniting all devotees of the truth, and a Herodotean display of cultural diversity. Greeks do not sacrifice camels because there are no camels in Greece, Jews and Phoenicians do not sacrifice pigs because there were once no pigs in their countries (*Abst.* 1.14.4); different cultures ban different animals as food (4.5.5). There are also exotic variants in the asceticism which expresses the purity, and the undistracted closeness to the gods, of the religiously committed. The Samaneans of India, for instance, abandon their families without a backward look; when their souls are ready, they may choose suicide, and climb onto their funeral pyres surrounded by their joyful companions who charge them with messages for those already in the other world (4.17.7–18.3). But all cultures have taught some kind of asceticism.

According to Augustine, Porphyry said at the end of *On the Return of the Soul*, book 1, that

> he had not yet found any one philosophical sect which provided a universal way of liberating the soul: not in any most true philosophy, nor in the ethics and discipline of the Indians, nor in the 'elevation' of the Chaldaeans, nor in any other way.
>
> (*City of God* 10.32)

Augustine was not out to give a balanced review of what Porphyry said, and in book 10 of *City of God* he was looking for ammunition. We need not accept his interpretation that Porphyry clearly acknowledges the existence of a universal way of salvation which he has not yet found: Porphyry might well have continued, in book 2, to expound the common Platonist truth which is adumbrated in other traditions.

But if a tradition was used to challenge Platonism, not to harmonise with it, Porphyry went onto the attack. Eusebius indignantly reports what he says is a quotation from Porphyry about Origen:

> Origen, a Greek educated in Greek literature, made straight for barbarism, putting himself and his literary training on the market; he lived like a Christian, lawlessly, but thought like a Greek about the divine and about things in general, insinuating Greek ideas into foreign fables. He lived with Plato; he was familiar with the writings of Numenius and Kronios and Apollophanes and Longinus and Moderatus and Nicomachus and the distinguished Pythagoreans; he used the books of Chaeremon the Stoic and Cornutus, from which he learned the allegorical interpretation used in the Greek mysteries and applied it to the Jewish scriptures.
>
> (*HE* 6.19.7)

Eusebius might well be annoyed. Quite what Porphyry meant by living *paranomôs*, 'lawlessly', is unclear. Iamblichus, in the persona of an Egyptian high priest, said that the Greeks are *paranomoi* in that they do not maintain religious tradition. Porphyry may have meant that Origen practised a religion which was actually forbidden by law, or more generally that his life as a celibate Christian was contrary to the *nomoi* of his society. But Porphyry himself challenged Greek social *nomoi*, and deployed allegory to find a Greek philosophical message in seemingly unphilosophical texts.

In *On Abstinence* (2.38–43), Porphyry regarded ancestral custom as strictly for the ignorant masses, and rejected animal sacrifice as a delusion imposed by greedy *daimones*. So far as the evidence goes, he declined to support his city and its gods by providing funds, cult and successors. But it would be too much to claim that he consistently rejected the *nomoi*. In the *Letter to Marcella* (18) he said that 'the greatest fruit of piety is to honour the divine in accordance with ancestral tradition, not because the divine has need of this, but because we are called to revere it by its awesome and blessed majesty'. (This need not mean acceptance of animal sacrifice: in *On Abstinence* (2.59.1) Porphyry argues that when the Delphic Oracle says 'sacrifice according to ancestral tradition', it means the tradition of the ancients, who made offerings of grain.) Philosophers do change their minds and see different aspects of a question (Smith 1987: 734–7). We do not know when Porphyry wrote *On Abstinence*: its extreme and isolationist tone suggests the depression of the late 360s for which Plotinus (according to Porphyry, *Life* 11) recommended a holiday, and Porphyry insisted (*Abst.* 2.3.3–4) that the way of life it commends is only for some philosophers.

It is less easy to defend Porphyry on the use of allegory. In *The Cave of the Nymphs* he allegorised Homer with the help of Platonised Mithraism (Lamberton 1986: 119–33; Turcan 1975: 23–43). According to the Christian theologian Didymus the Blind, he said that the conflict of Achilles and Hector was a more appropriate symbol than the conflict of Christ and Satan (Sellew 1989). Porphyry was on shaky ground when he complained that Christian allegorisation distorted a straightforward, but morally suspect, narrative. Homer, of course, is a Greek 'mystery', and therefore a suitable case for allegory, but here too Porphyry was not consistent in opposition. Numenius (O'Meara 1989: 13) had said that Jewish scripture, like Pythagoras, taught that God is non-material, and both Eusebius and Augustine cite Porphyry on the wisdom of the Hebrews and its relationship to the universal tradition (Eus. *Preparation for the Gospel* 9.10.1–5; Aug. *City of God* 19.23). But for Porphyry in polemic mode, the Old Testament is the wrong sort of text for allegorical interpretation because Christians put forward their sacred text, and their new claimant to divinity, not in support of Greek philosophical tradition but in deliberate rivalry. There were limits to pagan oecumenism.

Porphyry acquired the reputation of Christianity's fiercest opponent, but he did not stop at Christianity. He remarked in the *Life* (16, with Igal 1981) that there were many Christians among the students of Plotinus, but he distinguished the 'many' from heretics who argued that Plato had not understood the depth of being. They had texts which they said were ancient and authoritative, including some ascribed to Zoroaster. Some of the texts that Porphyry names have been found at Nag Hammadi, and it would not be difficult to give them a Platonist interpretation (Tardieu 1992). Why did Porphyry reject them, whereas he wrote commentaries on the Chaldaean Oracles? As with Christian allegory, the problem was that the 'Zoroastrian' texts were being used to challenge Plato, not to support him. Plotinus, according to Porphyry, often refuted these people, and Amelius and Porphyry showed that their texts were modern fabrications. These Gnostic opponents also appear in *On Abstinence* (1.42.1), claiming that their profound understanding frees them from ordinary concerns about purity, just as the depth of the sea absorbs all the impurities that enter it. Porphyry calls them *barbaroi*: these are the people he regards as aliens in terms of the Hellenic tradition they have studied but fail to understand, and who utter incomprehensible noises.

Porphyry, then, identified himself with the Greeks, who either marginalised or venerated non-Greek cultures, including the traditional culture of Phoenicia. His Greek education fitted him to share in the common culture of philosophy. This culture taught him that Greek and barbarian meet in the return to the divine, that the spiritual elite of barbarian peoples are far superior to the ordinary Greek, and that their barbarian language may express an awareness of the divine which is superior even to that of the philosophical Greek. Philosophy also taught him to be detached from his city, to travel in search of the right teacher, to resist the concerns of householding and politics; and to define his identity not as a Phoenician or Greek or Roman, but as a soul working for return to God. Porphyry, the pure intellectual, did have a true fatherland:

> Our fatherland is where we have come from, and our father is there. How shall we get there, how shall we escape to it? Not on foot, for our feet carry us here and there over the earth, from one land to another; nor should you hire horses or sea-transport, you must let all that go, not look at it, and as if you had closed your eyes awake another kind of sight

which everyone has, but few use.

(Plotinus, *Ennead* 1.6.8)

We are like those who, whether involuntarily or voluntarily, have gone away to another people, and not only are excluded from what is their own, but are filled by the foreign land with alien passions and habits and customs, and have acquired an inclination towards them. A man who is preparing to return from there to his homeland not only is eager to be on the journey, but also, so that he may be accepted, practises putting aside any alien way that he has acquired, and reminds himself of what he once had but has forgotten, without which he cannot be accepted among his own people.

(*Abst.* 1.30.2–3)

The foreign land might be Rome as much as Phoenicia, Athens as much as Egypt. The true philosopher is in exile even in the place of his birth, and perhaps especially there because he has more to hold him there. The fatherland is common to people who are, in this life, resident foreigners in any number of countries. For Porphyry, its language is the Greek of the highly educated, but he allows for other, translatable, expressions of shared understanding. The real barbarians are those who cannot, or will not, speak the language of the fatherland.

Acknowledgements

It is a particular pleasure to acknowledge a debt to Fergus Millar: immediately to the paper cited as Millar 1997, and more generally to prompt and benevolent help over many years. I am also indebted to Linda Jones Hall for advice on the survival of Phoenician, to Tom Harrison for an advance copy of Harrison 1998, and to Simon Swain for helpful comments on an earlier draft.

Notes

1 All translations are my own; translations of *On Abstinence* are from Clark fc.
2 My translation differs from Millar 1997: 254 in emphasising *logos*, which in Porphyry's argument is both reason and the articulate speech which expresses reason.
3 Prophyry uses *phônê* both of voiced sound, as in the first sentence of this quotation where it is (twice) translated 'speech', and of language, as in the second sentence.

4 Egyptian is a *patrios phônê* or *patrios dialektos*; the Magi speak as *epichôrios dialektos*. Latin is a *dialektos* in 4.16.5; so is Greek, *Hellênis dialektos*, as well as Porphyry's *patrios dialektos*, in the passage from the *Life of Plotinus* translated at the beginning of this chapter.

Bibliography

Athanassiadi, P. (1981) *Julian and Hellenism*, Oxford: Oxford University Press, reprinted as (1992) *Julian: an intellectual biography*, London: Routledge.

—— (1993) 'Persecution and response in late paganism: the evidence of Damascius', *Journal of Hellenic Studies* 113: 1–29.

Blumenthal, H. (1996) 'On soul and intellect', in L. Gerson (ed.) *The Cambridge Companion to Plotinus*, Cambridge: Cambridge University Press.

Bowersock, G. (1990) *Hellenism in Late Antiquity*, Ann Arbor: University of Michigan Press.

—— (1994) *Fiction as History: Nero to Julian*, Berkeley, CA: University of California Press.

Brisson, L. (1982) 'Prosopographie' in L. Brisson et al. (ed.) *Porphyre: La Vie de Plotin*, tome 1. Paris: Vrin.

—— (1992) 'Plotin: une biographie', in L. Brisson et al. (ed.) *Porphyre: La Vie de Plotin*, tome 2. Paris: Vrin.

Clark, G. (1999) 'Porphyry and Iamblichus: philosophic Lives and the philosophic life', in T. Hagg and P. Rousseau (eds) *Greek Biography and Panegyric in Late Antiquity*, Berkeley, CA: University of California Press.

—— (fc) *Porphyry of Tyre, On abstinence from killing animals*: translation and commentary. London: Duckworth.

Copenhaver, B. (1992) *Hermetica*, Cambridge: Cambridge University Press.

Dillon, J. and Hershbell, J. (1991) *Iamblichus: On the Pythagorean way of life*, Atlanta: Scholars Press.

Edwards, M.J. (1994) 'Plotinus and the emperors', *Symbolae Osloenses* 69: 137–47.

Festugière, A.J. (1944) *La Révélation d'Hermès Trismégiste I: l'astrologie et les sciences occultes*. Paris: Gabalda.

Fowden, G. (1982) 'The pagan holy man in late antique society', *Journal of Hellenic Studies* 102: 33–59.

—— (1986) *The Egyptian Hermes: a historical approach to the late pagan mind*, Cambridge: Cambridge University Press.

Frede, M. (1997) 'Celsus' attack on the Christians', in J. Barnes and M. Griffin (ed.), *Philosophia Togata II: Plato and Aristotle at Rome*, Oxford: Clarendon Press.

Harrison, T. (1998) 'Herodotus' conception of foreign languages', *Histos* 2: http://www.dur.ac.uk/classics/histos/. [Electronic publication.]

Igal, J. (1981) 'The Gnostics and the "Ancient Philosophy" in Porphyry and Plotinus', in H.J. Blumenthal and R.A. Markus (ed.) *Neoplatonism and Early Christian Thought*, London: Variorum.

Kaster, R. (1988) *Guardians of Language: the grammarian and society in late antiquity*, Berkeley, CA: University of California Press.

Lamberton, R. (1986) *Homer the Theologian: Neoplatonist allegorical reading and the growth of the epic tradition*, Berkeley, CA: University of California Press.

Madec, G. (1974) *Saint Ambroise et la philosophie*, Paris: Etudes Augustiniennes.

Majercik, R. (1989) *The Chaldaean Oracles: text, translation and commentary*, Leiden: Brill.

Millar, F. (1993) *The Roman Near East 31 BC–AD 337*, Cambridge, MA: Harvard University Press.

—— (1997) 'Porphyry: ethnicity, language and alien wisdom', in J. Barnes and M. Griffin (ed.) *Philosophia Togata II: Plato and Aristotle at Rome*, Oxford: Clarendon Press.

O'Donnell, J. (1992) *Augustine, Confessions: text and commentary*, 3 vols, Oxford: Clarendon Press.

O'Meara, D. (1989) *Pythagoras Revived: mathematics and philosophy in late antiquity*, Oxford: Clarendon Press.

Rankin, D. (1987) *The Celts in the Classical World*, London: Routledge.

Saffrey, H. (1992) 'Pourquoi Porphyre a-t-il édité Plotin?', in L. Brisson (ed.) *Porphyre: La Vie de Plotin*, tome 2, Paris: Vrin.

Sellew, P. (1989) 'Achilles or Christ? Porphyry and Didymus in debate over allegorical interpretation', *Harvard Theological Review* 82: 79–100.

Shaw, G. (1995) *Theurgy and the Soul: the Neoplatonism of Iamblichus*, University Park, PA: Penn State Press.

Smith. A. (1987) 'Porphyrian Studies since 1913', in *Aufstieg und Niedergang der Römischen Welt* II.36.2, Berlin and New York: De Gruyter.

Sorabji, R. (1993) *Animal Minds and Human Morals: the origins of the western debate*, London: Duckworth.

Swain, S. (1996) *Hellenism and Empire: language, classicism and power in the Greek world, AD 50–250*, Oxford: Clarendon Press.

Tardieu, M. (1992) 'Les Gnostiques dans la *Vie de Plotin*', in L. Brisson (ed.) *Porphyre: La Vie de Plotin*, tome 2, Paris: Vrin.

Turcan, R. (1975) *Mithras Platonicus. Recherches sur l'hellénisation philosophique de Mithra*, Leiden: Brill.

7

AUTOBIOGRAPHICAL IDENTITY AND PHILOSOPHICAL PAST IN AUGUSTINE'S DIALOGUE *DE LIBERO ARBITRIO*

Simon Harrison

> The scholar must still struggle hard to catch a glimpse, behind the reassuring familiarity of a story told continuously in Western Europe from the fifth century onwards, of the outlines of a world profoundly unlike our own, in which the decisive changes of this period took place.
>
> (Brown 1995: 26)

I take Augustine's dialogue *De Libero Arbitrio* (*On Free Choice of the Will*) [*Lib. Arb.*] as the subject of this chapter because it provides us with something of the kind of 'glimpse . . . of the outlines of a world profoundly unlike our own' that Peter Brown speaks of in the closing words to his first Tanner Lecture. There is, to put it briefly, contrary to the editions and translations of the text that have made it familiar, no 'philosophical past' in *Lib. Arb.*, and no straightforward 'autobiographical identity'. What I mean is that in the dialogue Augustine does not give any indication of the provenance of the arguments he deploys. He does not, as a modern commentary will do, and as he does elsewhere, tell us whether his arguments are 'Stoic' or 'Platonic'. He does not refer us back or on to works by (say) Plotinus, Porphyry, Seneca, or Epictetus. The dialogue is entirely free standing; no previous grounding in philosophical or literary culture is required or presupposed. This is an obvious feature of the dialogue and of its philosophical strategy, obvious but all too easily obscured by the kind of information supplied by modern editions and discussions. This is what I mean by the absence of any 'philosophical past'. Again almost all modern editions and translations of the text print the names of the two speakers of the dialogue in the margin as 'Augustine' and 'Evodius'. At one point 'Augustine' tells a story in the first person singular about an episode of his intellectual development and claims that the dialogue as a whole recapitulates that episode. Moreover this episode is closely related to part of Augustine's life-story as told in the *Confessions*. However, what modern scholarship has obscured is that the speaker 'Augustine' isn't really Augustine. The dialogue that Augustine wrote, and I will put the case for this claim here, did not identify Augustine and Evodius as speakers. Evodius, in short, is not 'Evodius', and 'Augustine' is not Augustine. Or, at least, we may catch our 'glimpse' through the gap between the two.

The glimpse will be of an unfamiliar *Lib. Arb.*, and hence of a world unlike our own. The unlikeness, I hope, will prove to be 'profound', or at least to bring us to the edge of profundity, because it will give us a view of Augustine going about thinking about the questions posed in this book. Augustine approaches and constructs the questions he asks about his cultural and personal identity by playing literary and philosophical games with the identity of his literary and philosophical creations. The strategies played out in the dialogue are, I would suggest, preliminary to the great literary and philosophical identity he creates for himself in his autobiography, the *Confessions*. It is in the *Confessions* that Augustine addresses at length and in depth the question of his identity. Nabokov, in his novel *Pale Fire* (1962), conceives of 'Man's life as commentary to abstruse/Unfinished poem' (ll. 939–40). In the *Confessions* Augustine has conceived of his life in terms of autobiography. He has attempted to make sense of himself by telling his own life-story. Augustine is aware that he owes everything he is to his past, to what he has been taught, to everything that has made him what he is. He owes his Christianity, we could say, to Cicero. He owes what he is now to his past. He is, he comes to see, his memory; and it is by investigating his memory that Augustine aims to ask and answer questions about his identity.

> Assuredly, Lord, I toil with this, toil within myself: I have become to myself a soil laborious and of heavy sweat. For I am not now considering the parts of the heavens, or measuring the distances of the stars, or seeking how the earth is held in space; it is I who remember, I, my mind. . . . But what could be closer to me than myself? Yet the power of memory in me I do not understand, though without memory I could not even name myself. . . . Great is the

power of memory, a thing, O my God, to be in awe of, a profound and immeasurable multiplicity; and this thing is my mind, this thing am I. What then am I O my God? What nature am I?

> (*Conf.* 10.16.25–17.26, trans. Sheed 1944)

Augustine's autobiography is his exploration of his memory, of how he became what he is. Looking back after his conversion and baptism, after his assumption of a new identity as a Christian, Augustine faces up to the contribution of what the world has given him to this new identity. The contribution of friends, events, and above all his education. He tells us, and alludes to what and whom he read: Virgil, Terence, Sallust, Cicero, Aristotle (e.g. *Conf.* 1.13.22; 1.16.26; 2.5.11; 3.4.7; 4.16.28).

A chapter on what the unconverted Augustine read might provide a simple and necessary answer to the core questions of this book: Augustine's debt to Cicero, for instance, or Plotinus. It would be good to know what educated and earnest Milanese intellectuals were reading in the 380s AD. Such work has been done and done well. (See e.g. O'Donnell 1992.) What I want to investigate in this chapter is the way that Augustine goes about thinking about his debt to what he read. Augustine knows he owes his ability to read and write, his ability to think, and some of his most profound insights to his non-Christian education, to the whole culture in which he grew up. This was a tension felt, and felt very strongly, by others across the late antique world. Recall, for example, Jerome waking 'trembling from a dream in which Christ had called him a "Ciceronian not a Christian"' (Brown 1967: 265). By contrast, as Brown sees, 'Augustine was untroubled by nightmares. He avoided them in a characteristic manner: by hard thinking and by the application of a few basic formulae' (*ibid.*). I hope, in this chapter, to explore some of this 'hard thinking' in detail.

Having said that an exploration of what Augustine read is a necessary part of an answer to our questions, it can only remain a part. Such investigations have their limits, such as the limited information that Augustine gives us. This is a rather striking feature of some of Augustine's accounts of what he read. Sometimes he simply doesn't tell us what it was. Most famously, he tells us in the *Confessions* that he was given and read 'some books of the Platonists' (7.9.13). Yet he does not tell us what these books were. He doesn't even tell us the name of the man ('puffed up with monstrous pride') who drew his attention to them. Plenty of good material for investigative scholarship of course, but Augustine simply doesn't let the books speak for themselves: 'There I read, not of course in these words, but with entirely the same sense and supported by numerous and varied reasons, "In the beginning was the Word"' (*ibid.* trans. Chadwick 1991). It is worth lingering for a moment on the oddness of this substitution. Augustine reduces his philosophical past to silence. It is assimilated to a Christian, biblical language, the language of Augustine's present. The past, the books he reads are silenced. And yet, as Augustine knows, and as his autobiography acknowledges, he owes so much to these 'books of the Platonists'.

The same feature can be observed in the dialogue *De Libero Arbitrio*. Augustine, in the text, makes no explicit reference or appeal to any other work, apart from the Bible (and even then this is not a straightforward appeal to the Bible as an authority). Open any scholarly modern edition or translation and you will find plenty of references to other writers, both pagan and Christian. But these are the tools and trophies of modern scholarship. *Lib. Arb.* itself is, by contrast, a book you could take to Roy Plomley's Desert Island. You do not need the works of Plato, or Aristotle, or Plotinus to hand to follow the course of its arguments. There are no references back to check up or pursue. It is self-contained. (The only exception is the Bible, on which see below.)

This does not mean, of course, that *Lib. Arb.* has no philosophical past. It does have a place in history. Its ideas, its terms, its language owe much to Platonism and Stoicism. But does its refusal to refer to, to engage with, to acknowledge even, the philosophical past, its own history, its own roots in non-Christian thought mean that *Lib. Arb.* is simply, and straightforwardly a 'Christian' work? A work written for Christians by a Christian? A work that seeks to forget, ignore, or replace non-Christian thought? After all not only does it refer only to the Bible, but its subject – the problem of evil – is expressed in Christian terms.

> For we have agreed to hold to the course prescribed by the prophet who says, 'unless you believe, you will not understand'. But we believe that all things which exist are from the one God, and yet God is not the author of sins. But the mind is troubled by this question: if sins are from souls which God has created, and those souls are from God, how is it that the sins are not, pretty much directly, to be blamed on God?
>
> (1.2.4. The prophet is Isaiah 7:9 LXX)

As the dialogue progresses the terms of reference become increasingly biblical and Christian. To take the most striking example, an argument that in book 1 was pursued in terms of 'wisdom' and 'folly' is, in book 3, rerun at much greater length in terms of the narrative of Genesis chapter 2. Is *Lib. Arb.* then a Christian work for Christians, a work that aims to forget its debt to, and to replace, non-Christian culture? The question I am trying to explore is this. How does Augustine construct cultural 'identity' as a question? I am attempting to approach it through two rather smaller questions: Who is the 'Augustine' of *Lib. Arb.*, and why is there no acknowledged philosophical past in it? This leads me to ask such general questions as: What is going on when Augustine writes *De Libero Arbitrio*? What kind of a cultural product is it? Why write, why publish on the subject of *Free Choice of the Will*? What kind of identity is Augustine the author claiming, or perhaps interrogating, for himself?

The work arose, as Augustine tells us in the *Retractations*, from conversations he had with his companions in Rome in the winter of AD 387–8.

> While we were still delayed in Rome, we wanted to find, by arguing it out, the origin of evil. And we conducted our discussion in such a way that the explanatory account, when examined thoroughly, should bring us to understand what we already believed, in submission to divine authority, about this question, if we were able, and as much as we, with God's help, were able by discussion, to do this. And since we came to the conclusion, having carefully examined the account, that evil had no point of origin other than the free choice of the will, the three books which that discussion produced were called 'On Free Choice'. I completed the second and the third books in Africa, as best I could at the time, having already been ordained a Presbyter at Hippo Regius.
>
> (*Retr.* 1.9 (8).1)

We know that the book was sent to Augustine's patron, Romanianus, and to Paulinus of Nola (*Ep.* 27; 31.7), that Evodius of Uzalis had a copy (*Ep.* 162) and that Pelagius read it. Augustine tells Jerome in 415 that it has 'gone out into the hands of many, and is in the possession of even more' (*Ep.* 166.3.7). Why publish, why send the work out into the world, into the hands of readers, beyond one's control? What was Augustine hoping to achieve? Let me return to the two features of *Lib. Arb.* I wish to discuss. The glimpse I want to offer may at first sight seem not so unreassuringly or profoundly different, but it is at least a glimpse that has been obscured in modern scholarship. It is a glimpse of two features of the work as it would have presented itself to a contemporary reader. The first is the self-contained nature of the work. It is a dialogue in direct speech, beginning without scene setting or introduction:

EVODIUS: Please tell me: isn't God the cause of evil?
AUGUSTINE: I will tell you once you have made clear what kind of
    evil you are asking about. . . .
    (trans. Williams 1993)

As the dialogue progresses all its terms are carefully introduced. No prior knowledge, as publishers like to put it on the back of books, is presupposed. Indeed at several significant points, it is made clear that the chain of reasoning starts from what is simply self-evident (1.7.17; 1.12.25; 2.3.7). There is to be no appeal to 'authority', there is no appeal to any 'belief', only to what can be known and grasped by 'reason' (see esp. 2.1.1–2.37).

The second feature is manifest in the two opening lines quoted above: the identity of the speakers. The identification of the two interlocutors as 'Augustine' and 'Evodius' is, I argue, a modern invention. Although this convention has been the accepted practice since 1679 (the date of the great Maurist edition), no reader before, say, 1506 (the date of Amerbach's edition) would have read this. I suggest that Augustine did not identify by name his two speakers. No names, personal, professional or descriptive, are given in the text itself. At most what a contemporary reader would have seen, I suggest, would have been some sort of diacritical mark indicating a change of speaker, such as the arrows (*spicula* or *ancorae*, one pointing up, the other down) found in some of the earliest manuscripts.

I offer this suggestion on a number of grounds: the manuscript evidence, contemporary practice, and a consideration of the uses of such anonymity. First the manuscript evidence. The manuscripts offer a variety of names and sigla. While Augustine's name features frequently (although not always as the second speaker), no manuscript at all gives that of Evodius. I set out the evidence below, which I have simply taken from Green's critical apparatus (Green 1956):

138

Table 7.1 Signs used for the interlocutors

Sigla	Green's interpretation	Manuscript (consensus)	Date (century)
↑ ↓	'spicula'	M, B, F^1: (F = γ)	9th, 9th, 11th
•I• •R•	Inquisitor, Responsor	A, T (α)	11th, 9th
Ad. Aug.	Adeodatus, Augustinus	C (& 1st p. T.) (α)	9th
⇒ ⇐	'iacula'	G (α)	11th
•D• •M•	discipulus, magister	X, L (β)	10th
•D• •A•	discipulus, Augustinus	K (β)	12th
•C• •ω•	[None]	V (γ)	12th
A R	Augustinus, Ratio	R (γ)	12th
•ω• •A•	Orosius, Augustinus[2]	Y, S (δ)	12th

Most combinations seem to derive either from a sensible interpretation of the text (*discipulus* and *magister*: 'disciple' and 'teacher'), or would seem to derive from other dialogues, and on equally objectionable grounds. Thus Adeodatus' name is probably suggested from *De Magistro* ('*On the Teacher*') (read in conjunction with *Conf.* 9.6.14), and 'Ratio' (Reason) from the *Soliloquies*.

Second, my suggested emendation accords with what we know about ancient practice in general.

> In texts of drama or prose dialogue changes of speaker were not usually marked by the name of the new speaker. Instead the ancient reader had a colon, sometimes combined with a paragraphus or stroke in the margin, to guide him.
> (Wilson 1970: 305 – of Greek texts)

Latin texts have a slightly more complicated history (Andrieu 1954: 303). Nonetheless it remains the case that an ancient reader did not expect, as we do, the identity of dialogue speakers to be given in, so to speak, the margin. Readers could therefore approach a written dialogue in much the same way as an audience a performance of a play. Writers could exploit this. Thus where in tragedy, tied as it is to its characters (Oedipus, Antigone), characters are usually identified swiftly, in comedy the author often holds back the naming of a character, and furthermore can give the characters a dramatically significant name (Barton 1990).

I give an example and two counter-examples: the only Ciceronian dialogue which is, like *Lib. Arb.*, in direct speech, and has no introduction, the *Partitiones Oratoriae*, begins thus:

CICERO: Studeo, mi pater, Latine ex te audire ea quae mihi tu de ratione dicendi Graece tradidisti, si modo tibi est otium et si vis.
PATER: An est, mi Cicero, quod ego malim quam te quam doctissimum esse?. . .

(ed. Wilkins 1902)

The identity of the speakers (as well as the subject-matter) is revealed immediately in the vocative ('mi pater . . . mi Cicero'). My two counter-examples are two texts, both written after *Lib. Arb.*, which do make use of deliberate extratextual indications of the identity of speakers. The first is Iunilius Africanus' Latin translation of a catechism, written in 551 for Primasius, Bishop of Hadrumetum. In his preface, Iunilius writes:

> Haec tu, pater, nescio qua ratione omnibus christianis erudiri volentibus necessaria iudicasti excusantemque me diu usque ad editionis inpudentiam conpulisti, unde in duos brevissimos libellos regularia haec instituta collegi, addens ipsius dicitionis, quantum potui, utilem formam, ut velut discipulis interrogantibus et magistro respondente breviter singula et perlucide dicerentur. Et ne aliqua confusio per antiquariorum, ut adsolet, neglegentiam proveniret, magistro *M* graecam litteram, discipulis *Δ* praeposui, ut ex peregrinis characteribus et quibus latina scriptura non utitur, error omnis penitus auferatur.[3]

This sixth-century innovation appears to have affected some manuscripts of Cicero's *Tusculan Disputations*, which identify the two speakers as M. and A. (Andrieu 1954: 297; Pohlenz 1911). An earlier example of innovation is presented by N.G. Wilson: Theodoret of Cyrus' *Eranistes* is a dialogue between two characters named 'Orthodoxus' and 'Eranistes'. The former, as his name suggests, is a defender of orthodoxy, the latter, a Monophysite. The names themselves, as Theodoret spells out in his prologue, convey information: the name 'Eranistes' (usually translated as 'beggar', or better 'collector') is used to suggest that the heretic has a somewhat rag-bag collection of doctrines. In his prologue Theodoret explains the form of the work. I quote from Wilson's paraphrase:

Theodoret contrasts his own practice with that of the ancient writers of dialogue . . . Whereas they wrote for a highly cultivated public, he wished to be readily intelligible to the ordinary man, and to help the reader who is not experienced in facing the difficulties presented by ancient books. This will be done by indicating the speakers' name in the margin at each point of change.

(Wilson 1970: 305)

Note further that the *Eranistes* is a polemical work of Christology. It is usually dated to 447, written in the controversies preceding the Council of Chalcedon (451), not a time for a bishop to be misquoted or misunderstood on such controversial and highly politically charged matters. Although there are only some fifty years between them, *Lib. Arb.* and *Eranistes* are worlds apart.

No manuscript, then, identifies 'Evodius' and 'Augustine'. Nor, second, is it likely that a contemporary manuscript would have done so. Where does this modern identification come from? The answer is slightly different in each case. Evodius' name is most straightforwardly misleading. It is derived from information which would have been unavailable to contemporary readers. In 414 or 415, some twenty years after the completion of *Lib. Arb.*, Augustine wrote to his old friend, Evodius, then Bishop of Uzalis:

> If you re-read those books which have been known to you for some time (or were, unless I am mistaken, known to you, as you have perhaps forgotten them), those books which I composed when you were in conversation and discussion with me [*quae te conferente mecum ac sermocinante conscripsi*], *On the Greatness of the Soul,* and *On Free Choice,* if you re-read them you will find how to resolve your doubts without my help.
>
> (*Ep.* 162.2)

This historical information is confirmed by Augustine's account of the composition of *Lib. Arb.* in *Retr.* already quoted above. The 'we' of the *Retr.* account, Augustine's companions, would include Augustine's son Adeodatus, his brother Navigius (*Conf.* 9.11.27), Alypius (*Conf.* 9.6.14) and Evodius (*Conf.* 9.8.17; 9.12.20). The phrase used in *Ep.* 162 need not, however, imply, I suggest, that Augustine had put Evodius' name in the margin. What after all would this have meant to a contemporary reader in the 390s? For all the difference it would make Augustine might just as well have put 'Estragon' and 'Vladimir' there. We now, thanks to centuries of scholarship, have a lot of information about Evodius (it can be found for instance in Mandouze 1982). But the kind of interpretative moves made by, for instance, De Capitani who links the anti-Manichaean themes of *Lib. Arb.* to anti-Manichaean works written later by the historical Evodius, were unavailable to contemporary readers (De Capitani 1987: 26ff). Hence it is not until the sixteenth century that the connection between the dialogue and the historical Evodius is discovered, and used to give an identity to the anonymous interlocutor.

But what of the relationship of the author to the character 'Augustine'? This identification would seem to be slightly less misleading. There would seem to be every sense in attributing the opinions and arguments of the character to the author. Indeed Augustine later, in the *Retr.* and elsewhere, defends these views as his own. Furthermore there are a couple of autobiographical passages, one explicitly so, the other implicitly. The implicit passage (*Lib. Arb.* 1.11.22) has been noticed by O'Donnell and described as one of the 'first confessions' of Augustine: Augustine is here 'recounting his life story, howbeit briefly, and howbeit veiled as a hypothetical case. . . . [The passage] reflects a rehearsed narrative that would be developed more fully in the writing of the *Confessions*' (O'Donnell 1992: i. xlviii; lii n. 103).

> What then? Should one think it a light punishment that lust dominates the mind, and drags it about in all different directions, stripped of the riches of virtue, helpless and in need; now assenting to the false as though it were true, now even defending it, now disapproving of what it had earlier approved, but nonetheless rushing into other falsehoods, now suspending judgement and fearing to trust plenty of crystal-clear arguments, now despairing of finding the whole truth and sticking deep within the depths of folly, now straining up into the light of understanding, and again, from weariness, falling back down. While at the same time this rule of lust rages like a tyrant and disturbs the whole mind and life of the man with diverse and contrary storms, fear on one side, longing on the other, anxiety here, inane and false joy there, here the torture of the loss of what was loved, there the passion for obtaining what is not possessed, here the pains of wounds received, there the fire of revenge, on all sides, avarice is able to constrain, luxury to

dissipate, ambition to enslave, pride to inflate, envy to tor-
ment, idleness to entomb, obstinacy to goad, subjection to
afflict, and the crush of whatever other innumerable things
that work in the service of the rule of lust.

(Lib. Arb. 1.11.22)

Not much of a narrative, perhaps, but O'Donnell is right to link it
to the kind of self-presentation in the *Confessions.* The explicit 'autobiographical' passage, however, contrasts slightly with the narrative
of the *Confessions.* By 1.2.4 Evodius' opening question ('is God
responsible for evil?') has been discussed, and taken on a more precise
form:

E.: Alright then, since you have done quite enough to force me to
admit that we do not learn to do evil, tell me what the source
of our evil actions is.

A.: You raise precisely that question which, when I was a young man,
worked me so very hard and which wore me out and cast me
down among heretics. And I was so wounded by this fall, and
so suffocated under heaps of empty myths, that had love of finding out the truth not obtained divine assistance for me, I would
not have been able to get out of there into that first freedom to
seek, and to breathe again. And since my case was so carefully
proceeded with, that I was delivered from that inquisition, I
will proceed with you following the same order as that which I
followed and so escaped.

The heretics are, presumably, Manichees. Note however that (in
keeping with the whole tone of the dialogue) they are not named.
This narrative seems to correspond to the experience of the young
Augustine, who was a Manichee for some 10 or so years. There is a
slight discrepancy between the two accounts. Here the speaker presents the question of the origin of evil as the cause of his becoming
a Manichee. Yet in the *Confessions,* the chain of events is rather
more complicated and, moreover, the question about the origin of
evil is first put to him by Manichees when Augustine is already
one of them.

The one thing that delighted me in Cicero's exhortation was
the advice 'not to study one particular sect but to love and
seek and pursue and hold fast and strongly embrace
wisdom itself, wherever found.' One thing alone put a

brake on my intense enthusiasm – that the name of Christ
was not contained in the book. [*sic!*] . . . (3.4.8)
 . . . I therefore decided to give attention to the holy scriptures . . . [But they] seemed to me unworthy in comparison
with the dignity of Cicero. . . . (3.5.9)
 . . . That explains why I fell in with men proud of their
slick talk, very earthly-minded and loquacious. In their
mouths were the devil's traps and a birdlime compounded
of a mixture of the syllables of your name, and that of the
Lord Jesus Christ, and that of the Paraclete, the Comforter,
the Holy Spirit. . . . (3.6.10)
 . . . I was unaware of the existence of another reality, that
which truly is, and it was as if some sharp intelligence were
persuading me to consent to the stupid deceivers when they
asked me: 'Where does evil come from? and is God confined
within a corporeal form? has he hair and nails? and can those
be considered righteous who had several wives at the same
time and killed people and offered animals in sacrifice?' In
my ignorance I was disturbed by these questions.
(3.7.12 trans. Chadwick 1991)

What is significant is that Augustine has the major speaker adopting
an autobiographical stance, and that this is adopted as the basic structure of the work: 'I will proceed with you following the same order as
that which I followed and so escaped.' But this should not blind us to
the fact that it is only a stance. The 'I' of *Lib. Arb.* 1.2.4 is a literary
product.

Evodius, then, is not Evodius, and Augustine is not straightforwardly Augustine. The contemporary reader, then, would encounter
a text with no explicit indication of who is speaking, or explicit indication of the origin of the ideas and arguments within it. Perhaps the
contemporary reader has even less knowledge of its author than we
have. How is the reader to make sense of the work? How is the
reader to work out who is speaking, what the relationship between
the speakers, and the relationship between author and reader is?
How is the reader to evaluate the ideas and arguments put forward?
The short answer is that this is something readers must work out for
themselves.

In Augustine's dialogue, the *Soliloquies*, the identity of one of the
speakers is made explicit only as the work progresses. The dialogue
opens in the first person singular:

> When I had been pondering many different things to myself
> for a long time, and had for many days been seeking my own
> self and what my own good was, and what evil was to be
> avoided, there suddenly spoke to me – what was it? I
> myself or someone else, inside me or outside me? (this is
> the very thing I would love to know but don't).
>
> (*Sol.* 1.1.1. trans. Watson 1990)

Watson's translation continues 'at any rate, Reason said to me', but
this is to pre-empt Augustine. The mysterious second speaker identifies itself later on at 1.6.12: 'You are right to be impressed. For
Reason who is talking with you [*Ratio, quae tecum loquitur*] promises
that she will display God to your mind just as the sun is displayed to
the eyes' (trans. Watson, adapted).

But the question of the identification of the two speakers is bound
up with the subject-matter of the dialogue. Reason is indeed 'the
very thing I would love to know but don't'. The relationship between
'I' and my 'reason' is complex and subtle, and it is this complexity
that Augustine is exploring by rewriting the philosophical dialogue
as a new kind of genre, the soliloquy: even the word is a deliberate
neologism.

Similarly the lack of identification of the speakers in *Lib. Arb.* contributes to the philosophical investigation there undertaken. *Lib. Arb.*
is a philosophical inquiry into freedom and responsibility: God is not
to be held responsible for all the evils that happen, because human
beings are responsible for the evil that they do. What Augustine
tries to do in *Lib. Arb.* is to bring his readers to see and to appreciate
for themselves their own responsibility. One way he achieves this is
by getting them to see that the identification of the speakers is *up to
them*, it is *their responsibility*. The anonymity of the interlocutors, then,
instantiates the philosophical theme of the dialogue: responsibility.
This is also instantiated in the lack of explicit philosophical past:
the reader is to weigh up and think through ideas and arguments
on their own terms. No clue as to how they are to be taken is
given by attributing to them the authority of Plato or Chrysippus,
or St Paul. Again the intellectual task of reading, thinking and
understanding is shown to be, in the last analysis, the task of the
reader. Like the character Evodius, the reader is – we, that is – are
invited to think through the problems for ourselves, from our own
'first-personal' perspective. 'I will proceed with you following the
same order as that which I followed and so escaped.'

It might at this point be helpful to give a very rough sketch of the structure of the dialogue. I give first a number of features indicative of the nature of the work (table 7.2), followed by a rough sketch of its structure and contents (table 7.3).

Each of the three books differs from its predecessor by (see table 7.2 below)

(i)   an increase in length,
(ii)   an increase in (average) sentence length,
(iii) a decrease in the proportion of words Evodius has to say,
(iv)   an increase in use of direct and indirect quotes from Holy Scripture,
(v)   an increase in the level of difficulty and in the complexity of the subject-matter.

Books 1 and 2 follow a single trajectory. Their structure is very clearly marked and signposted. The structure of book 3 is, however, less obvious and much more complex. Certainly my map hardly does it justice. That said, as long as the procedure and results of the previous two books are kept in mind, book 3 can be navigated. The first two books have what we can call introductions. These are the sections which open each book and in which Evodius' original questions and concerns become modified and set out as a procedural series of distinct questions (1.1.1–1.3.6; 2.1.1–2.3.7). Augustine then sets out a procedure for reaching the answer required. Thus he says that in order to understand the origin of our doing evil ('unde male faciamus') we must first know 'what doing evil is' (1.3.6). In order for Evodius to find this out, Augustine says, if, that is, he can't give a definition of evil action already, they should begin from examples of evil actions (1.3.6). A definition of evil action (i.e. what it is about an action that makes it evil) is arrived at, at the end of the first book (1.16.34), by which time it has become clear that in the process of giving this

Table 7.2

		Bk 1	Bk 2	Bk 3
(i)	No. of words	7,312	12,659	15,647
(ii)	Average no. of words/sentence	16	21	24
(iii)	Evodius' words as a percentage of the total	27	16	6
(iv)	No. of direct (and indirect) biblical references	1 (7)	16 (4)	19 (20)

Table 7.3

Book 1			
Overall problem:	(i)	Is God responsible for evil?	(1.1.1)
specific question	(ii)	whence do we do evil?	(1.2.4)
answered via prior question	(iii)	what is evil?	(1.3.6)
Answer to	(iii)	turning from divine to temporal things	(1.16.34)
	(ii)	by free choice of the will	(1.16.35)
This gives further problem	(iv)	is God responsible for evil in virtue of giving us the means to do evil?	(1.16.35)

Book 2		
Question (iv) *is answered via three prior proofs:*		(2.3.7)
that	(v)	God exists
	(vi)	all good things are from God
	(vii)	free choice of the will is a good thing
hence answer to (iv):		God is responsible for will being a good thing, we are responsible for using it for evil
Resulting problem:	(viii)	but whence the bad will? (2.19.54)
Answer to (viii):		There is no 'answer', as what is not from God has no being and is unknowable. (2.19.54)
Enough has been said . . .		

Book 3		
. . . but now that the overall answer is in place, other problems can easily be dealt with.		
Further problems	(ix)	things have their natures *necessarily*
answer to	(ix)	difference between the natural and the voluntary (3.1.3)
	(x)	God's foreknowledge seems to make the future *necessary*
answer to	(x)	God foreknows the *will* (3.4.11)
General problem	(xi)	Is God not necessarily reponsible for everything?
general method of answer:	(xi)	The Rule of Piety: adopt attitude of gratitude and praise (3.5.12)
Further problems	(xii)	Necessity and our condition (3.19.51)
answer to	(xii)	whatever the truth about the human condition and how we got here, we can be more certain that we have free will.

definition, the answer to the '*unde*' question has also been given (1.16.35). Book 2 resumes the discussion with the question which remains at the end of the first: is God not responsible for evil, given that he created us with the wherewithal to commit evil (1.16.35)? The overall problem of the relationship between God and evil (1.1.1; 1.2.4) has not yet been resolved. In the introduction to the first book it was made clear that Evodius had this problem because he already believed certain things. The problem was given by what Evodius believed. The problem of evil is, of course, a problem for the theist. In this second introduction much more time is spent on the relationship between what one believes and what one understands; this discussion makes it clear that Evodius is after understanding, which is something more than belief. It also makes it clear that there can also be a question about what one *ought* to believe. Further the introduction subjects Evodius' formulation of the problem to examination. What Evodius actually asks is first '*why*' God gave us free choice of the will ('*quare*'), and then '*whether*' God did in fact give it us ('*utrum*') (2.1.1), and then this becomes the question whether God '*ought*' to have given it us ('*debuisse*' 2.2.4). This formulation of the question is the one fundamental to the rest of the book. Augustine sets out a procedure ('*ordo*') for answering the question: 'Was it right of God to give man free choice of the will?'; it is to be answered as the conclusion of (let us say) a syllogism, the premises of which are given by the propositions, each of which will first be shown to be true:

1   God exists.
2   All good things have their existence from God.
3   Free choice of the will is a good thing (2.3.7).
    Now for a syllogism, (1) is not essential. The conclusion
4   free choice of the will has its existence from God

completes a valid syllogism from (2) and (3). Why then does Augustine spend so much time on (1) (2.3.7–2.15.40)? The answer has to do with the way (1) is demonstrated. What Augustine puts as the first step in the order ('*ordine*', 2.3.7) is the question 'how it is manifest that God exists' (2.3.7). The proof that God exists of 2.3.7–2.15.40 (inasmuch as it is a proof, and not everyone has been happy to call it a proof of God's existence) is designed to make it clear that God's existence is presupposed by the very ability to ask questions about how things '*ought*' to be. God's existence is the existence of standards by which we make judgements. These standards derive, Augustine argues, from truth (argued to be absolute and eternal). Hence the importance of the time spent in the introduction on questions of what God *ought* to have done. Note, moreover, that, as in book 1, the answer to the overall problem is found to be already contained in the answer to the intermediary questions. God is not the author of evil, because in ascertaining that he has given us free will, we have thereby ascertained that the nature of this free will is such that it absolves God from this responsibility. Book 2 ends with Augustine's account of the unintelligibility of sin. The will is something we can know, and we can understand how it is the 'cause' of sin. But 'why' we will to sin (or why, at least, the first sinner willed to sin in a perfect universe) is, he says, an unanswerable question. It is unanswerable because it is the antithesis of everything an intelligible answer should be: it is without order and structure; it is a movement away from God, who is responsible for all intelligibility. Again the way God's existence has been proved is of the first importance for understanding this claim.

The trajectory of the first two books here has completed its rather elegant curve. Yet a third book remains. What we have here is a series of exercises. We take the conclusions that we have gained from the first two books and by elaborating upon and using them to respond to these excuses, we come to understand them in ever-increasing depth. The idea of 'necessity' can be used to characterise all the further problems upon which our hard-won gains are brought to bear. First of all Augustine argues that while nature may imply necessity, we can distinguish our will from our nature (3.1.1–3). The next problem raised is that of God's foreknowledge (3.2.4–3.4.9). Does not this determine our actions? Augustine argues that if God foreknows a will, then what he foreknows is thereby (jolly well) going to be a will. This problem then turns into a general question about all necessity. Up to now we have been dealing with the idea of the necessary as being opposed to the voluntary. But there are plenty of things in the universe which *do* happen of necessity. Here Augustine brings in a different kind of answer: the 'rule of piety' (3.5.12–3.12.35). Again this can be seen to derive from the 'how' (*quomodo*) of book 2 ('*quomodo manifestum est Deum esse*', 2.3.7). Because God is the source of all intelligibility and goodness, whatever he is responsible for must be good and (ultimately) intelligible. Augustine deals with a number of objections to this rule. He then gives a succinct summary from first principles (3.13.36–3.16.46). Again Evodius raises the basic fundamental question (3.14.47–3.18.50), not because he is stupid, but in order to bring up a fourth challenge from necessity, the necessity of the condition we are born into (3.18.51–3.25.77). Here we return to the territory of book 1. As at 1.11.22 (quoted above) our punitive condition is described under two headings, which are here named 'ignorance' and 'difficulty'. This time round, however, we are in a position to give a really sophisticated set of answers to the problems raised. Augustine first shows that our present condition is punitive. He then goes on to show how the question of the soul's origin is strictly irrelevant to the problem, as all its possible answers are perfectly compatible with God's goodness and justice (3.30.56–3.31.62). (At 1.11.24 he had merely told us that it was not relevant.) He is able to show that God's goodness and justice would not be compromised 'even if' our present condition were 'natural' as opposed to punitive. He then returns to the problem of the intelligibility of the account of the very first entry of sin into the universe in terms which are both philosophical ('appearances', 'middle states', 'envy') and biblical (the devil, pride). The book, he concludes, could go on for ever, but must come to an end at some point (3.25.77).

This then is a quick run through *Lib. Arb.* There is one further relevant feature, which again has to do with the first person. Augustine uses an interesting kind of argument as a 'starting point' in three places: 1.7.17; 1.12.25; 2.3.7. It is a very significant kind of argument as he shares it with the founder of modern philosophy, Descartes. It is an argument that works from the first person. Descartes's argument is known as the *cogito*: '*cogito ergo sum*', I think therefore I am. This argument is something that 'each person must administer . . . to himself in the first person' (Anscombe 1975: 45). Descartes 'therefore' only works when one thinks from one's own point of view. (Further on Augustine and Descartes, see Matthews 1992).

Augustine gives a version of this argument at a key moment in the dialogue by the idea that 'I oughtn't to give you an answer to your question unless you want to know the answer' (1.12.25). The thought behind this idea is that understanding is something that, in the last analysis, the teacher cannot do for the pupil: it is something that pupils must do for themselves. My understanding is my understanding, I can only acquire it by thinking for myself. This is a theory of knowledge explored in Augustine's dialogue *De Magistro* (*On the Teacher*), a dialogue which argues that 'no one can teach another person'.

This much can words do, to attribute to them as much as

possible. They merely prompt us to look for things. They do
not show them to us so that we know them. He teaches me
who puts before my eyes, or any bodily sense, or even my
mind itself, those things which I want to know.

(*Mag.* 11.36)

This gives rise to Augustine's theory of illumination, when the
same idea is given in rather more theological terms:

But as for all the things which we understand, we do not
consult someone speaking externally, but inwardly the
Truth which presides over the mind, prompted, perhaps
by the words. And it is he who is consulted that teaches,
that is, Christ who is said to dwell inside a man, who is
the immutable and eternal Wisdom of God. It is Wisdom
that every rational soul consults, but Wisdom is available
to each soul only as much as each soul is able – on account
of its own good or bad will – to receive.

(*Mag.* 11.38)

This is a thoroughly Platonic epistemology, contrasting 'knowledge'
(as understanding) with 'belief' (Burnyeat 1987). It is an account of
knowledge that Augustine has made his own, and which he takes
very seriously. 'When we speak properly' Augustine writes in a
famous passage, 'we say we know only that which we grasp by
firm reasoning of the mind.' This is in contrast with 'what we perceive by our bodily senses and what we believe on the authority of
trustworthy witnesses' (*Retr.* 1.14.3 quoted from Burnyeat 1987:
6). These last two may be true, and may have justification. But
what justifies knowledge as knowledge is something else: the
'grasp of the mind's firm reasoning'. This Augustine can also call
'understanding'. Plato illustrates the distinction by means of the
example of the difference between the jury and the eyewitness (*Theae-
tetus* 201A–C): While the jury may reach the right verdict, they
cannot know what happened, in the same way as the eyewitness
can. Augustine will take up the use of direct first-hand vision in
his accounts of what makes knowledge knowledge in his account
of knowledge as 'illumination'.

Education, then, what one learns, is not something passively
acquired. A *bon mot* from another dialogue makes the point well.
In the dialogue *Contra Academicos*, Augustine (it is a dialogue in
indirect speech, and so the scene is carefully set and the interlocutors

clearly identified) is getting his two pupils to think about scepticism. Licentius, one of the younger and less experienced interlocutors, protests that he is hardly in a position to defend Academic scepticism against the arguments of Augustine. 'But have I', he asks, 'either read the writings of the Academics, or have I been instructed in as varied knowledge as you, who come thus prepared against me?' To which Augustine replies: 'Neither had those who first defended your case read the Academics' (*c. acad.* 2.7.17 trans. O'Meara 1951). The point is, for Augustine, that to understand, one has to think for oneself. Philosophical arguments are simply philosophical arguments. Those who thought them up in the first place were in much the same position as those who are ignorant of them now.

Furthermore, the truth of such arguments does not derive from those who put them forward, but from Truth (with a capital T). This is the 'hard thinking' (Brown 1967: 265) that allows Augustine to come up with the educational programme of the *De Doctrina Christiana* (*On Christian Education*):

> Since correct inferences may be made concerning false as well as true propositions, it is easy to learn the nature of valid inference even in schools which are outside of the Church. But the truth of propositions is a matter to be discovered in the sacred books of the Church. However, the truth of valid inference was not instituted by men; rather it was observed by men and set down that they might learn or teach it.
>
> (*Doctr. Chr.* 2.31.49–32.50)

Augustine, as Peter Brown, making the connection with the *City of God*, so clearly sees,

> is the great 'seculariser' of the pagan past. Areas of Roman life, in which the gods still seemed to lurk, reassuring the conservative and frightening the Christian, are stripped of their religious aura for both sides. They are reduced to purely human dimensions: they were only 'traditional forms laid down by men; adjusted to the needs of human society, with which we cannot dispense in this life' [*Doctr. Chr.* 2.24.37]. Augustine will even treat the Roman Empire in this way. . . . In the *City of God* . . . Augustine will judge the Empire on its merits as a purely human insti-

tution: he will reduce it to the level of any other state . . .
[Augustine] had already come to regard a unique culture
and a unique political institution as replaceable, in theory
at least.

(Brown 1967: 266)

This 'secularisation' of Augustine's world has its philosophical roots
in his understanding of knowledge and truth. *Lib. Arb.* explores, in
book 2 (2.3.7–2.15.39), the notion of truth, just as *Lib. Arb.* as a
whole explores the notion of human responsibility.

When Descartes sat 'by the fire, wearing his winter dressing-gown
holding' his piece of paper in his hands, and set out 'once in the
course of my life, to demolish everything completely and start
again right from the foundations' (*First Meditation, CSM* II 12) the
argument he used as his foundation, the *cogito*, immediately
reminded his contemporaries of St Augustine, and in particular of
Augustine's *Lib. Arb.* One of the first people to refer to the connection between Augustine and Descartes was Arnauld, who begins his
(*Fourth*) *Set of Objections* by quoting Augustine:

> In Book II chapter 3 of *De Libero Arbitrio*, Alipius, when he is
> disputing with Euodius, and is about to prove the existence
> of God, says the following: 'First, if we are to take as our
> starting point what is most evident, I ask you to tell me
> whether you yourself exist. Or are you perhaps afraid of
> making a mistake in your answer, given that, if you did
> not exist, it would be quite impossible for you to make a
> mistake?' This is like what M. Descartes says: 'But there is
> a deceiver of supreme power and cunning who is deliberately
> and constantly deceiving me. In that case I too undoubtedly
> exist, if he is deceiving me.'
>
> (*CSM* II 139)

(Note, by the way, yet another identification of the interlocutors,
this one not found in any of the manuscripts, and made while, I pre-
sume, the Maurists were preparing their edition.) Arnauld says
nothing more on the subject, and Descartes's *Reply* is entirely to
the point.

> I shall not waste time here by thanking my distinguished
> critic for bringing in the authority of St Augustine to sup-
> port me, and for setting out my arguments so vigorously

that he seems to fear that their strength may not be sufficiently apparent to anyone else.

(CSM II 154)

The point is, of course, that Descartes's arguments can look after
themselves. Indeed they are intended precisely to be arguments
which can, which must, do without assistance from authority. Likewise, the arguments of *Lib. Arb.* are to stand on their own two feet, so
to speak. The interlocutors are to proceed without referring to
'authority', but by thinking everything through for themselves. It
is Augustine's version of the *'cogito'* argument that provides *Lib.
Arb.* with a foundation, a starting point from which to start this
process of reconstruction. Augustine encounters and formulates his
culture – his education, himself as an educator, everything that education has given and made him – as a philosophical problem in a
similar way to Descartes. It is not just the basic argument that
Augustine shares with Descartes, but the attempt to rethink from
fundamentals, and from fundamentals revealed by the *'cogito'* type
of argument, everything that he has learnt and has taught. Augustine, moreover, like Descartes, undertakes a first-person inquiry, an
inquiry that takes the nature of the inquirer as an 'I' seriously.
Such an inquiry leads Augustine, like Descartes, not only to write
autobiographically, but also to think through a family of arguments
that resembles Descartes's *'cogito ergo sum'*.

As Arnauld's quotation shows, the argument of *Lib. Arb.* 2.3.7 is
to be employed as a 'starting point' and as something 'most evident'.
To characterise the argument that begins from this point as a proof of
God's existence, while correct, fails to capture its revisionary status.
It is not just that the interlocutors in the dialogue are to work to a
proof of God with any recourse to 'authority', without relying on
what they believe about God. Rather this working to a proof of
God is to re-educate the interlocutors about what they believe. It
is to bring them to relearn for themselves about their own selves
and their relation to God. It is to give them that correct Christian,
'secularising', perspective upon which the political programme of
the *City of God*, and the hermeneutical rules of *Christian Education*
depend. God's existence is proved, it is 'learnt' by investigating
the nature of truth, the standard by which we are able to judge
whether something is the case or not (*Lib. Arb.* 2.12.34; 15.39).
When Augustine, in the passage from *On the Teacher* quoted above,
talks of consulting 'Truth which presides over the mind' he is
referring to the same feature of our mental life that he discussed in

154

De Doctrina under the heading of logic ('the truth of valid inference' – quoted above). What his *'cogito*-like' argument reveals in *Lib. Arb.* is a mind that depends for its ability to learn wholly upon truth, wholly upon God. The mind, when it understands, when it grasps something rationally, works along the laws of 'valid inference', or at least the laws of valid inference represent man's achievement in coming to terms with the nature of the universe. But the *'cogito*-like' argument also reveals that in order to come to understand its dependence upon God, in order to learn about the nature of itself, it must begin from the perspective of the first-person singular, from the 'I' that inquires and which desires to understand. It is this perspective which enables Augustine to rethink clearly the nature and role of his education and his culture. It is this perspective which Augustine uses to make sense of his own identity over against the culture which made him what he was.

The work of the two features of *Lib. Arb.* that I have highlighted is to help the reader make this change of perspective. With minimal assistance from the author, readers are to work out for themselves the identity of and the relationship between the two interlocutors. Without any clue as to the provenance of any particular idea or argument they are to think through the argument for themselves. In both cases the readers are thrown back on their own resources, they are thrown back on their first-person perspective. But this is precisely what the dialogue aims to get us to understand: our own responsibility, what it is that is up to us, and it is precisely when we understand this, that we can begin to think about our identity and its relationship to the culture we were born into.

Augustine formulates the question of his cultural identity as part of a complex of philosophical questions about his identity. The absence of explicit references to other authors does not mean that Augustine is ignoring or rejecting his philosophical past. On the contrary, it is the way that Augustine attempts to come to terms with that past. Similarly the anonymity of the speakers, and Augustine's experimentation with the literary conventions of philosophical dialogue, and with the literary presentation of the self, instantiate the philosophy of this attempt. It doesn't matter, from his perspective, whether one's ideas are Platonic or Stoic, pagan or Christian; it doesn't matter what the names of the speakers are. What matters is the attempt to get to the truth.

I have tried to catch a glimpse of Augustine working at the questions that form the core issue of this book by trying to catch a glimpse of what the manuscript of *Lib. Arb.* that, we may imagine,

Pelagius held in his hands in Rome in the 390s, looked like. Faced with a text which, fully within the conventions of its time, does not identify its speakers, or refer to its philosophical past, the late antique reader is forced to work out how to take the text only by reading it. *Lib. Arb.* does not distinguish between pagan and Christian, it does not seek to reject or attack the world it belongs to, but as readers work through it, they find themselves thinking themselves into a world that is increasingly articulated in biblical Christian terms, and adopting the perspective that will provide the breathtaking vision of *Christian Education* and *The City of God*.

The culture in which *Lib. Arb.* is written is, however, a culture that is, as the quotation with which I began recognises, changing. While we have no manuscript of *Lib. Arb.* dating from before the ninth century, there survives a sixth-century edition of *The City of God*, which makes 'a clear attempt to distinguish quotations from Christian and pagan authors by different marks' (Bischoff 1990: 172 n. 60).

Notes

1 These would appear also to be the signs which are used in a ninth-century fragment of *Lib. Arb.* in the library of University College London (Römer 1972), as described to me by Professor E.W. Handley.

2 This is also the attribution of the *editio princeps* (Parma, 1491), and of those that derive from it (Venice, 1491 and Paris, 1520). It is of course impossible as an historical attribution, in view of the fact that Augustine did not meet Orosius until 414.

3 As quoted by Pohlenz 1911: 629. There is nonetheless still some *confusio* in the manuscript tradition – the *Mu* can be taken as the first letter of *magister*, or as the first letter of the Greek *mathêtês*, the *Delta* as the first letter of *discipulus* or *didaskalos*, and the student can be presented as asking the questions ('a press conference style') or answering them ('the catechism that the work was originally intended to be') (O'Donnell 1979: 248). Further information and translation at http://ccat.sas.upenn.edu/jod/junillus.html.

Bibliography

Editions and translations quoted (other translations are my own)

Augustine

CONFESSIONES [CONF.]

Sheed, F.J. (trans.) (1944) *The Confessions of St. Augustine*, London: Sheed & Ward.

Chadwick, H. (trans.) (1991) *Saint Augustine: Confessions*, Oxford: Oxford University Press.

CONTRA ACADEMICOS [C. ACAD.]

O'Meara, J.J. (trans.) (1951) *Against the Academics* (Ancient Christian Writers 12), New York: Newman Press.

DE LIBERO ARBITRIO [LIB. ARB.]

Green, W.M. (ed.) (1956) Corpus scriptorum ecclesiasticorum Latinorum 74, Vienna: Hoelder-Pichler-Tempsky.
Williams, T. (trans.) (1993) *Augustine: On Free Choice of the Will*, Indianapolis: Hackett.

SOLILOQUIORUM LIBER [SOL.]

Watson, G. (1990) *Soliloquies and Immortality of the Soul*, Warminster, Aris & Phillips.

Cicero: Partitiones Oratoriae

Wilkins, A.S. (ed.) (1903) Oxford Classical Texts. Oxford: Oxford University Press.

Arnauld and Descartes

[CSM] *The Philosophical Writings of Descartes,* 3 vols, trans. J. Cottingham, R. Stoothoff, D. Murdoch (and for vol. 3, A.J. Kenney). Cambridge: Cambridge University Press, 1984, 1985, 1991.

Secondary literature

Andrieu, J. (1954) *Le Dialogue antique*, Paris: Les Belles Lettres.
Anscombe, G.E.M. (1975) 'The First Person', in S. Guttenplan (ed.) *Mind and Language*: 45–65. Oxford: Oxford University Press.
Barton, A. (1990) *The Names of Comedy*, Oxford: Oxford University Press.
Bischoff, B. (1990) *Latin Palaeography*, Cambridge: Cambridge University Press.
Brown, P.R.L. (1967) *Augustine of Hippo: A Biography*, London: Faber & Faber.
—— (1995) *Authority and the Sacred: Aspects of the Christianization of the Roman World*, Cambridge: Cambridge University Press.
Burnyeat, M.F. (1987) 'Wittgenstein and Augustine *De Magistro*', *Proceedings of the Aristotelian Society* 61: 1–24.
De Capitani, F. (ed. and trans.) (1987) *Il 'De Libero Arbitrio' di S. Agostino. Studio introduttivo, testo, traduzione e commento*, Milan: Vita e Pensiero.

SIMON HARRISON

Mandouze, A. (1982) *Prosopographie chrétienne du bas-empire 1. Prosopographie de l'Afrique chrétienne (303–533)*, Paris: C.N.R.S.

Matthews, G.B. (1992) *Thought's Ego in Augustine and Descartes*, Ithaca, NY: Cornell University Press.

O'Donnell, J.J. (1979) *Cassiodorus*, Berkeley: University of California Press.

—— (ed.) (1992) *Augustine: Confessions* (3 vols, vol. 1: Introduction and text, vols 2, 3: Commentary). Oxford: Oxford University Press.

Pohlenz, M. (1911) 'Die Personenbezeichnungen in Ciceros Tusculanen', *Hermes* 46: 627–9.

Römer, F. (1972) *Die handschriftliche Überlieferung der Werke des Heiligen Augustinus. Band II/2: Großbritannien und Irland – Verzeichnis nach Bibliotheken.* Österreichische Akademie der Wissenschaften, Philosophisch-Historische Klasse, Sitzungsberichte, Band 276. Vienna: Verlag der Österreichischen Akademie der Wissenschaften.

Wilson, N.G. (1970) 'Indications of Speaker in Greek Dialogue Texts', *Classical Quarterly* 20: 305.

8

THE DESTRUCTION OF STATUES IN LATE ANTIQUITY[1]

Peter Stewart

Ponamus exemplum, ut quod dicimus manifestius fiat, si
quando tyrannus obtruncatur, imagines quoque eius depo-
nuntur et statuae, et vultu tantummodo commutato,
ablatoque capite, eius qui vicerit, facies superponitur, ut
manente corpore capitibusque praecisis caput aliud com-
mutetur.

[Let us cite an example to clarify what we are saying: when a
tyrant is cut down, his portraits and statues are also
deposed; then only the face is changed and the head
removed, and the face of the victor is placed on top, so
that the body remains, and another head is substituted for
those that have been removed.]

Jerome *In Abacuc* 2.3.14ff

What happened at Antioch in the spring of 387 deserves to be less
well known. When protests following the imposition of at least
one new levy developed into an organised riot, the ultimate victims
of the violence were the images of the emperor Theodosius and his
family. The insurrection was quickly suppressed, and the Antiochenes held their breath while they awaited the emperor's response.

The Riot of the Statues (with capital letters) has come to be
regarded as the single most significant act of secular iconoclasm in
late antiquity. The sacrilege was outrageous. For A.H.M. Jones it
was 'an unprecedented defiance' born of utter desperation (Jones
1973: 163); Williams and Friell see it as treasonable destruction of
images that were 'the most sacred political icons of the empire, the
holy objects in the universal cult of the godlike Augustus, whose
sanctity Christianity had never succeeded in diminishing' (Williams
and Friell 1994: 44f).[2] It is certainly true that the destruction of

imperial images during the emperor's established reign represented one of the worst forms of *maiestas*. The shock of seeing his own images destroyed in conjunction with those of Maximian was enough to finish Diocletian off, according to Lactantius; for it was a fate that had never befallen any emperor, 'quod nulli umquam imperatorum accideret' (Lactantius *De Mort. Persec.* 42). The riot at Antioch had significant repercussions, attracting the comment of Theodoret and Sozomen (Theodoret *H.E.* 5.20.1; Sozomen *H.E.* 7.23). But the event has acquired a somewhat exaggerated place in history because of the graphic accounts in the surviving *Homilies on the Statues* (*De Statuis*) of the young (Saint) John Chrysostom and in the speeches of the pagan rhetor Libanius (*Or.* 19–23). It was in their interests to imply that such violence was unique, evil, and mindless.

Sometimes historians give the Antioch riot a place at the end of a long Roman tradition of statue-destruction (e.g. Browning 1952: 20; Hopkins 1978: 226; Oliver 1996: 152f; Pekáry 1985: 140f). From this point onwards it is the religious iconoclasm of Christians against pagans or other Christians, or else the less ideological depredations of Lanciani's declining Rome, that attract most attention.

This chapter has two main aims. First, to survey the secular iconoclastic tradition and to highlight its conventions and topoi, its rules of violence and disorder, as the imperial sources in general, and the late Roman sources in particular, articulate them. This is a classicist's view of late antiquity in which the particular events at Antioch are neither so surprising nor so novel as they may at first seem. My second aim is to review both secular and Christian statue-destruction in the later empire, and to reveal the common ground from which new forms of Christian iconoclasm grew.

Portrait statues and their destruction are obviously highly relevant to the construction of identity in the Roman world. But this chapter does not focus on that aspect of the portrait. It is concerned, rather, with the iconoclastic tradition as a cultural thread joining late antiquity with the earlier empire (in the eyes of ancient as well as modern commentators), and as a cultural language shared by pagans and Christians. 'Languages', of whatever kind, are crucial in the creation and manipulation of cultural identity. Separate groups are associated in the common use of a language, but dialect and usage also serve to cultivate difference or to separate communities and promote internal cohesion – often in extremely subtle and variable ways. The ancient evidence examined here is part of that process of definition.

Damnatio memoriae and the rules of disorder

From the beginning of the first century BC to the end of the fourth century AD, in the city of Rome and throughout the empire, there was no generation that had not witnessed the symbolic destruction of statues and other portrait images. Many had participated. This was the practice most commonly referred to today as *'damnatio memoriae'*. In the strictest sense it involved the annihilation of a traitor's social persona. The outcast who had fallen from power or favour was executed, and anything that might preserve his or her memory or identity was erased. Property was sold off; the victim's *praenomen* might be lost to his family, as the Claudian *gens* lost the name Lucius (Suetonius *Tib.* 1); burial was forbidden; portrait images were destroyed; the name was removed from inscriptions. Such punishments, recorded in the early empire, are still to be seen in AD 399, in the terms of Eutropius' *damnatio* included in the Theodosian Code (9.40.17):

> Omnes res Eutropi . . . aerarii nostri calculis adiunximus, erepto splendore eius et consulatu a taetra inluvie et a commemoratione nominis eius et caenosis sordibus vindicato . . . Omnes statuas, omnia simulacra, tam ex aere quam ex marmore seu ex fucis quam ex quacumque materia quae apta est effingendis, ab omnibus civitatibus oppidis locisque privatis ac publicis praecipimus aboleri.

> [We have added all the possessions of Eutropius to the accounts of our treasury; his distinction has been removed; the consulate has been delivered from his abominable filth and the commemoration of his name and from that foul taint . . . We have decreed that all his statues, all his images, should be banished from all the cities and towns, in private places as well as public ones, whether they are bronze or marble, or paintings, or any other material that can be crafted.]

Although the term *damnatio memoriae* is a modern invention, it is well suited to this kind of socio-legal annihilation, and indeed, it is based on ancient juristic references to *'memoria damnata'* or *'memoriam accusare'* (Vittinghoff 1936: 64ff; Pekáry 1985: 135).[3] *Damnatio memoriae* as a legal practice has received much detailed discussion in the past (esp. *RE* 4.2059–62; Vittinghoff 1936: 13ff; Mommsen

1887). Frequently, however, we encounter the term in connection with the more famous and more graphic condemnations of fallen emperors. The emperor defeated by his enemy was declared *publicus hostis* and the usual measures were ordered by the senate. We have numerous mutilated inscriptions that bear witness to the widespread execution of the decree. But the most vivid impression is created by literary accounts of the destruction of images. The imperial image was ubiquitous, so the officially sanctioned destruction of this image affected every part of the empire with a massive spectacle of symbolic violence. The large and prominent statues of emperors in public places must have made a particularly forceful impression when, as in Antioch, crowds pulled them from their bases and dismantled them, abused them, and dragged them through the streets. Such violence, as we shall see, was inflicted upon the victim's body itself; but there was only one corpse and thousands of statues. Statues gave greater exposure to the annihilation of the enemy, as they did to the emperor's ruling presence before his fall: this role played by the statue as representative of the emperor is mentioned by Ambrose when he discusses access to the spiritual through the material (Ambrose *Expos. Psalm.* 118.10.25). It was also usual for the same fate to befall the emperor's family.

Such displays are very familiar to contemporary Europe, and countless parallels can be found in other cultures at other times.[4] But while it may be possible to find common, recurring social or psychological factors to explain iconoclasm (Freedberg 1989: 378–428), it is important to discuss the specific and unique. The forms of disorder discussed here belong to Roman culture, and it is within the evolving Roman cultural tradition that they are exploited, adapted and defined. We must be careful to avoid the tidy, oversimplified view of statue-destruction which is fostered by an awareness of recent history. In particular, we should remember that the destruction of statues did not merely follow the destruction of rulers, though the emperor's images were more prominent than anyone else's. Many 'private' individuals suffered *damnatio* throughout the empire: Sejanus is the most famous example (Juvenal 10.58ff), but there were others. Moreover, it is easy to overlook those occasions on which angry crowds, acting spontaneously, and not according to any official decree, inflicted violence upon the emperor's images. This happened to 'good' emperors as well as 'bad', but history – the Romans' history, that is – irons out these irregularities so that only a few conspicuous exceptions remain: the statues of Poppaea in Rome (Tac. *Ann.* 14.61; 'Seneca' *Octavia*

PETER STEWART

780ff); those of Tiberius in Gaul during his Rhodian exile (Suet. *Tib.* 13); Constantine's also (Nazarius *Pan. Con.* 2–5), and of course, the imperial images at Antioch (John Chrysostom *De Statuis* 21.11).[5] Those examples suggest another complication which is crucially important. The violence towards statues takes the same form as that of the official *damnationes,* but it belongs to the field of what has been called 'spontaneous statue-destruction' (Pekáry 1985: ch. 19 and esp. 139–42). In fact, there is generally very little indication as to whether the destruction of statues mentioned in a literary source is 'spontaneous' violence or the result of a decree. It is usually the urban populace – the mob – who are said to carry out the destruction, but that need not make it spontaneous. When we hear of the fall of a 'bad' emperor, accompanied by mob violence, it is likely that an official decree was issued by the senate; the crowd may act simultaneously, or in anticipation of the decree, but they may also be serving as the agents of the senate.[6]

This point is essential. As with so many Roman institutions, *damnatio* was deputised. There is some evidence for centralisation: the decree itself and the legal process (SHA *Maxim.* 12.11);[7] senatorial deliberations on the form of Commodus' *damnatio* (SHA *Commod.* 18.12ff); a fragmentary papyrus of AD 212 from Egypt recording an edict of the prefect Baebius Iucinus, passing on the order from the senate for the *damnatio* of an unmentioned, unmentionable victim, who must be Geta (BGU 2056 in Maehler 1968: 77f; Pekáry 1985: 137). There is also a third-century dedicatory inscription from Pannonia which may record the mission of an officer sent to deal with troops who had refused to remove the imperial images of a defeated regime from their standards: 'ad eradendum nomen saevissimae dominationis missus' (*AE* 1935: no. 164, 48f; Pekáry 1985: 136f). Yet the sources say little about the military execution of the decree (except in regard to military property). Though we do not know who chipped away inscriptions, the portrait statues fell at the hands of ordinary populations throughout the empire. The effects of this common effort of annihilation were much more pervasive than any centrally organised destruction. Even papyri and coins show the marks of *damnatio* (Pekáry 1985: 137; Crawford 1983). In theory at least complicity was enforced on pain of death (Dio 78.12.5; *Octavia* 611). Sources are explicit about the requirement to remove images in public *and in private* (Tac. *Ann.* 11.38.3; *Cod. Theod.* 9.40.17). Private participation was taken for granted – a fact exemplified by the relative scarcity of intact portraits of 'bad' emperors, and by other archaeological fragments: a statue base of

THE DESTRUCTION OF STATUES IN LATE ANTIQUITY

Diadumenianus found in the *latrina* of the vigiles' barracks at Ostia (*ILS* 465; *AE* 1947: 7; Pekáry 1985: 134); a head of Domitian from a well at Munigua in Andalusia (*Lo Sguardo di Roma*: 51).

We now recognise, especially in the light of Zanker's work, that Roman imperial propaganda functioned in the same way (Zanker 1988). The widespread reproduction of centrally created imagery was, at first, a response to the dominant ideology, and represented adherence to it. The destruction of images in public and private would have had a similarly cohesive effect. The notion of public execution of justice in particular was deeply ingrained in Roman culture, as Nippel clearly shows (Nippel 1995). The devolution of violence was always familiar.

In many of the statue riots recorded in the sources rumour and uncertainty seem to play a role. The destruction of statues provided a symbolic clarification of the situation, and it is little wonder that this form of signal was exploited, occasionally, in a vain attempt to influence events. Such was perhaps the case when Tiberius' images were toppled, and it may also help to explain Antioch. According to Dio (63.25.1f), Nero's officer Rufus was urged by his troops to take the throne, 'for he was a man of action, with a strong force behind him, *and the soldiers had pulled down Nero's images and shattered them, and they were calling him Caesar and Augustus*'.

In the accounts of all these iconoclastic activities a number of common features recur, and they give a remarkable impression of continuity from the early empire to late antiquity, which belies the social and *artistic* changes which occurred in the meantime. A brief survey follows.

Chanting. Chanting gives a common voice to the dissatisfied crowd. The games were a suitable setting for addressing the emperor directly in this way (Vanderbroeck 1987: 143). Chanting was a normal activity, led and manipulated by professional claques (Vanderbroeck 1987: 78; Browning 1952). By the fourth century the theatrical claques could be seen as an independent, influential and subversive force, and they may even have been responsible for the progress of the Antioch riot (Browning 1952). Chanting could serve as the ritualised statement of relations between the emperors and their subjects, including the senate. The Theodosian Code begins with an extract from the minutes of a meeting of the senate in AD 438. Statements are interspersed with repeated declarations of approval by the senators, and they are rounded off with a chorus of acclamations: 'per vos honores, per vos patrimonia, per vos omnia [28 times]' and so on. This practice has been seen as a typical feature of the later empire (e.g. Matthews 1989: 248), but it must have existed earlier, for Dio describes such acclamations during Severus' funeral oration for Pertinax (Dio 75.5.1). The perversion of such acclamations often provided a prelude to statue-destruction or lynching, as in the SHA account (*Commod.* 18.12ff) of Commodus' *damnatio*: 'delatores ad leonem . . . statuae detrahantur' etc.[8]

Toppling the statue. The actual destruction of the statues is rarely discussed in detail, but ropes and crowbars were required (*Octavia* 796–9; Juv. 10.58f; Libanius *Or.* 22.8).[9] Stoning occurred only occasionally,[10] perhaps on account of the Roman preference for large (basalt) cobble stones. The process was not particularly easy and must have created an impressive spectacle, as we can imagine from the Via Paisiello painting discussed below and from modern experience.[11]

Mutilation. The mutilation and dissection of the statue was symbolically much more important and it is a recurring feature. The actions seem to be derived from the treatment of the victim's corpse (Plut. *Cic.* 49; Dio 58.11.5; 72(73).13; 74.2.1; Tac. *Hist.* 3.74; 3.84; Suet. *Vitell.* 17; Orosius 7.88; Procopius *Anec.* 18.12–21; SHA *Commod.* 6.2; 18.3; Herodian 1.13.6).[12] Elagabalus' case is extreme but typical: he and his mother had their heads cut off, they were stripped, and their bodies were dragged through the city, the emperor's being dumped in the Tiber (Dio 80.20.2; SHA *Elagab.* 17). In the fourth century the same fate befell Theophilus, Montius and Domitianus (who, after all, had an ill-omened name), and Bishop Georgius of Alexandria (Ammianus Marcellinus 14.7.6; 14.7.15f; 22.11.8f). The treatment of statues followed the same pattern (Seneca *De Ira* 3.15.1; Tac. *Hist.* 3.84; Dio 58.11.1; 74.2.1; Pliny *Pan.* 52). In Roman thought, *nomen* (name) and *facies/caput* (face/head) were closely associated, and the portrait head's role in identifying a standard sculptural body arose from the so-called 'appendage aesthetic' (Brilliant 1963: 10, 26–31) – the separate conception of body and limbs. Decapitation, and the replacement of heads (Blanck 1969), was therefore the particular kind of mutilation that served *damnatio* and related violence best. That is clearly illustrated by Jerome's statement at the head of this chapter.

Dragging. An important recurring part of the display. At Antioch, according to Libanius (*Or.* 22.8), the imperial statues were dragged through the streets. Corpses and statues had been dragged by rioters for centuries, particularly, in Rome, to the Gemonian Steps by the

Capitol – the place where traitors' bodies were traditionally displayed (Tac. *Ann.* 14.61; Dio 72(73).13; Tac. *Hist.* 3.74; Suet. *Tib.* 75; Tac. *Hist.* 3.84; Suet. *Vitell.* 17; Juv. 10.66f; Dio 74.2.1; SHA *Commod.* 18.12; Herodian 1.13.6; SHA *Elagab.* 17; Amm. Marc. 14.7.15f; Dio 59.30.19; *Octavia* 797; Suet. *Nero* 24.1). Bishop Georgius' remains suffered in the same way (Amm. Marc. 22.11.8f).

Refuse disposal. Bishop Georgius' body ended up in the sea. The bodies of Montius and Domitianus were thrown into the Orontes at Antioch (Amm. Marc. 14.7.16). Disposal of assaulted statues and human remains in the sewage system – and that usually meant the river – was the norm. The statue base from Ostia mentioned above provides good material evidence for the dragging of monuments 'in latrinas'.[13]

The world turned upside down. From all these features of statue destruction a trend emerges. The normal order is reversed. *Damnatio memoriae* and parallel activities subvert the position of honour in which an individual and his or her honorific images are held. Sometimes there is an explicit contrast between the treatment of the ascendant and the defeated individual, while the irony of the fall from a great social height is a recurring topos (Pliny *Pan.*; Tac. *Ann.* 14.66; Juv. 10.58ff and see Whittaker 1969: 86, n. 1). Dragging of statues might be seen as a reversal of the normal honorific procession, and we have seen the perversion of the honorific chant. Eusebius refers to the condemned Maximian as 'δυσσεβάστατος' – very ungodly or un-august – but also un-Sebastos, un-Augustus, un-emperor (Eusebius *H.E.* 8.13.15). A similar term, contrasted with the 'εὐσεβάστατος' Caracalla, is applied to Geta in the Egyptian decree already mentioned.

These 'rules of disorder' are literary topoi. The author imposes order on his perceptions. The same phrases recur. But more than this, the literary sources provide ostensibly truthful historical narratives, sometimes by eye-witnesses, and supported by archaeological finds. I do not wish to suggest a material reality of which the essential elements are conveyed by the sources, in spite of a little rhetorical embroidery. Rather, what we detect, hardly surprisingly, are topoi constructed by *actors on the ground* as well as by writers. There is no clear division between the reality and the rhetoric of these accounts. In the rest of this chapter the texts are taken primarily as samples for the history of ideas and representations, but the rituals of iconoclasm were very real for those who experienced them; the numerous actors had their own ideologies, and that fact is important for an

PETER STEWART

accurate assessment of the role of iconoclasm in the later Roman empire.

At this point one misrepresentation should be exposed. *Damnatio memoriae* was not exactly about the destruction of memory, though ancient sources insist that it was:[14] the statue or portrait image is a means of obtaining immortality; its destruction reverses the process; no written trace of the victim should remain; the name must not be uttered (Cicero *Pis.* 93; Dio 60.22.3; Suet. *Nero* 24.1; SHA *Commod.* 19.1; SHA *Elagab.* 17; the Egyptian decree, above; Nazarius *Pan. Con.* 5). The face and the head, as the key to visual recognition and identity, are the focus of violence (Tac. *Hist.* 3.74; Pliny *Pan.* 52.4; Dio 72(73).13; SHA *Maxim.* 23.6; Nazarius *Pan. Con.*; John Chrysostom *De Statuis* 21.11). Yet what actually occurred was a highly symbolic, universal display of pantomime forgetfulness. Caracalla decreed that the very name of Geta should not be uttered, but it was literally vital that everyone should remember whom to keep quiet about. People went through the motions: 'don't mention you-know-who!' Of course, *everybody* knew who. Consequently, whenever it was felt necessary, the removal of statues could be carried out discreetly, at night, and without triggering the conventional train of violence (Dio 60.4.5; cf. 79.19.2). The point of secular iconoclasm was not that violence should be done, but that violence should be seen to be done.

The other ostensible motive for iconoclasm was the desire for revenge and the satisfaction of bloodlust (Cic. *Pis.* 93; Juv. 10.67; Dio 59.30.1a; Pliny *Pan.* 52; SHA *Gord.* 13.6; cf. Gregory 1994: 95f). In particular, joy, celebration and mockery are the characteristics of the riotous mob (people like Pliny quite understand, though they would not act that way themselves).[15] The sources often associate riots with the mindless violence of the crowd (Vanderbroeck 1987: 187f). The idea of the mindless Roman mob has prevailed (Hannestad 1994: 18, n. 19; Price 1984: 194 'orgies of destruction'), and indeed, the cliché of 'mindless violence' is often misused today in other contexts, in spite of long-established and clearly argued sociological objections (Turner and Killian 1957: esp. 16–19, 157–61; Couch 1969: esp. 109f and 114). Andrew Gregory (1994) has used a different sociological framework to alter misconceptions about statue-riots in particular, pointing to the 'expressive' and 'instrumental' dimensions of such collective behaviour. It is enough to recognise here that even the most emotional outburst can follow conventional patterns, and that the syntax of *damnatio* examined above may help to explain apparently 'illegitimate' or accidental statue-destruction,

167

as in the cases of Poppaea (*Octavia* 792ff; Tac. *Ann.* 14.61), Favorinus the sophist (Philostratus *Vit. Soph.* 489–92; [Dio Chrysostom] *Thirty-Seventh Discourse*; Gleason 1995: 3–20 and 146ff), and the praetorian prefect Plautianus (Dio 76.16.2–5; SHA *Severus* 14). And perhaps even Antioch. The destruction of imperial images during an emperor's established reign was certainly outrageous. But the fourth century was not such a stable period. Just over a year after the Riot of the Statues there were disturbances in Constantinople triggered by the false rumour of Theodosius' defeat by Maximus (Socrates *H.E.* 5.13; Sozomen 7.14; Ambrose *Ep.* 40.13; Browning 1952: 13). Browning notes that according to John of Nikiu such a rumour also spread before the Riot of the Statues, but he rejects the notion because 'his chronology is hopelessly confused' (Browning 1952: 13, n. 7). There *may* be some kernel of truth in the report; but the important fact is that such a sequence of events is seen as plausible. In all of these cases it is possible to imagine communities acting according to their expectations of the political situation; in other words, waiting for signals from above, before clarifying the new socio-political circumstances with the conventional sequence of iconoclasm.

But the myth of mindless violence existed in antiquity also, and it is even possible that the representation of some statue-destructions as misguided initiatives of provincials or mistaken mobs is the result of imperial hand-washing after the event, or an ancient misunderstanding of the underlying logic. In any case, the mob that threw down the statues of Poppaea, believing her to have fallen from grace, is driven by *furor* and *rabies* in *Octavia*; the destruction of Constantine's images before his victory is described by Nazarius as blind madness, 'caeca dementia' (Nazarius *Pan. Con.* 12); and the idea of mindless violence is even more explicitly propagated in an early fifth-century inscription from Rome (*CIL* 6.1783 (*ILS* 2948); De Rossi 1849; *PLRE* 1: 345–7). It comes from a statue base found in front of the Basilica Ulpia. This was set up by a relative in AD 431 to bear the statue of Nichomachus Flavianus the Younger. He was the son of the more famous pagan Nichomachus and had been a close associate of the 'usurper' Eugenius, yet he survived to serve under Theodosius. The inscription quotes a letter from Theodosius II and Valentinian III to the senate, redeeming the memory of Nichomachus, recently deceased, and condemning what had been done against him as the result of a 'caeca insimulatio' and against the will of the *princeps*. This may be another example of citizens acting in accordance with their expectations of the emperor's will, apparently by toppling

Nichomachus' portrait. But mindlessness (or 'blindness') is invoked to correct the family's social position.

Finally, Libanius goes to great lengths to avoid the conclusion that Antioch was guilty of the highest treason. Demons were responsible for the trouble. The subversive alien claque-leaders were to blame. The actions of the Antiochenes were literally mindless in that they were stimulated by alcohol: the violence was παροινία. Libanius also seems astonished that images of the emperor's family should suffer in the riot, although that was typical of iconoclastic violence.[16] Libanius utterly condemns the rioters, and yet to suggest that they acted thoughtfully – perhaps inspired by the curial class – would have had much more serious implications.

Late antiquity

By the fourth century AD the features of Roman iconoclasm were completely familiar to educated writers. Although Juvenal had presented *damnatio* as a well-known sequence of events (in his generic, 'descendunt statuae restemque secuntur'), it is in late antiquity especially that the pattern of iconoclasm is presented as a regular practice, most notably in Jerome's description of *damnatio* and form-changing, or *metarryuthmêsis*. SHA *Commod.* 17.5 tells of the replacement of the head and inscription of the Roman colossus in the accustomed manner, 'more solito'. At Antioch the imperial statues were dragged through the city as people insulted them 'in the usual way' (Sozomen *H.E.* 7.28). Many of our accounts of *damnatio* come from the *Historia Augusta* which describes each event anew but also recognises the recurring pattern. Novel and bizarre practices stand out against this background, as when the statue of Celsus is crucified: 'novo iniuriae genere imago in crucem sublata persultante vulgo, quasi patibulo ipse Celsus videretur adfixus' ('in a new kind of punishment, his image was hoisted onto a cross, and the crowd danced around as if they were looking at Celsus himself fastened to the stake').[17]

This latter example, with its obvious allusion to the Crucifixion, highlights one new feature of statue-destruction in the later empire.[18] Portraits were more explicitly represented as tokens of an absent and intangible ruler, and this relationship mirrors the connection between the mortal Christ and God. Setton discusses a number of Christian writings – notably by Athanasius and Basil – in which the emperor and his images serve as a theological exemplum (Setton 1967: 196–211; cf. Freedberg 1989: 392–5). The present image of the absent emperor is likened to Christ who is the physical manifestation of God. The imperial image is repeatedly treated *as* the emperor, which is why the events at Antioch seem so shocking. This is naturally a complex and ambiguous relationship, as Ambrose makes clear (*Expos. Psalm.* 118.10.25).[19]

The analogy of the portrait and the ruler to explain the relationship of God, Christ and the created world casts the adoration and abuse of imperial statues in a new light, while the analogy was no doubt facilitated by the extreme reverence with which the emperor was treated in late Roman ceremony. (The emperor is continually compared with God or Christ (Setton 1967: esp. 194f).) And yet in spite of the wealth of evidence for the treatment of the imperial image as *deus praesens*, the function of the portrait had not radically changed, and Hopkins points to many examples of the earlier imperial statue serving as a stand-in for the distant and venerated monarch; it is within this context that he discusses *damnatio* and the riot at Antioch (Hopkins 1978: 221–31).

The really noticeable change between the statues of the Principate and those of late antiquity is a formal one. The trend in the direction of the abstract and schematic seems to be best exemplified by the portraiture of the Tetrarchs and the successors of Constantine, the latter being characterised by the same patterned fringe of hair, large, staring eyes, frontality and lack of individualised physiognomical features (figure 8.1). There is greater variety in private portraiture, but in the representation of the emperor after Constantine, the Constantinian image itself provides the model for rulers who are portrayed as a *class* rather than as individuals. R.R.R. Smith gives a standard explanation: 'The desire for dynastic consistency and less concern for "recognizability" should explain why we cannot identify the sculptured portraits and also suggests there was probably little or severely reduced use of centrally provided models for making them' (Smith 1985: 220). In fact, the difficulty of distinguishing late Roman imperial portraits is notorious (they are recognised as emperors through the presence of the diadem). We cannot assume that the ancient viewer would not have *seen* them as individualised images, but the extraordinary similarity among them makes it surprising that the idea of mimetic likeness continues in late Roman texts (Basil, for example, says that the imperial image represents its subject μιμητικῶς – by imitation (Basil *De Spiritu Sancto* 45, ap. John of Damascus *Or.* 1)). In particular, it makes it surprising that Jerome can write of the replacement of one face with another. What was the difference? Such an exchange may have

Figure 8.1 Statue of a late Roman emperor at Barletta.

taken place within the late Roman *damnatio*, but of the many late examples of reworked heads in Blanck's catalogue (Blanck 1969), as far as we can tell, all are adaptations of much earlier imperial sculptures rather than the heads of contemporaries or immediate predecessors. Blanck himself believes that Jerome is thinking at least partly of the necessarily numerous *damnationes* of the third century.

Regardless of formal change, the statue, being obviously analogous to the human body, continued to serve the rituals of honour and dishonour in late antiquity, and the representation of secular iconoclasm did not change in any obvious way throughout the empire. The *idea* of the statue's symbolism was important; the idea of its symbolic destruction served the same function, in the same way, as long as emperors were honoured with prominent public images. And it is easy to imagine that in the fourth century the patterns of statue-destruction were widely familiar, not from the literary tradition, but from experience; for the destruction of imperial and private portraits must have been a regular occurrence throughout the third-century empire and secular iconoclasm is recorded several times in the fourth century. It is with this continuous tradition in mind that we must re-examine the practices of Christian iconoclasts in the same period.

Christians and idols

The fourth century did bring a new kind of statue-destruction. The security of the Christian Church under Constantine emboldened Christians to launch an offensive against the trappings of paganism – the temples and the cult statues within them – and to reinforce by violence the principles of the long apologetic tradition. Iconoclasm from now on has new associations for historians.

There is no doubt that the destruction of idols took place, though we could easily over-estimate its impact. The destructive and triumphalist zeal of Eusebius or Jacob of Saroug is mitigated by the controversial prominence of pagan practice late in the fourth century (notably in the disputes over the Victory statue of the Roman Curia). In the fifth century Augustine himself had reservations about the destruction of pagan statues; he and others were certainly hostile to spontaneous iconoclasm (Thornton 1986: 126f).

We can be sure, however, that with the ascendency of Constantine the Church changed its attitude to iconoclasm. In AD 306 the Council of Elvira (Canon 60) affirmed that the destruction of idols was neither sanctioned by the Gospels nor by the actions of the apostles, and that those who died for it were not to be considered martyrs. In the reign of Constantine, writers such as Firmicus Maternus and Eusebius present it almost as a Christian duty (Thornton 1986: 123). We cannot safely say much about the extent to which the Christian population of the empire performed this duty, and most of the sources lay greater emphasis on the demolition of temples and disruption of worship than on the idols themselves. But what we can detect is the impression that idol-destruction belongs in some sense to the ancient tradition of secular iconoclasm (and its representation) discussed above. Yet the academic division of labour has obscured this fact, separating the cultures and the histories of pagans and Christians, and ignoring the common cultural vocabulary which various groups and individuals in late Roman society adopted and adapted for their own activities. This is vividly illustrated by a remarkable but barely discussed catacomb painting in Rome.

In the first few days of 1865 the famous explorer of catacombs G.B. De Rossi inadvertently discovered this unique representation of iconoclasm. He was looking for the catacombs of St Pamphilus, but instead, crawling through a series of underground tunnels, he found himself in what turned out to be an isolated hypogeum.[20] In one cubiculum, which is still intact beneath the Via Paisiello, he discovered painted wall decorations, including figured scenes from the usual repertory of early Christian art: Jonah thrown into the ocean, the raising of Lazarus, the healing of the paralytic, the Good Shepherd (?), Noah in his chest-like ark, Jonah under the gourd tree, Moses striking the rock, Abraham and Isaac (?), the three young Hebrews in the fiery furnace (figure 8.2). There is no obvious programme in the location of these extant scenes. There are a few iconographic anomalies such as the stonework of Lazarus' tomb: the closest parallels suggest a date in the second half of the fourth century. These paintings were part of the redecoration of the cubiculum, which apparently occurred when two new loculi were roughly cut into the plaster of each side-wall. Although their content is mostly conventional, their form is extremely unusual, for they seem to be amateur sketches, abnormally small and rapidly painted on coarse plaster with brown pigment (and a little green for Jonah's gourd). Some of the subjects are only identifiable because of their loose adherence to the familiar catacomb repertory. All of this suggests that the anonymous hypogeum of the Via Paisiello was a private catacomb outside the control of the Church. That is Ferrua's explanation for the *unica* in the Via Latina catacomb (Ferrua 1960: 95–101; Carletti 1971: 117; Tronzo 1986: 71f, n. 2.).

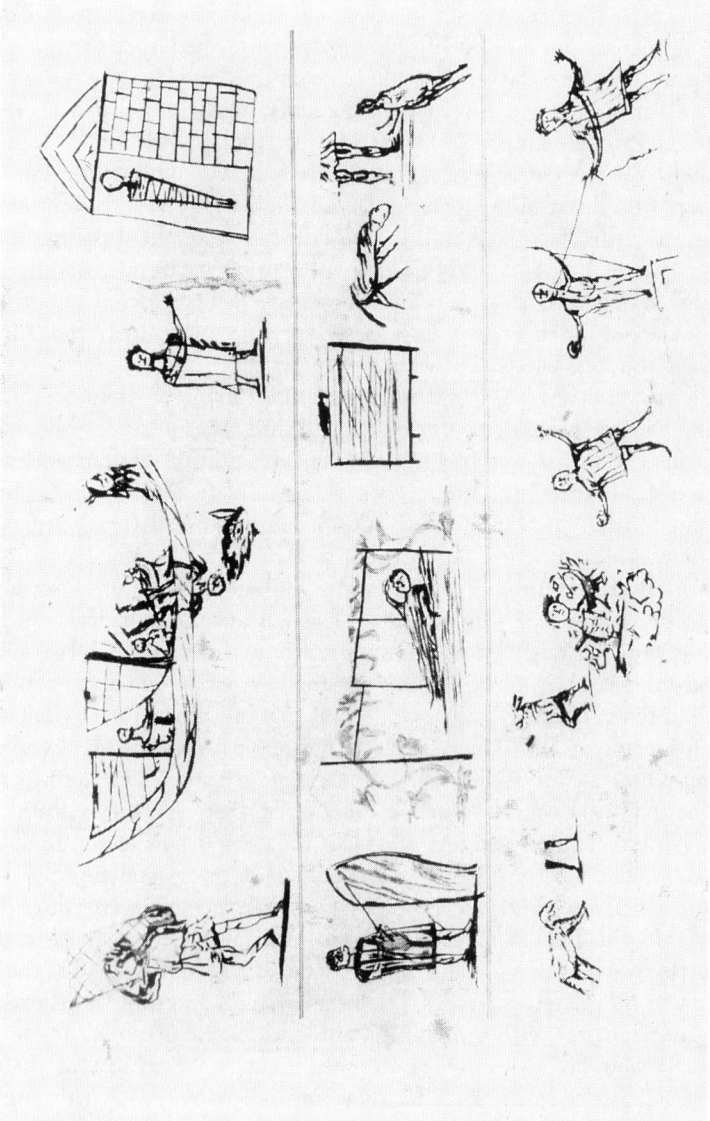

Figure 8.2 De Rossi's drawing of paintings in the anonymous hypogeum of the Via Paisiello, Rome.

But there is one more extraordinary anomaly in the tomb (figure 8.3). Next to the fiery furnace, between the loculi on the left wall, there is a scene of statue-destruction. The statue in question appears to be a naked male figure on a pedestal. In the left hand it holds a sceptre or staff; in its right there is a circular object, most probably a patera. The iconography of the statue could suggest an emperor's portrait statue, but De Rossi rejects this interpretation on the grounds that naked imperial statues belong to the earlier empire. If it represents a particular deity then Jupiter is the most likely choice. The statue is flanked by two men in short tunics. All commentators have taken the man on the left to be a stone-thrower. The right-hand figure is clearer: raising his arms in the air he clutches a rope which is attached to the statue's neck. Given the context for the painting there can be no doubt that this is the only extant ancient depiction of Christians destroying a pagan idol.[21]

This scene has been viewed in the context of the Theodosian backlash against paganism, and in a recent exhibition it was represented with a caption from the Sirmondian Constitutions (an imperial order for the destruction of idols in AD 407). But removed from its context it could mean something else. No visual representation of *damnatio memoriae* survives. But if it did, it might look just like this. There is no iconographical indication that the statue is not that of an emperor. Naked portraits *had* existed, and if we wished to identify a close iconographical parallel for the figure we might settle upon the famous statue of Claudius 'as Jupiter' from Lavinium.[22]

The Via Paisiello hypogeum shows how tenuous the distinction between secular and Christian iconoclasm could be, at least in terms of visual representation, and there is enough literary and archaeological evidence to suggest that the separate rituals themselves, and their symbolism, were closely associated in the minds of Christian iconoclasts and their observers.

At first much of this seems to be circumstantial evidence. At Trier in the time of Gratian, at the sanctuaries of the Altbachtal, the statues were apparently destroyed by Christians; the sculptures were left standing but without their heads, a road was constructed over part of their sanctuary and a few temples were converted into dwellings (Wightman 1970: 229). A broken torso of a Venus statue used to stand near the church of St Matthias as a target for stones thrown by passers-by; a medieval inscription claims that it had been made an object of ridicule by St Eucharius (Wightman 1970: 229; Espérandieu 1915: 272, no. 5037; Kempf and Reusch 1965: 17, no. 1). These objects are reminiscent of the statues

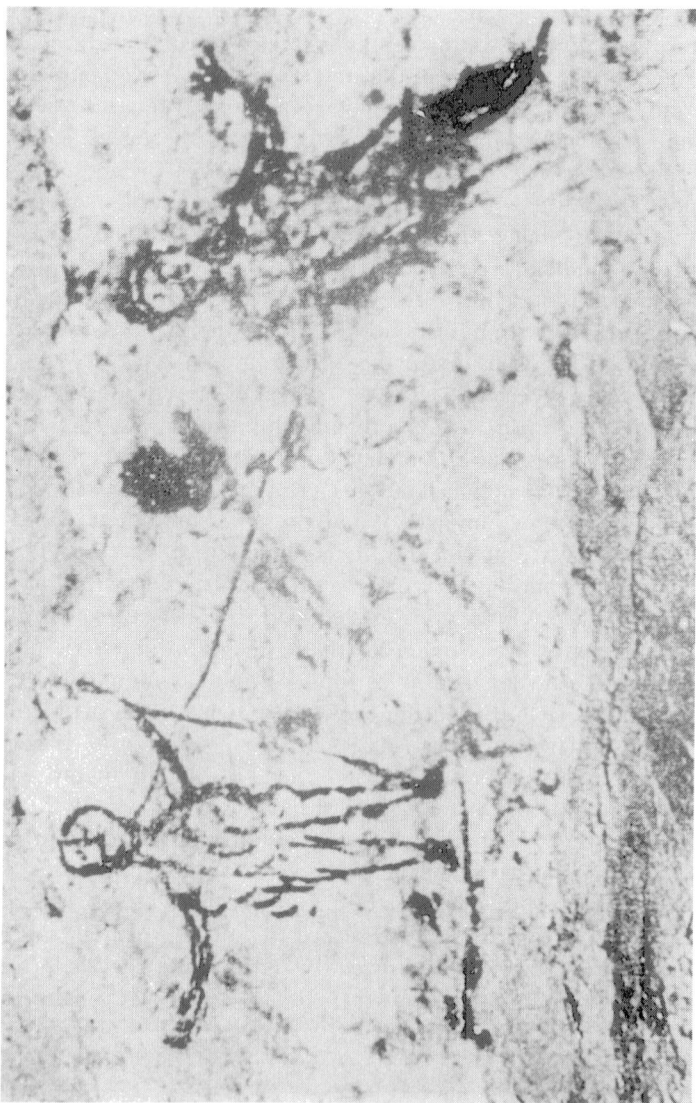

Figure 8.3 Painting of the destruction of an idol from the Via Paisiello hypogeum.

mutilated and mocked by iconoclastic crowds (see p. 000), and beheading in particular could be seen as an attempt to remove the image's identity in the tradition of *damnatio*. It *could* be argued that the desire to mutilate and behead an effigy is universal and natural, but it is hard to avoid the Roman secular precedents. And there are other instances of decapitation. The well-known bronze head of Sulis Minerva from Britain seems to have been wrenched off its body (Cunliffe 1969: 34, pl. 11).

Ralph Merrifield's inquest on the sculptures of Londinium reveals that, while Christian iconoclasm is not a satisfactory explanation for all ancient damage to cult images, there are nevertheless some secure examples: the sculptures buried for safe keeping in the Walbrook Mithraeum include a head of Mithras – presumably part of the main cult image – that had already been lopped in half at the neck (figure 8.4), apparently with a right-handed blow from something like an axe (Merrifield 1977: 376–8, pl. 17).[23] The headless body of a deity, possibly Mercury, was also found in the fill of a ditch at Bow in association with material from the first half of the fourth century, and seems to have been the victim of iconoclasm (Merrifield 1977: 394, pl. 17.V(a)).[24] If these fragments hint at decapitation and mutilation as a common feature of the two kinds of iconoclasm, then some of the literary accounts suggest an association of the two in the minds of the authors: a kind of *interpretatio Christiana*, perhaps, of traditional statue-destruction.

Eusebius' panegyric delivered at Tyre, which is included in his *Historia Ecclesiae*, proclaims the triumph of God over evil (10.4.10– 16). Christ, who is the slayer of tyrants (τυραννοκτόνος), is the teacher of piety and destroyer of evil (εὐσεβείας; ἀσεβῶν: cognate words recur); the devil is explicitly associated with godless tyrants, who are his agents (ἀσεβῶν τυράννων; δυσσεβῶν ἀρχόντων); and he has deceived people through idols. Now Christ has made evil vanish, and so completely that it seems never to have had a name: 'ὡς μηδὲ πώποτε ὠνομάσθαι δοκεῖν'. And now thanks to Him the most exalted of emperors can 'spit upon the faces of dead idols . . . and laugh at old, inherited deceits'. Some of Eusebius' vocabulary is strikingly reminiscent of *damnatio* as we have formulated it. The reference to oblivion is particularly significant, as are the clear references to Constantine's 'tyrannical' predecessors and rivals. The victory of Christianity involves a kind of *damnatio* of evil, and this is manifested in the abuse of pagan cult images. In the *Vita Constantini* Eusebius addresses the theme of iconoclasm more directly. In 2.45, 4.23 and 4.25, Constantine is presented as a

Figure 8.4 Marble head of Mithras from the Walbrook Mithraeum in London.

PETER STEWART

destroyer of idols. Iconoclasm is described in detail in 3.54ff. The terms are interesting. The statues are broken up and stripped of their precious material, melted down and exposed to ridicule (ἐπὶ γέλωτι καὶ παιδιᾷ); the bronze idols are pulled down with ropes and dragged. The dismemberment of the statue and its dragging are familiar from secular iconoclasm, though Eusebius presents their 'mutilation' as a practical measure, designed to expose the cult images for what they are – mere stone and metal.[25] Mockery, as we can see from Antioch, was also a feature of secular iconoclasm and the lynchings that accompanied it (see the imagery of reversal discussed above and: Libanius *Or.* 22.7; Plut. *Pomp.* 1.2 (καθυβρίσαντες); Suet. *Vitell.* 17 (*ludibria*); Josephus *A.J.* 19.357 (ἀφύβριζον); Dio 74.2.1 [ἐξυβρίζειν]; Herodian 1.13.6 (ἐνυβρίσαντες)). When Eusebius describes the *damnatio* of Maximinus in the *Historia Ecclesiae* (9.11.2), he refers to the toppling and destruction of his statues, and the mockery of the crowd (γέλως . . . παιδιὰ . . . ἐνυβρίζειν). This is reminiscent not only of the passages in the *Vita Constantini*, but also the *Triennial Oration*, in which Constantine is said to have sent out his friends to end idolatry; they supervise the destruction of statues which takes place with much laughter and degradation: 'πολλῷ γέλωτι καὶ σύν αἰσχυνῃ' (8.3; cf. Origen *Contra Celsum* 8.41 where Christians are accused of mocking pagan statues). Then again, at 8.4, the idols are said to have been stripped of their valuable materials and led off with ropes.

We can find other hints and resonant phrases in Christian writings of the period. In *De Concensu Evang.* 1.16, Augustine says that the third-century Christians would have liked to see the destruction of temples and cult statues and the '*damnatio*' of sacrifices: 'eversio templorum et damnatio sacrificiorum et confractio simulacrorum' (though of course, '*damnatio*' was not the specific word for *damnatio memoriae*). Prudentius appeals for someone who will close the temples and condemn their thresholds – 'damnet limina' (*Peristeph.* 2.479). The fifth-century Syriac sermon of Jacob of Saroug is a triumphalist declaration of the death of idolatry which begins with the death of Christ. Again, the dismemberment of idols is associated with mockery and derision:[26] they become a pile of fragments 'made to arouse laughter and scorn' (l. 185); the demons reproach Satan (ll. 220ff), saying 'your statues, your busts, the instruments of your cult have all been overturned – they lie on the ground and everyone laughs at your deceptions'; in ll. 260ff, 'the crucified man defeats the giants, humiliates them and turns them into an object

179

of mockery'; Christ's shattering of all kinds of pagan statue is described at length in ll. 230ff, and then, at 325ff, in a passage that recalls Eusebius, 'men begin to strip their gods; they remove from their idols the gold that covers them; they break them and take away the bronze and silver; they denude them and load them with shame and scorn'. Finally, in 375ff, Satan laments the breaking and stripping, the burning and crushing of his idols' statues, saying '[Christ] has disfigured our portraits and annihilated them [Martin: 'anéantis']'.

If the apparent fusion of secular and religious iconoclastic imagery in these texts seems to amount only to circumstantial evidence, we must return to the passage of Jerome with which we began. This quotation is taken out of context as a detailed ancient reference to the process of *damnatio* (e.g. in Blanck 1969; cf. Price 1984: 194, with more concern for context). But Jerome is not *exactly* concerned with imperial power and its symbolism. He is explaining chapter 3, verses 13–14 of the Septuagint Book of Habbakuk (the Hebrew/Vulgate text is quite different): *Divisisti in stupore capita potentium* (You have divided in wonder the heads of the powerful). Christ is the head of the Church, while Beelzebub is the 'princeps daemoniorum' and his squadrons each have a head. Christ has separated the heads from their subjects, like removing a head from a body, and 'in the place of the worst of heads he places the best of heads. Let us cite an example to clarify what we are saying' ('ubi caput pessimum fuerat, ibi caput optimum reponatur. Ponamus exemplum, ut quod dicimus manifestius fiat'); and so the analogy of *damnatio memoriae* is introduced.

Further explanation follows, and then Jerome returns to the analogy:

> Possumus hoc versiculo uti, si quando reges et duces eorum Christianum viderimus sanguinem fundere, et postea ultionem Domini consecutam, quod dudum in Iuliano, et ante eum Maximiano, et supra in Valeriano, Decio, Domitiano, Nerone perspeximus, et dicere ad Dominum in exsultatione et oratione cum cantico . . .

> [We can appreciate this verse if we think of when we have seen their kings and leaders shedding Christian blood, and afterwards, the resultant vengeance of the Lord; we saw this recently with Julian, and before him Maximian, and

before that Valerian, Decius, Domitian, Nero; and [we spoke] to the Lord in exultation and in speech and singing.]

Then Jerome thinks back to his school days, when he heard of the death of Julian the Apostate. In this extended comparison, the downfall of Paganism and Evil and the rise of Christianity and the Church fostered by Good Emperors are explicitly likened to, and associated with, the downfall of tyrants (who were persecutors of Christians) and their subsequent *damnatio*. And the same comparison is to be found in Lactantius' *De Mortibus Persecutorum*, for God has shown His retribution by extinguishing and deleting the enemy of His name: 'in extinguendis delendisque nominis Sui hostibus' (1.7). The downfall of the persecutors/Bad Emperors is described, with particular attention to the *damnationes* of Domitian and Maximian. In Domitian's case (3.2f),

nec satis ad ultionem fuit quod est interfectus domi; etiam memoria nominis eius erasa est. Nam cum multa mirabilia opera fabricasset, cum Capitolium aliaque nobilia monimenta fecisset, senatus ita nomen eius persecutus est, ut neque imaginum neque titulorum eius relinquerentur ulla vestigia, gravissime decretis etiam mortuo inureret ad ignominiam sempiternam.

[nor was it sufficient revenge that he was killed at home; even the memory of his name was erased. For although he had constructed many wonderful works, and although he had built the Capitol and other noble monuments, the senate persecuted his name to the extent that no traces were left of his portraits or his inscriptions. Even when he was dead, in the most severe of punishments, by its decrees it branded him for eternal infamy.]

It is unclear whether or not the author recognises the paradox of 'memoria erasa . . . ignominiam sempiternam' that is inherent in *damnatio*. Now Good has triumphed and God has punished the tyrants with death and *damnatio*. 'Nempe delevit ea Dominus et erasit de terra' (52.3). In the texts examined here, the destruction of pagan cult statues and the demise of pagan emperors, with their honorific statues, are part of the same process: the fall of the tyranny of Evil, and the rise of the kingdom of God.

Conclusion

I do not wish to replace the existing simplifications and categorisations of historians with a new edition of the facts. A general survey of patristic responses to the imperial image, for example, reveals some of the subtleties, contradictions, ambiguities and complexities of the late Roman literary corpus (see Setton 1967: 196–211). *Damnatio memoriae*, spontaneous statue-destruction and Christian iconoclasm were not the same thing. Fourth-century Christians did not simply live pagan culture. And yet, when it came to the destruction of statues, there was a continuity of imagery, a common vocabulary which could be used to articulate differing beliefs and perspectives. This vocabulary extended beyond literature to the very rituals through which statues were addressed.

I have proposed two new views of statue-destruction. First, the tradition of *damnatio* and parallel activities thrived without obvious change as long as the use of honorific statues in the Roman empire. The representation of this iconoclasm suggests a repertory of symbolism which remains constant. The destruction of portrait statues in late antiquity conforms to a long tradition, and represents one strand of cultural continuity from the late Republic to the fifth century AD. Second, it is against the background of this tradition that Christians of the fourth century began to destroy idols in greater numbers. It was almost inevitable that their actions would owe something to the continuous conventions of iconoclasm, especially since the imperial statues that were most obviously the victims of *damnatio* had been (and continued to be) venerated in places as cult images. The selection of evidence reviewed here suggests that the familiar and ubiquitous rituals of portrait-destruction were adapted by iconoclastic Christians, and especially, that some commentators more or less consciously applied the imagery of secular iconoclasm to the downfall of paganism and the destruction of idols.

In one sense, these sources resist our efforts to identify cultural change between the conventional periods of the Principate and the later Roman empire. They defy evidence for social, cultural and artistic transformation with symbols of continuity. At the same time, writers like Lactantius and Jerome, who associate the fall of tyrants with Christian ascendancy, have a part to play in shaping late antiquity as a discrete period, and their Christianising use of the well-worn vocabulary of tyrannical downfall and iconoclasm declares the perceived novelties of the times in which they lived. This need not have been an aggressive appropriation of 'secular',

pagan imagery: to some the new significance of traditional iconoclasm must have seemed obvious, and the language of damnatio
would have come easily to the minds of Roman Christians who
thought about the place of statues and images of power in their
imperial world.

Naturally, the shared cultural vocabulary of iconoclasm could be
used in many different ways, and our sources give us only a glimpse
of that complexity. The imagery of *damnatio* remained in use much
later, in the sixth century, when statues themselves were increasingly
rare in the cities of the empire. My final examples of cultural continuity and appropriation belong to that setting.

In the *Secret History* (*Anecdota* 18.12–21) Procopius innocently
describes the one statue of Domitian that was allowed to stand in
Rome after the tyrant's death. This was a portrait based on the
emperor's remains which his wife had dutifully sewn together. It
provided the best indication of Justinian's appearance. Procopius presents the background to the statue's production as an odd and
unfamiliar digression. It was the image of Domitian – the son of
Vespasian, that is – and he was so bad that the Romans meted out
a remarkable punishment: they could not satisfy their rage by
ripping him to pieces; so the senate decreed that his name should
be removed and that his images should not survive anywhere; so
his name was chiselled out of inscriptions and only the one statue
survives anywhere in the empire. This is far from an innocent explanation. By the time of Lactantius, Domitian (whose name is almost
an anagram of *damnatio*) seems to have become an archetypal fallen
emperor. More sources survive for his *damnatio* than for any other
emperor. Procopius must have been aware of this, and beneath his
description of the tyrant's bizarre fate lie the elements of *damnatio*:
the destruction of the name or identity, the dismemberment of the
body, the removal of images; and the one surviving statue stood, incidentally, 'on the way up to the Capitol, on the right as you go up
from the Forum': therefore on or near the site of the Gemonian
Steps. The point is that this statue, representing the 'appearance
and the fate' of Domitian, also conveys the appearance and implies
the condign fate of Justinian. By innuendo Procopius inserts
Justinian into a recognised, traditional paradigm of the fallen tyrant
(cf. Cameron 1985: 58f).

Not long before, in the 530s, Cassiodorus had formulated two
enthusiastic pleas for the preservation of Rome's sculptural heritage
(*Variae* 7.13 and 15). Divorced from the social and religious circumstances of their creation, the city's statues were at risk: the balance

between intrinsic and symbolic value had tipped in favour of the lime-kilns and furnaces. In one of these appeals, the *Formula Comitivae Romanae* (*Variae* 7.13), Cassiodorus calls for the protection of Rome's 'population of statues', for they are suffering a 'gravissimum damnum'; he is contemptuous of those who prey on the public sculptures, 'who mar the elegance of the ancients with the removal of limbs and do those things with public monuments that they should be suffering' ('qui decorem veterum foedant detruncatione membrorum faciuntque illa in monumentis publicis quae debent pati'). It is not too fanciful to identify an echo of the old iconoclasm in 'the dismemberment of limbs' which the thieves themselves should suffer. Why should meaningless antique statues be linked to the *damnum* of imperial traitors? Perhaps simply because it does imply meaning. For Cassiodorus uses the resonant language of an ancient tradition to reanimate forgotten statues, and to suggest that their destruction is more meaningful than it is. Perhaps it was a last-ditch attempt; for the kind of statue-destruction that prevailed from this point on represented a genuine break from the iconoclastic tradition. For the first time statues were destroyed without order or meaning. Byzantine iconoclasm focused on different objects in different ways, and we must wait until the Renaissance for the revival of the statue (designated as such) and for the reappearance of symbolic destruction in its ancient form.

Notes

1 The initial research for this article was carried out in the British School at Rome, where I benefited from discussions with Dr Robert Coates-Stephens.
2 For ancient late Roman sources on the inviolability of the imperial image see Browning 1952: 20.
3 The term was used by Schreiter-Gerlach as the title of a dissertation in 1689.
4 Parallels in Mayor 1881: 87; Pekáry 1985: 135; cf. Freedberg 1989: 246–82 and 378–428; Bahrani 1995. For further bibliography: Gregory 1994: 96f.
5 However, Gregory (1994: 95) suggests that the Tiberian example represents a response to the emperor's clear feelings towards the exile.
6 Gregory (1994: 95) points out that violence in anticipation of an emperor's fall seems to have been limited to the army (who were in an inherently better position to influence events).
7 Note Dio 79.17 on Macrinus' reluctance to risk an official *damnatio* of Caracalla; Tac. *Ann.* 11.38.3; Dio 60.4.5 on Claudius' resistance to an official *damnatio* of Gaius.
8 This is allegedly copied from the earlier account by Marius Maximus. Dio (48.31.4) writes of the shouted protests at the games which preceded the

PETER STEWART

toppling of statues of Antony and Octavian. The Roman crowd famously
called for the dragging of Tiberius at his death: 'Tiberium in Tiberim'
(Suet. *Tib.* 75). Cf. Vitellius: Tac. *Hist.* 3.74; Domitian: Suet. *Dom.*
23.1; Commodus: Dio 74.2.1.

9 Cf. Verres' embarrassing, bungled attempt to remove a statue of Hercules
in Sicily: Cic. *Verr.* 2.4.95.
10 But see Dio 78.2.6; John Chrysostom *De Statuis* 21.11; Dig. 47.10.27. Cf.
Nippel 1995: 43.
11 Cf. Freedberg 1989: 391, fig. 179 (a photograph of the toppling of an
equestrian statue in Iran in 1979).
12 Cf. Nippel 1995: 43f (on the topos of the crowd tearing the body limb
from limb).
13 Care is taken to avoid proper burial: SHA *Commod.* 20. For bodies thrown
in rivers see Suet. *Tib.* 75; *Vitell.* 17 and Orosius 7.8.8; Dio 58.11.5; SHA
Elagab. 17; Herodian 1.13.6. For statues: Suet. *Nero* 24.1; possibly other
heads found in rivers: Oliver 1996: 152f.
14 As Gregory (1994: 97) also suggests.
15 And it is with some surprise that Suetonius (*Dom.* 23) records the more
active involvement of the senate on the death of Domitian.
16 For references and discussion see Browning 1952; note esp. Libanius *Or.*
22.7.
17 SHA *Trig. Tyr.* 29.
18 The crucified Christ, like the emperor's corpse or statue, is mocked and
mutilated, e.g. in Matt. 27:30ff; Mark 15:24ff; Luke 23:34ff. As in the
case of the fallen emperor, the rituals of kingship are inverted (e.g. the
crown of thorns). This probably suggests a common feature of Roman
execution rather than a direct association with *damnatio*.
19

Qui enim coronat imaginem imperatoris, utique illum honorat
cuius imaginem coronavit, et qui statuam contempserit imperatoris, imperatori utique cuius statuam contempserit fecisse videtur
iniuriam. Gentiles lignum adorant, quia dei imaginem putant; sed
invisibilis dei imago non in eo est quod videtur, sed in eo utique
quod non videtur.

[For whoever crowns the emperor's image necessarily honours him
whose image he has crowned, and whoever scorns the emperor's
statue must appear to have harmed the emperor where statue he
has scorned. The gentiles worship wood because they think it is
the image of a god; but the image of the invisible god resides
not in that which can be seen, but rather in that which is not seen.]

20 The hypogeum has been affected by subsequent building work. After De
Rossi's visit it was lost again until 1918. It receives no mention after that
until 1954 when a proper study was conducted for the Pontificia Commis-
sione. Carletti's 1971 publication is the result. See also De Rossi 1865: his
speed in publishing his find (in a matter of weeks) is exemplary! De Rossi's
drawing appeared in the 1996 touring exhibition *The Gaze of Rome* (*Lo
Sguardo di Roma*: p. 50 in catalogue – see bibliography).

185

21 The destruction of the idol of Dagon depicted in the synagogue at Dura-Europos is a representation of iconoclasm by divine agency. In this frontier town it may, however, hint at *damnatio*, for the cult statue seems to resemble the painted cult image from the temple of Adonis across the road, which itself suggests the iconography of the Roman emperor. See Mesnil de Buisson 1939: 77; Moon 1995: 299.

22 Vatican, Museo Gregoriano Profano, inv. 243; Amelung-Lippold III.1: no. 550, 137–40, pls 40–2. It is also worth noting that the rope-puller at least has his arms in the orant pose. If this evoked any sense of *pietas* (as some of its iconographical precedents did: Klauser 1959), it may hint at acts of piety (towards humans or gods) that followed the destruction of an enemy's images: Tac. *Ann.* 14.61; SHA *Maxim.* 23.6f; Dio 63.25.1. A more direct association with the emperor's images may be suggested by juxtaposition with the Three Hebrews. The Apocryphal version of their story (*Daniel, Bel and the Snake*) ends with the destruction of the graven image, while some early representations of the story depict the cult image as the bust of an emperor (recalling the refusal of contemporary Christians to worship the imperial image (e.g. Mathews 1993: 81–3, fig. 60)).

23 The head was not repaired, which suggests that the sculptures were buried quickly after the assault. This possibly took place in the first quarter of the fourth century AD.

24 Also 390–4 on the famous decapitated statues from Britain (which are not obviously attributable to Christians). A marble eagle, possibly deliberately decapitated, found in a military rubbish pit of the late first century in Exeter, may have been part of a statue of Nero as Jupiter which would have been assaulted at his fall: Toynbee 1979: 130–2, fig. 44, pl. 20.

25 There is also the even more practical motive of raising revenues, e.g. in Firmicus Maternus (see Bowder 1978: 80).

26 I rely on the text and translation of Martin (1875).

Abbreviations

AE	*L'Année Épigraphique*, in *Revue Archéologique* and separately, 1888– .
Amelung-Lippold III	Lippold, G. (1936) *Die Skulpturen des Vaticanischen Museums*, vol. III.1, Berlin and Leipzig: Walter de Gruyter & Co.
CIL	*Corpus Inscriptionum Latinarum* (Berlin, 1863–).
ILS	Dessau, H. (1892–1916) *Inscriptiones Latinae Selectae*.
PLRE	Jones, A.H.M., Martindale, J.R. and Morris, J. (1971) *The Prosopography of the Later Roman Empire*, vol. I, AD 260–395, Cambridge: Cambridge University Press.
RE	Pauly, A., Wissowa, G. and Kroll, W. (1893–) *Real-Encyclopädie der klassischen Altertumswissenschaft*.

Bibliography

Bahrani, Z. (1995) 'Assault and Abduction: The Fate of the Royal Image in the Ancient Near East', *Art History* 18: 363–82.

Blanck, H. (1969) *Wiederverwendung alter Statuen als Ehrendenkmäler bei Griechen und Römern*, Rome: Bretschneider.

Bowder, D. (1978) *The Age of Constantine and Julian*, London: Elek.

Brilliant, R. (1963) *Gesture and Rank in Roman Art: The Use of Gesture to Denote Status in Roman Sculpture and Coinage*, New Haven: Connecticut Academy of Arts and Sciences.

Browning, R. (1952) 'The Riot of AD 387 in Antioch: The Role of the Theatrical Claques in the Later Empire', *J. Roman Studies* 42: 13–20.

Cameron, A. (1985) *Procopius and the Sixth Century*, London: Duckworth.

Carletti, C. (1971) 'Ipogeo anonimo di Via Paisiello', *Rivista di archeologia cristiana* 47: 99–117.

Couch, C.J. (1969) 'Collective Behavior: An Examination of Some Stereotypes', in R.R. Evans (ed.) *Readings in Collective Behavior*, Chicago: Rand McNally and Co.

Crawford, M.H. (1983) 'Roman Imperial Coin Types and the Formation of Public Opinion', in C.N.L. Brooke et al. (eds) *Studies in Numismatic Method Presented to Philip Grierson*, Cambridge: Cambridge University Press.

Cunliffe, B. (1969) *Roman Bath*, Oxford: The Society of Antiquaries.

De Rossi, G.B. (1849) in *Annali dell'Instituto di Corrispondenza Archeologica*: 351ff.

—— (1865) 'Un Esplorazione sotteranea sulla via Salaria vecchia', *Bullettino di archeologia cristiana*, Jan. 1865.

Espérandieu, E. (1915) *Recueil général des bas-reliefs, statues et bustes de la Gaule romaine*, vol. VI, Paris: Imprimerie Nationale.

Ferrua, A. (1960) *Le pitture della nuova catacomba di Via Latina*, Vatican City: Pontificio Istituto di Archeologia Cristiana.

Freedberg, D. (1989) *The Power of Images: Studies in the History and Theory of Response*, Cambridge and London: University of Chicago Press.

Gleason, M.W. (1995) *Making Men: Sophists and Self-Presentation in Ancient Rome*, Princeton and Chichester: Princeton University Press.

Gregory, A.P. (1994) '"Powerful Images": Responses to Portraits and the Political Use of Images in Rome', *J. Roman Archaeology* 7: 80–99.

Hannestad, N. (1994) *Tradition in late antique Sculpture: Conservation, Modernization, Production*, Aarhus: Aarhus University Press.

Herodian (1969) *Herodian* (Loeb translation), vol. I, trans. and ed. C.R. Whittaker, London and Cambridge, Mass.: Heinemann and Harvard University Press.

Hopkins, K. (1978) *Conquerors and Slaves*, Cambridge: Cambridge University Press.

Jones, A.H.M. (1973) *The Later Roman Empire 284–602: A Social, Economic and Administrative Survey*, Oxford: Blackwell.

Juvenal (1881) *Thirteen Satires of Juvenal with a Commentary*, vol. II, 3rd edn, trans. and ed. J.E.B. Mayor, London and Cambridge: Macmillan.

Kempf, T.K. and Reusch, W. (1965) *Frühchristliche Zeugnisse im Einzugsgebiet von Rhein und Mosel*, Trier: Landesmuseum.

Klauser, T. (1959) 'Studien zur Entstehungsgeschichte der christlichen Kunst II', *Jahrbuch für Antike und Christentum* 2: 115–45.

Maehler, H. (1968) *Ägyptische Urkunden aus den Staatlichen Museen Berlin: Griechische Urkunden*, vol. XI, *Urkunden römischer Zeit*, Berlin: Verlag Bruno Hessling.

Martin, M. l'Abbé (1875) 'Discours de Jacques de Saroug sur la chute des idoles', *Zeitschrift der deutschen morgenländischen Gesellschaft*: 107–47.

Mathews, T.F. (1993) *The Clash of Gods: A Reinterpretation of Early Christian Art*, Princeton: Princeton University Press.

Matthews, J. (1989) *The Roman Empire of Ammianus*, London: Duckworth.

Merrifield, R. (1977) 'Art and Religion in Roman London: An Inquest on the Sculptures of Londinium', in J. Munby and M. Henig (eds) *Roman Life and Art in Britain: A Celebration in Honour of the Eightieth Birthday of Jocelyn Toynbee*, vol. 2, Oxford: British Archaeological Reports.

Mesnil de Buisson, Comte du (1939) *Les Peintures de la synagogue de Doura-Europos, 245–256 après J.-C.*, Rome: Pontificio Istituto Biblico.

Mommsen, T. (1887) *Römisches Staatsrecht*, Leipzig: Hirzel.

Moon, W.G. (1995) 'Nudity and Narrative: Observations on the Synagogue Paintings from Dura-Europos', in W.G. Moon (ed.) *Polykleitos, the Doryphoros, and Tradition*, Madison and London: University of Wisconsin Press.

Nippel, W. (1995) *Public Order in Ancient Rome*, Cambridge: Cambridge University Press.

Oliver, A. (1996) 'Honors to Romans: Bronze Portraits', in C.C. Mattusch et al. (eds) *The Fire of Hephaistos: Large Classical Bronzes from North American Collections*, Cambridge, Mass.: Harvard University Art Museums.

Pekáry, T. (1985) *Das römische Kaiserbildnis in Staat, Kult und Gesellschaft, dargestellt anhand der Schriftquellen*, Berlin: Gabr. Mann Verlag.

Price, S.R.F. (1984) *Rituals of Power: The Roman Imperial Cult in Asia Minor*, Cambridge: Cambridge University Press.

Setton, K.M. (1967) *Christian Attitudes towards the Emperor in the Fourth Century, especially as shown in Addresses to the Emperor*, New York: A.M.S.

Lo Sguardo di Roma: Ritratti delle province occidentali dell'impero romano dai musei di Mérida, Toulouse e Tarragona (various authors, 1996), Tarragona: Edicions El Mèdol.

Smith, R.R.R. (1985) 'Roman Portraits: Honours, Empresses, and Late Emperors' (review article), *J. Roman Studies* 75: 209–21.

Thornton, J.C.G. (1986) 'The Destruction of Idols – Sinful or Meritorious?', *J. Theological Studies* 37: 121-9.

Toynbee, J.M.C. (1979) 'A Note on the Sculptured Torso of a Bird', in P.T. Bidwell et al., *The Legionary Bath-House and Basilica and Forum at Exeter, with a Summary Account of the Legionary Fortress*, Exeter: Exeter City Council.

Tronzo, W. (1986) *The Via Latina Catacomb: Imitation and Discontinuity in Fourth-Century Roman Painting*, University Park, Penn.: Pennsylvania State University Press.

Turner, R.H. and Killian, L.M. (1957) *Collective Behavior*, Englewood Cliffs: Prentice-Hall.

Vanderbroeck, P.J.J. (1987) *Popular Leadership and Collective Behavior in the Late Roman Republic*, Amsterdam: Gieben.

Vittinghoff, F. (1936) *Der Staatsfeind in der römischen Kaiserzeit*, Berlin: Junker & Dünnhaupt.

Wightman, E.M. (1970) *Roman Trier and the Treviri*, London: Hart-Davis.

Williams, S. and Friell, G. (1994) *Theodosius: The Empire at Bay*, London: Batsford.

Zanker, P. (1988) *The Power of Images in the Age of Augustus*, Ann Arbor: University of Michigan Press.

9

WOMEN AND LEARNING

Gender and identity in scenes of intellectual life on late Roman sarcophagi

Janet Huskinson

Cultural identities are very much to do with relationships and how we perceive ourselves and each other in terms of particular social signifiers: for example, do we work on similarity or difference? Gender is one instance where this kind of relativity is used to shape identities, and in many recent studies of Roman women notions of 'same' and 'other' have provided a useful key to understanding the construction and dynamic of their social roles. Add to the discussion further variables to do with the representation of particular cultural qualities (in this case, the value of learning) and religious change (to Christianity), and a multiplicity of possible identities emerges.[1]

How these possibilities pan out for the representation of women in activities of learning is the subject of this chapter. Taking images which appear on sarcophagi that were made in and near the city of Rome during the third and earlier fourth centuries AD, I will argue that women become increasingly visible as participants in such scenes, both in terms of straightforward numbers and also in relation to men. In art of the earlier empire women were often represented as a counterfoil to men in terms of virtues that were physical and domestic rather than intellectual, and the change that is traced here is towards a figure which is more independent and self-referential.

Scenes on sarcophagi are a rich source of information about Roman society as Romans had a long tradition of commemorating their dead in terms of the *res gestae* and *virtutes* of their past lives. From the late Republic and early Empire memorials used portraits as a means of conveying life experiences and social values, and developed a vocabulary of significant attributes and codes of dress or gesture to indicate status and profession. Sarcophagi of the later second and earlier third centuries AD added some other forms of expression: old subjects were opened up to new meanings (Koortbojian 1995, on myth), and new ones created to celebrate the life of the professional man (e.g. Kampen 1981) or victory in battle or the hunt (Koch and Sichtermann 1982: 90–107). In another significant development scenes which once represented exclusively upper-class interests were taken up by the widening social clientele who bought sarcophagi. Some of the most popular showed intellectual activities – learning, reading, declamation, or music-making, represented by groups or by particular figures (Marrou 1937; Zanker 1995; and Paduano Faedo 1970a: 442 for Muse sarcophagi). Although many of these figures are essentially generic (philosophers, for instance), they were often given an individual value through the addition of portrait heads, or by being set as full-figures or as busts within those standardised schemes of decoration on strigillated or '*clipeus*' sarcophagi which proliferated in the mid- and later third centuries; and on the earliest Christian sarcophagi this practice continued with the figures often (literally) set within the new context of biblical events. This kind of emphasis allows us to consider the individual in an intellectual setting.

But before the content of these images can be evaluated, the context of their production needs to be understood (as well of course as their final survival rate, which is important to remember here in the rather basic attempts at quantification which form some of the argument). There are various reasons to be wary of taking such images at face value. For instance the pragmatics of sarcophagus production often led to figures being carved in a highly stereotypical form which could be adjusted on customer demand or recut for subsequent use (Squarciapino 1944); and few sarcophagi have inscriptions which can reliably identify the person (or persons) who used them. Then there are art-historical factors: in this case we should note how compositions change over the course of time in response to new contexts. They may be adapted, or conflated, or even misunderstood, affecting in turn the role of particular figures that are represented. Ideology may colour the assessment, especially in terms of modern attributions or interpretative assumptions. The desire (understandable but not always appropriate) to label images and sarcophagi as 'Christian' or 'non-Christian' is an example of this, as are the snap identifications of female praying figures as 'souls', of philosophical-looking men as 'apostles', or of a male and female couple as necessarily 'man and wife'.

But beyond these factors is the issue of how these representations relate to an historical social reality. Noting that 'it remains the case that Christian writers of the period . . . do show an emphasis on women that would have been unusual in pagan texts' Cameron (1989: 192) observed 'Yet it will usually be found that the relationship between "realistic" and texual elements in any individual case is not simple.' And this is something which must be anticipated here. Like the written texts these images on sarcophagi are part of a contemporary rhetoric about women which was primarily based on traditional hierarchies: women were defined in terms of a male society, as potential reinforcements or as threats to its values (e.g. Kampen 1988, 1996).[2] This is summed up in words that have a particular relevance to this study:

> The relational character of gendered imagery conveys as well its hierarchical nature. Thus, a woman by taking on selected attributes of men became more virtuous. A man, taking on attributes of women, became suspect unless he was a youth or a god in whom androgyny was permissible. The visual images help to make viewers aware, over and over, of this 'fact': Men and women are different and unequal. The very reiteration helps to make it into a fact.
>
> (Kampen 1996: 18)

In the images to be explored here women are shown taking on attributes traditionally assigned to men in representations of intellectual pursuits; yet the presence of powerful female models suggests that women were also idealised for qualities of their own.

These two themes – women in relationship to male roles, and to female ideals – are central to this study. The material is presented in three main groups of examples which progress through the third and early fourth centuries: first, scenes which show men and women with the Muses, then scenes which show women without men, and finally, scenes on Christian sarcophagi.

Men, women and Muses

The images of men and women with the Muses which form the first examples introduce some important features of composition and content which recur throughout the whole body of material; and in particular they raise questions about the relationships that exist between the figures in terms of identity and power. These scenes start to appear quite regularly on sarcophagi in the earlier third century when imagery of the intellectual life became popular to commemorate even quite ordinary people. The emergence of this theme, with its promotion of cultural interests so valued in the Roman empire, was the subject of Marrou's seminal work on the man of culture, the 'Mousikos Aner' (Marrou 1937), and most recently Zanker (1995) has charted its development within the wider context of intellectual imagery across classical antiquity. His chapter entitled 'The Cult of Learning Transfigured' looks at scenes on Roman sarcophagi and is especially relevant here, first because it moves the classical imagery into Christian experience, constructing a particularly seamless glide, and second because he considers the role of women in these scenes and the part played by the Muses.

As Zanker shows, the intellectual life was a theme which offered a range of ideals for contemporary Romans, not least for their everyday concerns. For men it offered a route to *auctoritas* and public office and allowed them to explore and develop other facets of their traditional social identity without yielding their Romanness (Zanker 1995: 272–82). For women it offered what Zanker records as a new '*integral* role in the commemoration of the intellect' (Zanker 1995: 271; my italics).

In images like figure 9.1 women appear to have an equal place with men for the first time in scenes of the intellectual life on sarcophagi.[3] This sarcophagus is typical of a number which express this by a symmetrical composition. The balance they set up between the couple and their companions (whether these are Muses on both sides, as here, or philosophers accompanying the man and Muses the woman, as on e.g. *ASR* v, iii, no. 160) implies an equality of status. This is strengthened by the apparently complementary nature of their activities: the woman who is usually shown playing the lyre does 'soft', more pleasurable things, while the man with his scrolls and philosopher companions is involved in 'harder' intellectuality. Taken together these figures and their attributes seem to reflect qualities of the companiate marriage, the balancing of sense and intellect that reflects well upon their household (cf. Cooper 1996), while the conspicuous presence of the Muses may signify 'the notion of marital *concordia* in the shared service of the Muses' (Zanker 1995: 275).

Yet this symmetry conceals an imbalance of status between the man and the woman in terms of their respective relationships with

Figure 9.1 'Married couple' with Muses, *c.* AD 260. Rome, Vatican Museums.

their Muse companions since the woman is of the same sex as the Muses whereas the man is not. This creates a potential gap between the two: as Zanker (1995: 272) puts it, 'This mythical overlay means . . . that the wife, unlike her husband, is distanced from the real world. There is thus no immediate spiritual rapport between the married couple.' This 'distancing' is shown even more acutely in those scenes of the couple with a group of Muses where the woman is often literally depicted as the ninth Muse (that is to say, eight Muses are shown, and her, as in figure 9.1), almost as 'her husband's personal Muse'. This imbalance may not alter the relative value of their different activities, but it certainly affects their individual status, for the woman is directly linked by her gender with the power of the Muses.

But men too could lay claim to this power by identifying themselves as Muses, as is shown on a few other sarcophagi where one of the nine Muses is depicted as a man or with a male portrait head (Wrede 1981: 285–92, nos. 239, 255 (here as figure 9.2), 256, 257). Given that 'A man, taking on attributes of women, became suspect' (Kampen 1996: 18, as quoted above), and that there were other specific male figure-types used to depict men amongst the Muses – as philosopher (e.g. *ASR* v, iii, no. 168) or as Apollo (cf. *ASR* v, iii, no. 219) for instance – this was obviously a particularly pointed choice of image. One reason for it may be suggested by the fact that most examples occur on child-sized sarcophagi. There in the specific context of a young man's cultural development a cross-gendered image could signify a formative stage by suggesting how he had taken on the discipline of the Muses; as Gleason (1995: 80–1) has suggested, 'Masculinity was . . . thought to be grounded in "nature", yet it remained fluid and incomplete until firmly anchored by the discipline of an acculturative process.'[4] But for men in general this image provided a way of expressing their intellectual status in the mythical terms which were more readily available to women through the coincidence of gender. In other words, women did not have an exclusive claim on this privilege, and men too could invest themselves with the Muses' power.

Yet despite the possible equality on this score it would be true to say that in this first group of examples, that is, scenes with men, women and Muses, the woman's role is usually defined by reference to the other two figures. Her activities complement the man's and her status relates to the Muses. So although women now start to be depicted quite regularly with this 'integral role in the

Figure 9.2 Front of sarcophagus showing young man as the ninth Muse, late third century. Verona, Museo Maffeiano.

commemoration of the intellect' (Zanker 1995: 271), it remains to be seen how much they have an intellectual existence of their own. The next group of examples considers this, by exploring through a number of images how women are shown in intellectual contexts without male companions, and how their roles are then defined.

Women without men

The first are images of women with the Muses, but this time depicted without male companions. Here too there is a close identification with the women shown surrounded by all nine Muses (for example, *ASR* v, iii, nos. 170 and 183), or by a token two (*ASR* v, iii, nos. 70 and 220), or even being portrayed themselves as the 'ninth Muse' (*ASR* v, iii, no. 57). These images are of course posthumous compliments paid to cultivated women, but they also hint at some kind of empowerment through the direct linkage of human woman with divine. An interesting example where this theme is developed in different ways is the sarcophagus in the Museo Nazionale Romano of *c*. AD 280 (*ASR* v, iii, no. 130; figure 9.3). This shows on the lid five small Muses and a woman holding a scroll, and on the coffin a conventional *thiasos* of Dionysiac cupids which includes (unconventionally) a figure of Psyche dressed in a *pallium* and holding a scroll. This collection of scenes seems to express the dead woman's learning – and perhaps her experience of the afterlife – in terms of two different types of apprehension, namely through intellect and through contact with the divine.

The image of a woman holding a scroll, as it appears in the portrait bust on this sarcophagus, represents an important development in the representation of women. In this case the portrait was set on the sarcophagus lid, but the popularity of '*clipeus*' and strigillated sarcophagi in the third century increased the scope for inserting busts and figures into their standardised schemes of decoration. These generally appear rather stereotypical in their poses and attributes, and indeed were often initially made to be so, with any individual features to be carved later if or when required. Common, if not ubiquitous, attributes for men were the scroll and scroll-box. During the third century they become equally popular in portraits of women; in fact a quick count of sarcophagi decorated with figures of Seasons (which were particularly common in the last three decades of the third century) reveals marginally more female portrait busts with scrolls than male (*ASR* v, iv).

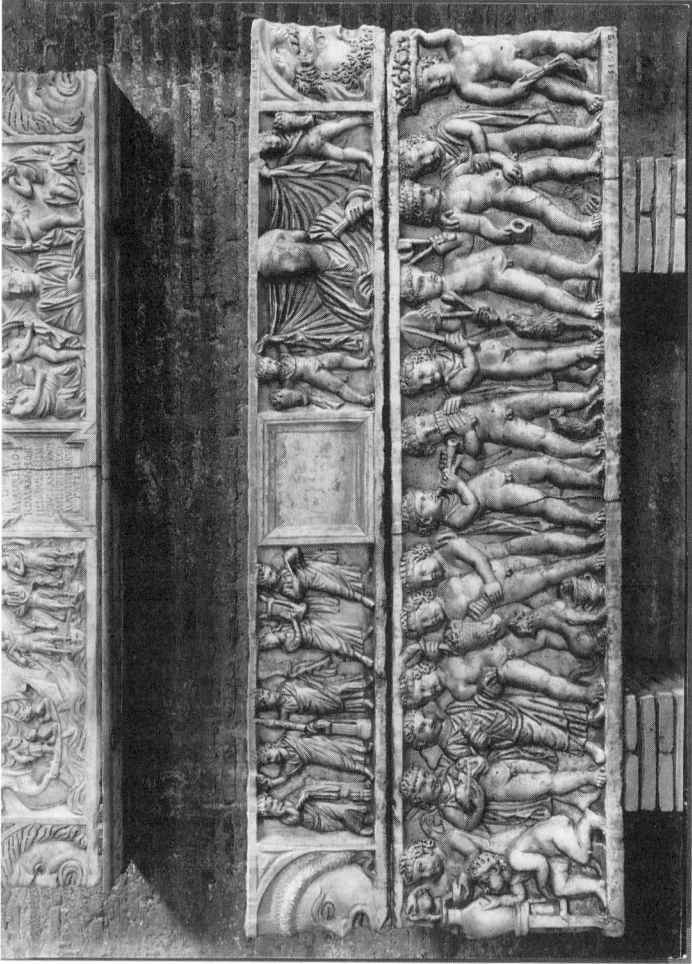

Figure 9.3 Sarcophagus, *c.* AD 280. Rome, Museo Nazionale Romano.

This development is particularly important as it represents a major change in the terms by which women had been commemorated, at least in comparison with the art of the first and earlier second century AD. There had been occasional signs that culture was valued in a woman, in scenes evoking leisured learning (e.g. Zanker 1995: 213–14, fig. 111) or depicting a young girl's reading lesson (Koch and Sichtermann 1982: fig. 76, lid), or in memorials of women as Muses (Kleiner 1987: no. 82; Wrede 1981: no. 238).[5] But overwhelmingly the funerary imagery for women in the early empire idealised domestic virtues and physical beauty (Kleiner 1981 and 1987; Wrede 1981; D' Ambra 1993b; Fantham et al. 1994: 369–71; cf. Lattimore 1962: 299–300). These qualities were expressed through images of women as Venus and through attributes like wool baskets which celebrated their household arts. This imagery was not just for family consumption but was considered central to the life of family and state and so its funerary use is paralleled in contemporary public art. In fact so deeply entrenched were these ideals that the casual equality with which the women on these Season sarcophagi seem to brandish their scrolls is even more surprising. The earlier image did not entirely fade,[6] but by the middle of the third century AD the image of the woman with a scroll became a regular occurrence.

At one level not too much should be read into this, for the scroll was so common an attribute as to be short on particular meaning when used in this kind of context. For men it may once have signified the marriage contract, or a particular profession, or practice in public oratory as much as private philosophy; but in these mid-third-century portraits it probably simply functioned as a sign that its owner claimed some kind of learning and the social status to go with it, and it was probably gratuitously used. Female busts may simply have acquired it by default, given the production processes at this time; after the convenience of unisex drapery unisex attributes could follow next (Squarciapino 1944). But on another level these stereotypes are important and revealing: they suggest a collective acceptance that this scroll-carrying image was also possible for the contemporary woman. 'The very re-iteration helps to make it into a fact' (Kampen 1996: 18).

Confirmation of this development is suggested by the increasing popularity in the late third century of yet another female image, the full-length figure with a scroll (e.g. *ASR* v, iv, nos. 75–9 and 89–90; *RS* nos. 74, 696, 837, 1004). In form this is related to the figure-types of the Muses Calliope and Polyhymnia and to some contemporary images of men,[7] but it becomes a regular and distinctive figure in its own right. The example shown in figure 9.4 (*RS* no. 696) is characteristic: the figure stands, with a scroll in her left hand and with her right hand held in the fold of her mantle (although sometimes, as on *RS* no. 1004, it is raised in an oratorical gesture). As on many other examples the facial features have been blocked out to await the carving of portrait details (yet essentially this is a type rather than an individual). The figure frequently occupies a central place in the decoration of the sarcophagus front, in a panel as here – but the statue-like figures of Muses are a unique accompaniment – or in friezes with pastoral or biblical scenes (*RS* nos. 14, 988), but it is also found in corner panels (e.g. *RS* no. 1022) or adapted for a central portrait roundel (as *RS* no. 1003).

A final set of images suggests a similar expansion in the visibility of 'the intellectual woman' at this time (and reintroduces a relationship with men). These are the various 'three-figure' groups with women as their centre. This type of composition is an effective space-filler, and as such gets repeated time and again most often as the central panel of strigillated sarcophagi; but although its figures are often little more than emblematic, their choice remains significant. In this case we can trace the increasing use of groups dominated by a woman. In two examples noted earlier she was flanked by Muses (*ASR* v, iii, nos. 70 and 220). In the more numerous Christian examples the Muses are replaced by two bearded men who usually carry scrolls (but cf. figure 9.4); *RS* records about a dozen instances of this group (roughly twice as many as those which have Christ as the central figure). By the 320s the same three-figure grouping appears at the centre of biblical frieze sarcophagi, and with a similar gender imbalance (*RS* has nine instances with a woman at the centre, compared to three images of Christ). The point of this crude statistical survey is to show how this female-centred group turns into a staple feature of sarcophagus decoration in the early fourth century; its strength is reflected in the fact that Christian sarcophagi have no comparable groups centred on the human male, while even the two bearded men who flank the women in these images appear little more than staffage figures.

Christian images

This selection of images has covered developments from the early empire to the emergence of Christian sarcophagi in the third century.

Figure 9.4 Front of a sarcophagus, late third century. Rome, S. Lorenzo fuori le mura.

Together they show that the representation of women moves from emphasising physical beauty and domestic ideals towards imagery of intellectuality which not only exploits the special association which women have with Muses, but also shares some common themes and compositions with men. The final group of examples illustrates some gender roles which emerge in the context of Christian sarcophagi of the late third and early fourth centuries. A key figure introduced in early Christian art is that of the *orans*, the woman at prayer. Her frequent appearance underlines the spritual element which develops as an increasingly prominent aspect of learning from the later third century (Zanker 1995: 284–90), and like the Muses she provides an obvious model for the representation of women.

In other respects there are many examples of continuity with themes and compositions used on non-Christian sarcophagi of a slightly earlier or near-contemporary date. Stock scenes are reproduced but often with a new Christian focus. This can be seen in two examples which depict men and women together. For instance the arrangement of a seated figure in each corner accompanied by Muses is still found, but now with the Good Shepherd as a central image (cf. *RS* nos. 817 and 945, 1). Other Christian sarcophagi take the group of seated philosopher and standing woman which derived from a popular third-century composition of philosopher and 'his' Muse and set it alongside specifically Christian figures. On a sarcophagus from the Via Salaria in Rome (*RS* no. 66) they flank a Good Shepherd figure and an *orans* who together thus seem to offer a Christian summation of the secular virtues represented at their sides. The seated philosopher and the *orans* appear on a sarcophagus in S. Maria Antiqua in Rome (*RS* no. 747, 1) where they are surrounded with Christian biblical and pastoral scenes on the theme of salvation. So, as Zanker notes (1995: 286–7), these old images of worldly learning are converted to depict study for inner peace and spiritual salvation.

But what of women in this? In answering this I want to look briefly at three sets of Christian material which seem to argue for an increased independence of women represented in Christian 'intellectual' contexts and an increase in their visibility. The image of the learned woman had become an acceptable stereotype by the late third century, and these Christian examples show a continuing use of and inventiveness on this theme; in fact their range and number suggests that Christian art opens up the intellectual role of women in relation to men even further than its recent antecedents had done.

The first set of material concerns the *orans* and her relationship to the figure of the standing woman which we considered earlier. Both these generic figures develop in the later third century but from different backgrounds: the *orans* was used in classical art as a symbol of *pietas* (Klauser 1959), while the other came from the secular world of learning where male values had prevailed. Yet on many Christian sarcophagi they are used interchangeably in a way which reinforces a collective female contribution (cf. *RS* no. 988, with 961; 17 and 25a; 80 and 75a). In particular, it is their intellectual aspect which is stressed; the prayerful activities of the *orans* are intellectualised to match the other, by the addition of symbols of learning and oratory, such as scrolls and scroll-boxes (e.g. *RS* nos. 4, 60, 780), or by juxtaposing her with philosophers (e.g. *RS* nos. 747, 1 and 912, 1).

Second, the scene of the woman standing by a seated male philosopher is also developed in Christian contexts, as we have seen. But their relationship, not to mention their identities, is not always clear. In describing the scene on the S. Maria Antiqua sarcophagus Zanker (1995: 286) refers to the philosopher and *orans* (who were both apparently intended to have portrait heads) as man and wife. Although this is an assumption which should be queried, it has the value of pointing back to the 'married couple' theme of Muse sarcophagi (like figure 9.1). But even in earlier non-Christian versions of the group there was often ambiguity about the respective roles of the figures (Paduano Faedo 1970b; Koch and Sichtermann 1982: 204): the woman might be a Muse (she is often shown in the pose of Polyhymnia: *ASR* v, iii, 135), or a human woman, or perhaps both simultaneously (for instance where a woman is depicted as the 'ninth' Muse: e.g. *ASR* v, iii, no. 133). This strong relationship with the Muses suggests that on non-Christian sarcophagi her role in relation to the philosopher must be one of inspiration, source of his power and guide to his learning.

But in Christian images it seems that this role was reversed. Although the woman is still posed as a Muse (e.g. *RS* no. 994 and Schumacher 1977: pl. 32a), the nature of the whole engagement has changed. She is not needed as the source of inspiration since the Christian philosopher receives his guidance direct from God; instead she performs the role of the learner who listens to the philosopher's exposition and affirms its truth. In other words, the Christian image has taken the existing figures and given a new value to their interaction. This is spelled out in greater detail on *RS* no. 811 (figure 9.5) where one panel shows an expanded scene

Figure 9.5 Sarcophagus (?) panel, late third or early fourth century. Rome, Capitoline Museums.

of learning which centres on an active exchange between a woman and a seated young philosopher. Here she is shown not like the usual listening 'Muse', but in the same purposeful 'intellectual' pose which we have met before, holding a scroll in her left hand, and raising her right in an oratorical gesture. The philosopher in his turn resembles the figure of the young Christ who appears in the pendant scene of the Raising of Lazarus. Amongst their audience is a second woman, and at the corners of the whole panel are the familar figures of standing male philosopher (l.) and female *orans* (r.). Overall the picture is of a woman receiving the learning that brings new life, which she too can practise through acts of prayer.

The third group of images shows that she can also practise it through a life of piety. These are the scenes that narrate episodes from the story of 'chaste Susanna' and her rejection of the lascivious elders (told in the Apocryphal book of Daniel and Susanna). This story was significant to fourth-century Christians for various reasons (Schlosser 1966), but is important here for the portrayal of Susanna as a woman of learning. For while later painters came to enjoy the possibilities that the story offered for sensuous depictions of her as she bathed, these early Christian sculptors (*RS* nos. 135,[8] 146, and 897 here as figure 9.6) showed her fully clad and carrying a scroll. This scroll has no place in the textual narrative, and so it is of major interest here as a signal to the viewer that Susanna should be identified with Christian women who have been empowered by their learning to live according to the precepts of their faith. The virtue which she consequently displays is in sharp contrast to the weakness of the men who have abused their positions of authority and shown sexual incontinence.

These three developments − the intellectualisation of the *orans* figure, the woman learning, and the learned Susanna − all show how Christian art depicted women with an intellectual status of their own. This reading is reinforced by a number of individual cases (often incidental) which reflect the confidence of this position, particularly in the relationship of the women with the men who are portrayed. Here are a few. The figures of a married couple on an early fourth-century sarcophagus lid warn against taking gender distinctions for granted in such portraits, as the man is shown as the *orans*, while the woman has the scroll and gesture of the 'intellectual' (*RS* no. 120). Elsewhere the strength of the woman's position is suggested by the relative placings of the figures: on *RS* no. 912 the *orans* (with scroll-box) occupies the centre, with the elderly philosopher and Good Shepherd at the far corners of the strigillations, while on

Figure 9.6 Fragment of a sarcophagus. Early fourth century. Rome, Camposanto Teutonico.

RS no. 696 (figure 9.4) the woman and Muses occupy the centre with the Good Shepherd to the sides. A sarcophagus in Saragossa (of local manufacture?) gives particularly strong confirmation of the woman's powerful role: here the upraised right hand of the *orans* is grasped by a hand apparently emerging from the heavens, while one of the two bearded men who flank her proffers her an open scroll (Sotomayor 1975: 159 ff). But a final word on female intellectual strength occurs on the lid of a biblical sarcophagus (*RS* no. 77) where in a highly unusual (unique?) version of a conventional arrangement, the drape behind the bust of a female *orans* is held back for her by two diminutive figures of philosophers.

What conclusions can be drawn from these representations about the workings of cultural identity?

It has been argued so far that during this period women come to occupy an increasingly visible and powerful role in scenes which may be described as 'intellectual': from the first examples where they are defined in terms both of men and of Muses they have come to stand as independent figures.

This development occurs in non-Christian and in Christian material. In other words the emerging identity seems common to these cultures and not restricted to one or the other, although historically speaking Christianity's general investment in intellectual discourse (Cameron 1991) may have been a factor in its promotion.

What is its value in terms of gender? The development involves the women in these images sharing many contexts and scene types with men. But in contrast to the '"fact": Men and women are different and unequal' which Kampen (1996: 18 quoted above, p. 192) finds repeated in visual imagery, these representations seem to depict a progressive equalisation, if sharing of attributes and activities is any guide. In many of the images we have discussed – for example the portrait busts and standing figure with scrolls – men and women appear to be of equal standing. In fact in certain images women come to predominate: this is exemplified by the three-person scenes on Christian sarcophagi where women, whether *orans* or 'scroll-holder', tend to outnumber their male equivalents[9] as the repertory of scenes moves relentlessly in the fourth century towards identifiable biblical narrative.

But it is important to look behind this appearance and in particular to consider how far it may reflect a real equality between men and women in terms of cultural identity, or whether these women have had to disguise their real selves and become 'the same' as men instead of developing their differences (cf. Aspegren 1990; Cameron 1989: 192). Interestingly it seems to have been the case on other monuments made for people of a similar social class to many users of these sarcophagi (that is, 'a narrow stratum below the aristocracy and rich merchants and gentry, but above the poorest members of the lower class'; Kampen 1993: 130), that men and women shared a common iconography for showing social and occupational roles; so it is possible that some issues of social status may underlie these cultural considerations.

In terms of a more exclusive intellectual culture, notions of a real equality may have been promoted by the belief held in some quarters that the soul itself was not sexed (Clark 1993: 121), and by the encouragement given in some philosophic households for their women members to practise philosophy too (Clark 1993: 132).

But although some female images we have considered are closely related to male figure-types,[10] the overall development does not seem to argue that women took on 'male' intellectual imagery as a means to social inclusion and empowerment. In fact many scenes suggest that men and women have roles which are positively complementary to each other. This is often conveyed through the depiction of couples: men and women, *orans* and philosopher. The woman's part in this is lifted from possible inferiority by the existence of particular female role models, the *orans* and the Muses. Since both of these are powerful figures in their own right (even attracting male identification), they give the women depicted in the scenes their own secure base from which to relate to their male counterparts. So on Muse sarcophagi (such as figure 9.1) the men and women together can be said to demonstrate marital *concordia*: her qualities reflect back on his standing and character,[11] while the philosophical strengths he displays help to counterbalance the *infirmitas* natural to her as a woman. As earlier she might have played Venus to his Mars (Kleiner 1981), in the third century she is more regularly Muse to his philosopher and in Christian examples a prayerful listener to his teaching. In other words, women make a consistent and distinctive contribution to this reciprocal arrangement. In doing so they do not seem to be denying their sex or acting somehow transgressively, but appear empowered to enjoy an intellectual identity of their own which is complementary to the men's.

An important factor in defining this identity is the intellectual activity itself. Whereas Venus represented more of an ideal 'identity *state*' to which a woman might aspire, now the emphasis seems to fall on *processes* of intellectualisation, of learning, reading and praying, in which women are shown to be expert practitioners. In Christian art the popularity of the *orans* figure for women confirms the value attached to her *pietas* and prayer. Above all she is properly active in pursuit of the texts that were a characteristic of contemporary Christian culture: she listens to them attentively as they are expounded by Christian teachers, and she holds, or reads from, a scroll or codex of her own. The content of what she reads and hears must be an important part of her self-formation, confirming her in her Christian identity.[12] Just as Proba abandoned the Muses' spring for the waters of the Baptistery as the source of inspiration for her Christian writing (Proba *Cento* lines 14–22; Rousseau 1995), so the book which Crispina/Susanna reads so avidly on *RS* no. 135 has been clearly marked with the monogram of Christ.

This leads to what seems the strongest argument, that in these images women are shown to have powerful qualities in their own right, and not because they have had to become 'male'. For these were not the only views of women to be depicted on sarcophagi. The traditional desirable qualities of physical beauty and fidelity still found expression, especially in representations which emphasise Venus-like charms.[13] Linking these with the theme of knowledge was another view, that women are essentially seductive and deceptive, and that knowledge in their possession is potentially dangerous: 'For if truth was clothed in words requiring interpretation, then equally falsehood came in seductive guises' (Cameron 1989: 191). This was a deep-seated element in the rhetoric about women which finds expression in mythological and Christian images to do with women as possessors of knowledge. The Sirens, defeated rivals of the Muses, are shown as women with attributes of learning in a scene of Ulysses' deafness to their song; as he sails resolutely past them he represents true wisdom rejecting the specious attraction of false knowledge (Koch and Sichtermann 1982: 169). In Christian scenes Eve represents a similar type of wrong knowledge which she reveals through succumbing to the serpent.

But this view of women as purveyors of false knowledge is specifically counteracted by the imagery we have been considering. In the case of each of these characters, the Sirens and Eve, there are female counter-figures who are shown able to redeem the situation: the Muses who physically overcome the Sirens (e.g. *ASR* v, iii, no. 61), and Susanna whose innocence can stand against the fault of Eve. This is pithily conveyed by the symmetrical arrangement of scenes on the sarcophagus lid *RS* no. 146 (cf. Clark 1986: 26). On the left Eve stands by a tree which separates her from Adam; below it

JANET HUSKINSON

uncoils the snake which is the cause of her action. On the right Susanna is watched by an elder through the branches of a tree; below it is the inspiration of *her* action, a large container of scrolls. Here, then, the powerful antidote to the negative intellectual image of women is now provided by characters who are themselves female, and not by men.

In fact the image of Susanna is a useful one on which to end: it involves sexuality as well as gender, and the abuse and assertion of power, moral and social. It shows a woman who has internalised the laws of the scriptures – as signified by the external symbol of the scroll – to such a degree that she resists physical temptation when at her most vulnerable, and subsequent wrongful accusation. She shows moral control and continence while the male elders display *infirmitas* and abuse their authority. Susanna has all the domestic virtues of a classical Roman *univira* (beauty, modesty, fidelity) which reflect back on to her husband; but they have an additional Christian value, of counteracting the fault of Eve. Like the Muses and Muse-like women, Susanna shows it is possible to be a woman with womanly characteristics and also to claim the empowerment of learning.

This chapter has shown how the identity of women depicted in these intellectual activities is multi-faceted and multi-layered. The process by which this came about is typical of the cultural dynamics of Late Antiquity, with its interaction of different social forces and accumulated traditions exposed to change. Also typical is an ambivalence to closure. As compared with the imagery of women in the early empire which fixed them in the mould of Venus, these late antique images open up new identities and roles for women, eliding and confusing existing gender differentiations. But on the other hand there is still a desire to close off the image in a time-honoured way, as the final stage in Susanna's story shows. For despite her empowerment through learning it is the wisdom and decisiveness of a man, Daniel, which ultimately vindicates her; and so her story ends by turning itself back to *his* reputation – 'And from that day forward Daniel was a great man among his people' (*Book of Daniel and Susanna* verse 64, *The New English Bible*). Not so far, perhaps, from the philosopher and his Muse-like wife (figure 9.1).

Notes

1 I am grateful to the Hugh Last Fund for an award at the British School at Rome which assisted in the preparation of this chapter. Thanks are also due to the participants in this seminar for their constructive comments.

2 See also for this rhetoric Hallett 1989; Aspegren 1990; Gould 1990; Cooper 1996; Staples 1997.

3 Cf. in painting: the mid-first-century AD portrait of the couple from Pompeii: Ling 1991: 160 fig. 170; Zanker 1995: 214.

4 The full importance of this phenomenon is suggested by the fact that while this kind of combination of human and divine is not uncommon in Roman funerary art, this is the only case which involves cross-gendering; furthermore the earliest of these examples (dated to the mid-second century: Wrede 1981: no. 239) is in fact the earliest known instance of the practice as a whole. The other examples all belong to the later third century, as does a comparable case in the Vatican Museums which shows nine boy Muses whose age and gender have both been manipulated to match that of the dead boy whom they commemorate (*ASR* v, iii, no. 139).

5 Also in inscriptions, e.g. Lattimore 1962: 297, n. 264. Cf. also Hallett 1989: 65–9.

6 E.g. a relief in Rome, Villa Albani *c*. AD 190–200: Kleiner 1981: 527–9; and *RS* no. 778, late third century.

7 Cf. *RS* no. 564; *ASR* v, iv, nos. 120 and 182. The seated version confirms how close is the relationship between male and female types: cf. *ASR* v, iv, nos. 181 and 183.

8 The figure group of a woman reading, between two trees watched by two men to the right, surely depicts Susanna spied upon by the elders, albeit in abbreviated form, even though the name CRISPINA is inscribed to the side of the woman.

   Schlosser 1966 raises the possibility that the cycle of Susanna scenes in early Christian art may itself come from illustrated books.

9 Obviously this does not relate to figures in biblical scenes.

10 See note 7.

11 Fantham et al. 1994: 349 draws attention to the neat encapsulation of this expressed in Pliny *Letters* 1.16.6: the wife cannot possibly have written the letters, but if she did, then credit must go to her husband who taught her.

12 Reading is not exclusive to women on these sarcophagi: men are shown on fragments *RS* nos. 231, 871, 943. For the 'continent heroine' as good listener and reader in the fourth century see Cooper 1996: 64–7.

13 See note 6 above.

Acknowledgement

DAIR   Deutsches Archäologisches Institut Rom

Bibliography

Abbreviations

ASR   C. Robert (ed.) *Die antiken Sarkophagreliefs* Berlin: Gebr. Mann.
——   v, iii M. Wegner, *Die Musensarkophage* (1966)
——   v, iv P. Kranz, *Jahreszeitensarkophage* (1984)
RS   F.W. Deichmann, G. Bovini and H. Brandenburg (eds), *Repertorium der christlich-antiken Sarkophage. Band I: Rom und Ostia*, Wiesbaden, 1967

Aspegren, K. (1990) 'The Male Woman. A Feminine Ideal in the Early Church', *Acta Universitatis Upsaliensis*, Uppsala: Uppsala Women's Studies.

Cameron, A. (1989) 'Virginity as Metaphor: Women and the Rhetoric of early Christianity', in A. Cameron (ed.) *History as Text*, London: Duckworth.

—— (1991) *Christianity and the Rhetoric of Empire. The Development of Christian Discourse*, Sather Lectures 55, Berkeley: University of California Press.

Clark, E.A. (1986) *Ascetic Piety and Women's Faith. Essays on late ancient Christianity*, New York: Edwin Mellen.

Clark, G. (1993) *Women in Late Antiquity: pagan and Christian life-styles*, Oxford: Clarendon Press.

Cooper, K. (1996) *The Virgin and the Bride: idealized womanhood in late antiquity*, Cambridge, Mass,. and London: Harvard University Press.

D'Ambra, E. (ed.) (1993a), *Roman art in Context*, Englewood Cliffs, NJ: Prentice Hall.

—— (1993b), 'The cult of virtues and the funerary relief of Ulpia Epigone', in D'Ambra 1993a: 104–14.

Fantham, E. et al. (eds) (1994) *Women in the Classical World: image and text*, New York and London: Oxford University Press.

Gleason, M. (1995) *Making Men: sophists and self-presentation in ancient Rome*, Princeton NJ: Princeton University Press.

Gould, G. (1990) 'Women in the Writings of the Fathers: Language, Belief, and Reality' in W.J. Sheils and D. Wood (eds), *Women in the Church*, Studies in Church History 27, Oxford: Basil Blackwell.

Hallett, J.P. (1989) 'Women as Same and Other in the Classical Roman Elite', *Helios* 16: 59–78.

Kampen, N.B. (1981) 'Biographical Narration and Roman Funerary Art', *American Journal of Archaeology* 85: 47–58.

—— (1988) 'The Muted Other', *Art Journal* 47: 15–18.

—— (1993) 'Social Status and Gender in Roman Art: the case of the saleswoman' in D'Ambra 1993a: 115–32.

—— (1996) 'Gender Theory in Roman Art' in D.E.E. Kleiner and S.B. Matheson (eds) *I Claudia: Women in Ancient Rome*, New Haven: Yale University Art Gallery.

Klauser, T. (1959) 'Studien zur Entstehungsgeschichte der christlichen Kunst II', *Jahrbuch für Antike und Christentum* 2: 115–45.

Kleiner, D.E.E. (1981) 'Second Century Mythological Portraiture: Mars and Venus', *Latomus* 40: 512–44.

—— (1987) *Roman Imperial Funerary Altars with Portraits*, Archeologica 62, Rome: Bretschneider.

Koch, G. and Sichtermann, H. (1982) *Römische Sarkophage*, Handbuch der Archäologie, Munich: Beck.

Koortbojian, M. (1995) *Myth, Meaning and Memory on Roman Sarcophagi*, Berkeley: University of California Press.

Lattimore, R. (1962) *Themes in Greek and Latin Epitaphs*, Urbana: University of Illinois Press.

Ling, R. (1991) *Roman Painting*, Cambridge: Cambridge University Press.

Marrou, H.-I. (1937) *Mousikos Aner, Étude sur les scènes de la vie intellectuelle sur les monuments funéraires romains*, Grenoble: Allier.

Paduano Faedo, L. (1970a) 'Contributo allo studio dei sarcofagi con Muse', *Studi classici e orientali* 19–20: 443–9.

—— (1970b) 'L'inversione del rapporto poeta–musa nella cultura ellenistica', *Ann. scuola normale di Pisa* 39: 377–86.

Rousseau, P. (1995) '"Learned Women" and the Development of a Christian Culture in Late Antiquity', *Symbolae Osloenses* 70: 116–47.

Schlosser, H. (1966) 'Die Daniel-Susanna-Erzählung in Bild und Literatur der christlichen Frühzeit' in W.N. Schumacher (ed.) *Tortulae: Studien zu altchristlichen und byzantinischen Monumenten*, Römische Quartalschrift 30. Supplementheft, 243–49.

Schumacher, W.N. (1977) *Hirt und 'Guter Hirt'*, Römische Quartalschrift 34. Supplementheft.

Sotomayor, M. (1975) *Sarcofagos romano-cristianos de España*, Biblioteca teologica Granadina 16, Granada.

Squarciapino, M.F. (1944) 'Sarcofagi romani con ritratti riadattati', *Rendiconti della pontificia accademia romana di archeologia* 20: 267–86.

Staples, A. (1997) *From Good Goddess to Vestal Virgins: sex and category in Roman Religion*, London: Routledge.

Wrede, H. (1981) *Consecratio in formam deorum*, Mainz: von Zabern.

Zanker, P. (1995) *The Mask of Socrates. The Image of the Intellectual in Antiquity*, trans. A. Shapiro, Berkeley: University of California Press.

10

CONSTRUCTING THE JUDGE

Judicial accountability and the
culture of criticism in late antiquity

Jill Harries

The administration and enforcement of law by judges, *iudices*, was a
high-profile activity in late antiquity. Governors of provinces,
whose main function was to act as judges of first resort, held their
hearings in public, in front of crowds. Private rooms, to which
access could be gained not by fair means but by bribery, were forbidden and judges were obliged to stay on their tribunals until all
cases pending had been heard (*Codex Theodosianus* 1.16.6, of AD 331).
As was traditional, they were supported by a council of their legal
advisers, or assessors. Christian bishops, too, administered their own
form of justice, with their own *consilium* of priests and other advisers.
Much is said about *iudices* in the sources and we might reasonably
expect from an examination of representations of judges by their
contemporaries, by legal sources, or by historians, to gain some idea
of the nature of late Roman justice and the legal culture within
which it functioned.

That task, however, is rendered more complicated than is often
realised by the nature of the evidence. Because the administration
of justice could not be separated from the politics of provincial
government in general, the figure of the governor as *iudex* became
in late antiquity the prisoner of highly tendentious rhetoricians,
whose various portraits of 'the Judge' are almost invariably conditioned by the wider purpose of their text. The judge who is
asked a favour will be credited by his correspondent with scrupulous
virtue, while the literary figure of the venal or persecuting judge was
a creation variously of imperial insistence on good behaviour on the
part of officials, as communicated in widely publicised imperial

legislation, or the polemic of the martyr acts. The various representations of this both feared and indispensable figure in Roman society are therefore often more relevant to the creators of texts and the cultural perceptions of late antiquity than to the actual functioning both of *iudices* themselves and, more broadly, of the judicial system of the time.

A distinction must also be drawn between generalised stereotyping of the *iudex* and particular cases. Individual bad governors did occasionally come under attack from disgruntled provincials, and names, some fictitious, were given to persecuting governors by the authors of the later martyr acts, but all too often criticisms are levelled at judges in general, in ways which make their accuracy impossible to verify. However, one consideration which supports the contention that what the sources contain is constructions of the judge rather than a reflection of reality should be noted at the outset. The different faces of the *iudex* in the sources, to be examined below, reveal a dichotomy between rhetorical portraits of past or present *iudices* as cruel and venal on the one hand, and the actual operation of some legal hearings, and the characters of some *iudices* who went on to be bishops, on the other. A closer look at late antique representations of the *iudex* will reveal the reasons for this dichotomy and perhaps assist in a reassessment of the impact of rhetorical stereotyping on ancient and some modern perceptions of the character of late Roman justice.

The ideal judge

Whatever the realities of the operations of late Roman justice, there existed always the notion of the ideal judge. The ultimate, all-powerful and infallible judge, for Christians, was God (e.g. at Augustine, *Sermon* 285.2 and 4), who, naturally, was assimilated to the best in late Roman jurisdiction. On the Last Day, according to Zeno of Verona (*Tractatus* 21 = PL 11.458–62), he would judge like a good paterfamilias, a figure whose authority over his family had been, under the Roman Republic, virtually absolute. God would act in a manner comparable with human 'iudicii forma'. But whom would he judge? Judgments were needed where there was doubt, 'ambiguitas', and there could be no doubt about the good or the very bad. The 'just' would not be judged but would themselves judge the world and the wicked would not require to be judged because they had already been condemned and were doomed to perish. There remained a third intermediate category of

Christian believers, who were willing to know the divine Law, but not to follow it, being instead led astray by 'worldly pleasures' and 'depraved habits'. God the paterfamilias would treat the virtuous man not like a servant but as a son. The wicked, 'whom he apprehended in adultery, in murder, in forgery, in evil magic, he would hand over to the executioner not for trial, but to suffer the torments of suitable punishments'. In dealing with the third, God would act like an examining magistrate and, after his investigation, he would reach his verdict, a procedure recognisable to every frequenter of a Roman court.

Ambrose of Milan perceived in the judgment of God features familiar in his own experience as a former *iudex*. As he read John 5.30, 'I can do nothing on my own; as I hear, I judge', he reflected on the immutability, as well as the ultimate rightness of God's judgments. Picturing a suppliant, falling at the knees of the heavenly *iudex*, he gives his reply:

> I can do nothing on my own; justice is what lies in the giving of judgments, not power. I do not judge you, your own actions pass judgment on you; they accuse you and they condemn you. The laws sit in judgment on you, which I as judge do not adapt but safeguard . . . I judge according to what I hear, not according to my own will; and thus my judgment is just [lit. true], because I do not act in accordance with my wishes but with what is right.
>
> (Ambrose, *Letter* 77.11)

This judge is not one to be swayed by considerations of mercy or leniency. While, as we shall see, judicial discretion in favour of leniency did exist in Roman legal practice, and could be invoked by bishops seeking amelioration of their clients' sentences, such *indulgentia* was not for Ambrose. However, his God was immovable precisely because he was not subject to the whims and failings of men. The Christ of John 5.30, 'as I hear I judge', is juxtaposed with the figure of Pilate, who is not named, at John 19.10, who tries to intimidate the captive Jesus by issuing arbitrary threats, 'Do you not know that I have the power to release you and the power to crucify you?' Reverting immediately to the earlier John passage, Ambrose asks, why could God not behave like that? His answer comprises the remainder of the John passage, 'my judgment is just, because I seek to do, not my own will but the will of him that sent me'. Therefore, concluded the bishop, the judgment of God is not subject to the will of man, but of God, which is the 'author of law, and the arbiter of justice'.

God differed from secular judges both because he knew everything and because the rich and powerful could not expect special treatment or any of the advantages they were perceived to enjoy, if brought to trial on earth. In a vivid evocation of the situation of the rich man confronting the Last Judgment, Basil of Caesarea (*Hom in Div.* 6 = *PG* 31.296) contrasted Dives' forlorn state with his situation in a secular trial, where he could hope to use his wealth and status to influence the outcome:

> What excuse will you offer, when those whom you have wronged stand round about you and shout their accusations against you before that righteous judge? What, then, will you do? What advocates will you bring forward? What witnesses will you produce?

The point of the contrast of the judges lay in the fact that an earthly judge, however honest he might be, could not know the truth – a point also made by Augustine, who argued that the ignorance of judges made torture necessary (*City of God* 19.6) – and could therefore be misled by a clever lawyer. 'How will you mislead a judge who cannot be deceived? There will be no clever pleader to hand. There will be no persuasive rhetoric capable of concealing the truth from the judge.' Nor could he exert pressure by the display of power: 'there will be no flatterers in attendance, no wealth, no regalia of high office. Bereft of funds, bereft of supporters, with no advocate, no defence, you will be exposed, shamefaced, downcast, wretched, alone, with no word to say.'

The three bishops shared a vision of the divine, infallible judge which owed much to their experience of the human, fallible, judges of their own day. Although Zeno did allow something for the *indulgentia* of the divine judge towards his doubtful group, the unworthy faithful, they emphasised the power of God, the sternness of his judgments of the wicked, the extremities of the torments awaiting the impious (Zeno) and God's unresponsiveness to the suppliant (Ambrose). Ambrose in particular laid stress on the lack of discretion available to the divine judge, who, as guardian of the laws, is therefore unable to change them. As such diverse sources as the imperial law-codes (e.g. *Codex Theodosianus* 9.10.1.4 of 390) and the *Relationes* of the Urban Prefect Symmachus reveal, judicial discretion was extremely difficult (although not impossible) to operate. Litigants had the right of appeal to higher courts, and governors were, as a group, vulnerable to complaints about them forwarded by disgruntled but influential provincials (cf. *Codex Theodosianus* 1.16.2, of Constantine) to their distant, and often poorly informed, imperial masters. Secular *iudices* therefore erred on the side of caution, forwarding consultations to emperors in cases of doubt, because of the weakness of their position. God's scrupulous observance of *aequitas*, by contrast, was the natural consequence of his omniscience.

The judge in court

By the time of Diocletian, court records could be taken down verbatim. The accuracy of these was essential to the functioning of the appeals system, which involved the assembling of all documents relevant to the case by the *iudex* and their prompt forwarding to the higher court, usually of the praetorian or city prefect. It was therefore important for the judge that the records showed that he had behaved with scrupulous fairness and conducted his cross-examinations properly, and it follows from this that the scanty court records that survive did provide a factual depiction of what the *iudex* said and did at work in his court.

The secular judge was not, of course, all-knowing, even in the matters of law which it was his duty to administer, nor was he expected to be so. While it was important for his credit that his decisions as *iudex* were in conformity with Roman law, he need not himself have been a legal expert. Law was not part of the standard education of the average Roman, who moved from the basic linguistic training offered by the *grammaticus* to the more advanced exercises in eloquence taught by the *rhetor*. Only at a later stage would a minority take advantage of the more specialist training offered by schools of law at Rome, Beirut and Constantinople, a training which was, in the fifth century, to become increasingly important as a qualification for service in the imperial administration in the East. Thus many provincial governors, presiding in their courts, would have had a little legal learning, reflecting a common and perhaps, by juristic standards, superficial legal culture acquired by experience in court, rather than through any profound study of abstract legal principles.

What was required of the *iudex* as part of his routine duties in court was an ability to cross-examine the witnesses and parties to a suit (cf. *Codex Theodosianus* 2.18.1 = *Codex Justinianus* 3.1.9). In civil cases, his interrogation aimed to establish the facts, and thus to enable him to deliver a verdict, but he had to reckon with the deviousness of the parties concerned and their advocates. In AD 250, representatives of the curia of the metropolis of Arsinoe in Egypt confronted a group of recalcitrant villagers before the prefect, Appius Sabinus (Skeat and Wegener 1935). The point at issue is whether the villagers are liable to carry out liturgies in the metropolis. Thanks partly to the diversionary tactics employed by both sides, the prefect is obliged to consult his legal advisers no less than four times. Gradually, the exchanges focus on a central point of law: is it 'lawful' to enrol villagers for liturgies in the metropolis? The villagers' advocate, Seleucus, insists, in response to a question from the *iudex*, that it is not, and proceeds to read out a law of Septimius Severus, by now some fifty years old. The prefect then turns to the advocates from the curia: 'read me a law too'. This the advocates for the curia are unable to do, but they respond that, 'while the laws are indeed to be admired and reverenced', prefects since (for whose decisions no documentation is offered) have had regard for the needs of the cities. Against Severus' ruling, they cite, as a principle, that 'it is the need of the cities which defines the force of the law'. When asked by the prefect what they think of the law of Severus, the party from the curia reply that circumstances have changed: Severus made the law in Egypt, while the cities were still prosperous. Appius Sabinus is unconvinced, pointing out that the argument from prosperity – or lack of it – applies to the villages too and, after a final consultation with his advisers, rules in favour of the villagers and, incidentally, of upholding the law of Severus: 'the force of the laws will increase with time'.

There is nothing cruel or threatening in Appius Sabinus' behaviour as a *iudex*. His duty to get at the facts through detailed interrogation of both parties emerges clearly from the record, which shows that correct court procedure had been followed and the grounds on which the decision had been reached. Appius never displays any profound knowledge of the law, nor does he need it. It was up to the disputants to establish their case, and produce their evidence and their arguments. Perhaps surprisingly, given the importance of the citation of imperial constitutions in some other known legal proceedings, the production of the Severan constitution was not in itself decisive. It was still open to the other side to produce another law, which they fail to do, or to establish that the law of Severus was no longer valid, not because of the passage of time in itself, but on the grounds that times had changed and prefects since had opted

JILL HARRIES

to invalidate Severus' decision by rulings of their own. In other words, a principle, 'the needs of the cities define the force of the law', could be cited against an imperial ruling with (perhaps) some chance of success and Appius, in theory, had the freedom to override an admittedly ancient constitution, if he believed the opposing principle to be valid (cf. Pearl 1971; more generally, Katzoff 1982).

The Egyptian hearing was a civil suit. Where criminal charges were entailed, such exchanges were less innocuous. In cases where the authenticity of documentation was in dispute, it was possible to interpose a criminal charge of forgery, which changed the rules of the hearing, by introducing the possibility of the interrogation of witnesses under torture, to establish the facts. In the *Acta Purgationis Felicis* (CSEL 26: Appendix 2), a hearing conducted by the proconsul of Africa, Aelianus, to investigate allegations that Bishop Felix of Aptungi was a *traditor*, a hander-over of sacred books to the persecutors, the turning-point arrives when a scribe, Ingentius, admits, under questioning, to forgery. Aelianus issues a formal warning about torture and the danger of telling lies and asks Ingentius more questions. Ingentius, apparently, lies again and the proconsul poses the ominous question, 'What is your status?', clearly a preliminary to the use of torture to decide the facts. Only then does it emerge that Ingentius is a decurion and therefore exempt from torture. Aelianus contents himself, for the moment, with taking Ingentius into custody, pending further investigations. Although the situation is more serious than the Egyptian example cited above, because of the forgery issue, Aelianus' conduct throughout is that of the correct, examining magistrate, showing himself to be an acute and persistent questioner, who carries out his duties in accordance with the rules. Neither he nor Appius Sabinus appear arbitrary, cruel or venal.

The corrupt judge

In sharp contrast to the 'real' judges of the court records are those represented through the medium of repeated imperial strictures on the 'arrogance', 'venality' and generally corrupt characters of provincial *iudices*. Constantine's attack on the corruption of the system, launched in November 331 (*Codex Theodosianus* 1.16.7; cf. ibid. 9.1.4; and, of Theodosius I, ibid. 1.5.9; 9.27.6), may be taken as representative: entrance to a hearing was not to depend on bribery and access should be available to rich and poor on equal terms. The attack is extended to the judge's apparitors and office staff, and opportunity is offered for victims of corruption or extortion to appeal, either to the governor himself, against his staff, or to the counts or praetorian prefects against the governors, 'so that we may be informed through their references to us and inflict punishment for such brigandage'. The violence of the rhetoric is characteristic of Constantine, the draftsmanship of whose laws is unknown, and, in this case, a serious distraction from the actual purpose of the law. The aim of Constantine, and other emperors, both before and after him, was to stamp out whatever corruption existed. They therefore acted to make provincial governors ever more accountable. Powerful language directed against the venality of judges was designed, not to convey anything about the extent of the abuse in the governance of the empire at large, but so that emperors would treat it severely, wherever it was found.

The rhetoric of imperial laws about *iudices*, therefore, expresses a concern about accountability, present from Augustus onwards, but now more emphatically expressed, in accordance with the linguistic conventions of the time, and stringently enforced. In the Theodosian Code, *iudices* were made liable to be punished under the *Lex Julia* on extortion (cf. *Codex Theodosianus* 9.27 *passim*), if convicted of theft or other crimes, if they act as 'sellers' of verdicts, if they sell judicial decisions, vary a penalty, or behave unjustly, and they were expected to respect the rights of decurions (not to be flogged) and to restrain the rapacity of tax collectors. The governors' office staffs were also held liable, and could be fined if they connived at law-breaking, or failed to keep the governor informed. On occasion, an example was made of a corrupt official: in 382, a former *dux*, Natalis, was to be escorted to his former province by soldiers from the imperial bodyguard, to restore what he and his staff had extorted, fourfold, 'in order that the punishment of one person may excite fear in many' (*Codex Theodosianus* 9.27.3). The public punishment of Natalis would serve the same purpose as the rhetoric of imperial laws against corrupt judges: it would prove that the emperor meant what he said.

None of this, of course, proves anything about the extent of corruption among judges. Nor, except in the language used, was there anything new about the holding of judges to account (MacCormack 1982). From the time of the Twelve Tables onwards, there had been mechanisms in Roman law to allow judges to be held liable to punishment by the state for improper conduct. Aulus Gellius, in the second century AD, recalled the provision in the Twelve Tables that exacted a capital penalty from judges who took bribes (*Noctes Atticae* 20.1.7), asking whether it was too harsh. By the second century BC, a second form of liability had been recognised, namely liability to the plaintiff; judges 'made the case their own' (*litem suam fecerunt*), if they turned up late or not at all to a hearing (Macrobius, *Saturnalia* 3.16.5 on a speech of 161 BC), and this allowed the plaintiff to claim damages against the judge. Over the first three centuries AD, the liability of judges both to litigants and to the state became more explicitly, and more widely, defined. The state's increasing concern with the behaviour of judges was expressed through amplification of ancient statutes on criminal law authored by the Dictator Sulla, Caesar and Augustus. Judges who resorted to the laying of false information or took bribes to secure a conviction were liable under expanded rules relating to the Sullan *Lex Cornelia de sicariis* – even if a conviction was not secured (Marcian at *Digest* 48.8.1 pr. and 1; Ulpian at *Digest* 48.8.4 pr.; Paul, *Sententiae* 5.23.11(10)). This liability was reinforced by the evolution of further sanctions under the *Lex Julia Repetundarum*, which penalised for bribery and extortion judges in both civil and criminal suits, with the added risk that a judge might be held liable for an unjust verdict, if 'impelled by anger' (cf. Macer at *Digest* 48.11.3; 7 pr. and 3; *Codex Theodosianus* 11.7.3; 12.1.61). Moreover, liability under this law extended to the 'companions' of judges, their *consilium* and, by extension, their office staffs (Macer at *Digest* 48.11.5). Predictably also, judges who ignored imperial constitutions which had been read out to them or brought to their attention, were liable to punishment, although they were in the clear if the constitutions were irrelevant to the case in hand (Marcian at *Digest* 48.10.1.3; Paul, *Sententiae* 5.25.4). All these failings on the part of judges rendered them liable to punishment by the state, and coexisted with a continuing liability to litigants, if procedures were not properly followed. These, by the second century, included not only failure to turn up, but also exceeding the limits set by the formula, failing to adjourn when required, and, most important of all, because of going beyond purely procedural matters, fraudulently reaching a decision which was against the letter or the spirit of the law (Ulpian at *Digest* 5.1.15 and Paul at *Digest* 1.3.29).

The steady encroachment of the state into trial procedures and outcomes was, then, a feature, not solely of late antiquity, but also of the early empire, under which the liability of *iudices* to litigants and the state, on substantive as well as procedural grounds, had been steadily increased. If the distractions of the rhetoric of Constantine's laws are ignored, it becomes clear that Constantine's insistence on the accountability of judges as an expression of the state's obligations to its citizens was nothing new. Already, by the time of Constantine, the liability of *iudices* was extensive. Already, too, the state took an active part in safeguarding the rights of litigants to a hearing that was both correctly conducted and fairly judged.

In the time of Constantine, the liability of the judge to the litigant was still a reality. In a law of 318 addressed to one Felix, governor of Corsica, Constantine issued a reminder of the rights of litigants where judges had acted improperly, whether through bribery or favouritism, leading to a wrong verdict, or by negligence, in face of repeated reminders, leading to the failure of a case through running out of time, for which the penalty would be that the plaintiff would be idemnified out of the governor's own resources for the amount involved in the litigation (*Codex Theodosianus* 1.16.3 and 2.6.2). However, there is little sign later in the fourth century of any further activation of *litem suam facere* and some evidence that the state took to itself responsibility for exacting redress for procedural irregularity. In legislation of the 380s and 390s, the state's right to punish criminal conduct by judges is expanded to encompass punishments for negligence, and governors or judges found to be 'lazy, negligent or idle' were to be dealt with by their superior, the praetorian prefect and substitutes appointed, if necessary (*Codex Theodosianus* 1.5.9). This further extension of the state's concern effectively removed the rights of litigants to seek direct redress for malpractice from the judge; in 385, the emperors ruled that if a litigant could prove that he had not been heard or his case deferred by the 'arrogance' or 'favouritism' of the judge, the judge would pay, not to the litigant but to the imperial fiscus, the estimated value involved in the case (*Codex Theodosianus* 2.1.6), and the heads of his office staff would be deported.

Accountability and the abuse of power

The rhetoric of corruption and the abuse of power obscures, for us and perhaps for contemporaries also, the fact of accountability. The *iudex* knew that he was doubly vulnerable. On the one side were provincials, some of higher status than he, and well able to express their views through their provincial councils, acclamations, or the reverse (*Codex Theodosianus* 1.16.6), public denunciations, such as those of Libanius of Antioch or Synesius of Cyrene directed against corrupt governors' oppression of their friends and clients (see MacMullen 1986/90), and the private representations of patrons at the court of prefect or emperor. On the other was the (in theory) ever-watchful state, armed with a formidable range of methods for bringing governors to account, and in the habit of advertising that accountability through the all-embracing moral denunciations of its official public pronouncements. For many a governor, still on the lower rungs of the imperial career ladder, the private pressures exerted by contumacious provincials and a suspicious emperor would have been fearsome indeed.

Moral strictures about the greed, arrogance or venality of judges, while designed to ensure accountability, must also have struck a chord with audiences. The power of judges, like that of all powerful men in late antiquity, was highly visible. Provincial *iudices* advertised their presence, with the full apparatus of state control, an apparatus designed to impress but also to terrify, as even schoolchildren could understand (Dionisotti 1982). Augustine, in whose experience the state was a useful ally, expressed his belief in the effectiveness of judicial ceremonial as a deterrent to the wicked and a protection to the good. The paraphernalia of justice, the 'right of the sword', the implements of torture and the armed guard, all were there for the positive purpose of underlining the *severitas* of the 'fatherly' judge: 'these things inspire fear, and the wicked are deterred and the good live more securely among the bad' (Augustine, *Letter* 153.6). Salutary or not – and the papyri show a willingness among the subjects to echo the rhetoric of their leaders (Bagnall 1993: 170) – the terror of the state judge affected guilty and innocent alike, while the demonstrations of power by the judges would further reinforce the conviction that, where there was power, there also existed the potential for its abuse. Observers would also infer, with good reason, that the most likely form of abuse was the exercise of *gratia*, favouritism or improper influence. As many involved in litigation had, at some point, resorted to the help of patrons, including bishops, who obliged with letters to the *iudex*, requesting his support for their client, accusations of *gratia* on the part of opponents and losers were inevitable, regardless of the fact that such had been the time-honoured operation of patronage in the Roman world.

Thus, whatever the actual conduct of judges, institutional aspects of their role and how they appeared to those they judged lent credibility to the rhetoric of the laws. However upright a *iudex* might be, the potential for the abuse of power was always present. That potential was rigorously and repeatedly suppressed by laws which reveal, not that abuses were extensive, but that emperors and subjects alike were profoundly – and publicly – aware that such abuses could and did exist and must be checked. It is this determination to discuss and criticise the abuse of power which is a distinguishing feature of the culture of late antiquity. Denunciation of abuse does not indicate that abuse of power was more widespread than at any previous time in Roman history, but rather that more and more articulate people were prepared to use the resources of their rhetorical training to denounce, and perhaps therefore check, official abuse of power.

The Persecuting Judge

Public awareness of the shortcomings of the judiciary and a rhetoric profoundly critical of power may go far to explain the emergence in late antiquity of the creation in martyr acts of the luridly tyrannical figure of the Persecuting Judge. Softer versions existed in earlier martyr acts and *passiones* but the determination of early Christians to guarantee the authenticity of their accounts gave less prominence to the judge as persecutor, and more to the irrationality of the mob, to which the governor, Pilate-like, gave way. Another effective means of ensuring the truth of the witness in interrogation was to use the court records, which preserved, at least in summary form, something approximating to the actual words of the martyr before the judge. For early Christians, of course, the prime interest of the documents was what the martyrs said and did and their steadfastness under pressure. Second- or third-century Christians, unlike their post-Constantinian brethren, lived with the reality of the threat of public shame, suffering and death, inflicted by judges who were themselves prisoners of the system they administered. Rules existed for the punishment of denounced Christians, which, as Pliny for one was aware, it was the duty of the governor to enforce.

It therefore in no way diminished the sanctity of the martyrs that the interrogating judge, the main figure in the supporting cast of some of the *acta*, was often not a sadistic and intemperate villain (as he was later to become) but an harassed and uncomprehending official, trying to do his job. The most reasonable interrogator of Christians to survive in the record, P. Vigellius Saturninus, proconsul of Africa, was confronted in his chambers by twelve would-be martyrs on 17 July 180. Saturninus' line was to insist on the observance of the religion of the state – 'if you start bad-mouthing our sacred rites, I shall not listen to you' – while at the same time urging these mad Christians to 'return to your senses'. When the arguments, sketchy as they are in the record, were exhausted, Saturninus asked a series of formal questions, which served to define the position of both sides: did the Christians persist? (Yes); did they wish time for consideration? (No); they were entitled to a reprieve of thirty days, would they take it? (No). The position having been agreed in the interrogation and duly recorded, the inevitable outcome was the prompt execution of the dissidents, an outcome which, thanks to the clarity of the record, could not subsequently be challenged.

Ideally, from the point of view of the accountable governor, the *acta* of court proceedings should demonstrate agreement as to the facts of the case and thus the correctness of verdict and sentence. While Christians might later adapt such records to allow martyrs more scope to state their case, most original *acta* were probably concise in form (Coles 1966: 24; for later, Teitler 1985: 5–26; 95–103), as were Cyprian's two hearings before two different proconsuls in the 250s. In both, a set of terse exchanges between bishop and proconsul establish the facts of the case. They begin, in correct legal fashion, with consular date, day and month, the place of the hearing and the names of the participants. At the first (Carthage, 30 August 257), the proconsul Aspasius Paternus and Cyprian make one speech each about religion. Paternus then asks if Cyprian persists and the bishop says he does. Would the bishop accept exile to the city of Curubis, in accordance with the emperor's command? Cyprian agrees to that. There follows an exchange reflecting the more active approach to persecution adopted by the authorities after Decius; presbyters are to be searched out, but Cyprian refuses to reveal their names on legal grounds, claiming, with doubtful accuracy, that 'in your laws you resolve rightly and usefully that there shall be no informers' (*Acta Cypriani* 1.5). The proconsul asserts, as he must for the record, that he will search them out anyway. He then concludes with a formal warning on the penalties for illegal meetings and entry to burial grounds; Cyprian responds that he has heard the order, implying, not that he will obey it, but that he knows and, by implication, will accept the consequences of disobedience. Apart from Cyprian's silence over the priests, the record shows that broad agreement was reached.

Cyprian's martyrdom a year later was equally consensual. On 12 September 258, the proconsul, Galerius Maximus, convenes his court in the hall of a country estate, Sauciolum, to judge Cyprian. The bishop is brought in and his identity formally established. Galerius reminds Cyprian of the emperors' orders to 'perform religious ceremonies'. Cyprian places his refusal on record with two words, 'Non facio' (I will not). After a brief warning from the proconsul, Cyprian instructs him to carry out his orders; deliberation on the case was unnecessary. Yet still Galerius refuses to rush to judgment. Following correct procedure, he takes advice from his *consilium* and finally, with obvious difficulty and reluctance, pronounces his decision and the grounds for it: Cyprian had for long held sacrilegious views, he had joined others to him in a 'conspiracy' and resisted the pressures on him from the emperors to conform. The reasons for punishment cited are the need to deter others by example and to ensure the good behaviour of the populace by imposition of the all-important *disciplina*; thus the death of a 'leading criminal' will deter those Cyprian has misled and the value of good order (*disciplina*) will be reaffirmed. Finally, the proconsul reads out the death sentence from his tablets and the bishop responds simply, 'Deo gratias'. Martyrdom and veneration duly ensue.

Acta Martyrum based on court records reveal a combination of confrontation over religious principle and consensus about the consequences. Not, of course, that court records in general would reflect such co-operation; most criminals condemned to execution were hardly likely to record acquiescence in their fate. It was accepted that *publica acta* were a genuine record of what happened. The simple style of the African interrogations is preserved even in more elaborate, late acts, such as those of Pionius, whose sayings are twice described as recorded by notaries in two separate interrogations (*Acta Pionii* 9 and 19), in a form noticeably more pithy than exchanges represented outside a formal juridical setting. Moreover, respect for public records as true, and therefore a potent weapon against adversaries who disputed facts, was evidenced, still, in the fourth and fifth centuries. Augustine, for example, and his contemporaries, ensured that outrages against Catholics committed by Donatists or pagans were recorded for future use in the *acta publica* and confessions of opponents, duly noted down in the records of their interrogations, were also useful potential propaganda (Augustine, *Letter* 133).

Brief and restrained exchanges between the parties and a respect for legal propriety are not, however, a feature of the martyr-stories of late antiquity. The supply of authentic court records of martyrs in the fourth and later centuries was, in any case, restricted by the lack of martyrs, and the spare, economical style of formal *acta* was incompatible with late antique literary tastes. Instead, the concise affirmations of their faith by the martyrs are replaced by speeches of, sometimes, unbelievable length, addressed to oppressive governors, whose main characteristics are sadistic cruelty in the invention of

227

tortures and a propensity to ungovernable rages. Asclepiades, for example, the torturer of the wordy martyr Romanus in Prudentius, *Peristephanon* 10, is labelled at the outset a 'tyrannus' (by contrast with Romanus, who speaks 'ore libero', as a free man), and is later described as 'incensus' and 'furens,' 'spewing out' his rage (after yet another long speech). Similarly, in the fourth-century martyrdom of Conon, a curious fantasy about a deserted city written in Greek, the Prefect is also described as 'tyrannos' (*Martyrdom of Conon* 4 and 5) while the martyrs Marianus and James first became the victims of the 'mad rage' (*furor*) of the 'bloodstained and blinded governor' at Cirta, then were transferred to Lambaesis to confront 'the frenzy of the crazed governor' (*Passion of Marianus and James* 2.4 and 10). The agent of the persecuting state displays all the tendencies of the standard bad ruler of the Graeco-Roman literary tradition, arbitrary tyranny, anger and lack of self-control.

Such literary portraits of judicial violence were not confined to the safely dead. Jerome's first letter, on a woman of Vercellae, tortured by the *iudex* for alleged adultery, owes much to the rhetorical stereotypes of the martyr-acts, but also claimed to be a true account of recent events, anchored in the reality of small-town Italian life. To start with, the hearing is represented as routine: the *iudex* was visiting the dilapidated town of Vercellae on his usual round. The woman was denounced for adultery by her husband, and the alleged lover 'confessed' his guilt. When the woman (whom Jerome presumes innocent) refused to confess, 'surpassing the strength of her gender', the *iudex* was, predictably, enraged and the tortures were carried out with great violence. Despite his failure to gain a confession, the judge, satisfied, we may assume, with the other proofs, ordered her execution and a crowd assembled, but the headsman was unable to do his job (his sword was bent backwards) and the crowd shouted that she be let off. However, the headsman made his own plea (his job was at stake) and the crowd wavered. A second attempt was apparently more successful, but the woman in fact survived and was given shelter by Christian religious women. Though alive, however, 'the laws still raged against her' and only after the intervention of an outside ecclesiastical patron, Evagrius, was a pardon finally granted.

While the mentions of Vercellae and Evagrius connect this story with a real incident, the failure to name any of the main participants in this local drama allow them to be subsumed into the rhetorical stock figures of the Judge, the Accuser, the Executioner and the Innocent. Although not in the end martyred, and tortured, not for her faith but to force a false confession of guilt, the woman of Vercellae testifies to her chastity with the conviction and endurance characteristic of the martyr. Similarly, the governor behaves in the cruel, enraged and oppressive manner of the persecutor. Jerome would expect his readers to recognise the stereotypes, but what, ultimately, was their source?

The Great Persecution of 303–11, followed within months by the conversion of Constantine, marked a watershed, not only in Christian history, but in Christian perceptions of that history (de Ste Croix 1954: 104 on exaggeration of its effects). Although the Tetrarchs were legitimate emperors, the two great historians of persecution, Lactantius and Eusebius, did not scruple to paint the main movers of persecution and their agents in the blackest of colours. Among governors, Urbanus, governor of Palestine, was singled out by Eusebius for especial criticism. On his entry to office, in 304, 'the war against us was waged more fiercely, the governor of the province being Urbanus' (Eusebius, *Martyrs of Palestine* 3.1). Within a few months, Urbanus was subjected, thanks to a security lapse, to a face-to-face confrontation with a Christian, Apphianus, who exhorted the governor not to sacrifice; the guards, perhaps to atone for their initial negligence, beat up the future martyr and subjected him to frightful tortures (ibid. 4.8). Later, after playing host to his friend, the 'tyrannus' Maximinus Daia, at games in Caesarea (ibid. 6.1), Urbanus' excesses grew yet worse: 'the same judge, being a terrible inventor of evil, . . . thought up unheard-of retaliation against the holy'. He condemned three men to fight against gladiators; Auxentius, a reverend and holy priest, was eaten by the beasts; others were castrated and condemned to the mines; and others, again, after cruel tortures, he shut up in prison. Then Urbanus made a futile attempt to convert a philosopher, by conducting an intellectual conversation with him; when the philosopher indicated his refusal to sacrifice, Urbanus' rage 'surpassed all bounds' and he ordered the infliction of 'the most harsh torments', behaving, as he did so, 'more savagely than a wild beast' (ibid. 7.4–6).

Equally loathed by Eusebius and Lactantius, because of his combination of persecution with intellectual attacks on Christianity, was Sossianus Hierocles (Barnes 1981: 22, 164–7). Early in 303, Eusebius had written a hurried refutation of Hierocles' attack on Christianity, in which personal abuse was scrupulously avoided (Conybeare 1912: 482–605). Very different was Eusebius' language four years later, when, as governor of Egypt, early in 307, the persecuting Hierocles 'raving like a drunkard and going beyond the

JILL HARRIES

bounds of right' humiliated respected men, holy women and conse-
crated virgins in numerous ways (Eusebius, *Martyrs of Palestine* 5.3).
Lactantius has a passing mention of Hierocles who, as governor of
Bithynia in 303, was one of the three governors to persecute the
dedicatee of the *De Mortibus Persecutorum* (16.4) and in his *Divine
Institutes* picks up Hierocles again in Bithynia, where he is seen corrupting his delegates, making friends with them, creating obligations under false pretences, bribing them into delivering corrupt
verdicts and denying redress to the victims (Lactantius, *Divine
Institutes* 5.2.3). This is recognisably the rhetorical figure of the
Corrupt Judge, enslaved to greed and dishonesty.

   Although these are the representations of the *iudex* so often
accepted as an accurate reflection of the terror of the late Roman judicial system, in fact, as complete or realistic portraits of judges, they
are seriously deficient. We never learn, for example, from the *passio* of
the African martyr, Felix of Thibiuca, that his interrogator, the
curator rei publicae, Magnilianus, was almost certainly also a generous
patron of his *municipium*, where he and his son restored and enlarged
the baths and held a three-day celebratory feast and theatrical shows
(*CIL* 8. 23964–5; Duncan-Jones 1974). Similarly, the procurator,
Hilarianus, the persecutor of Perpetua, may be identified with one
P. Aelius Hilarianus, who dedicated two altars in Spain, and whose
religious convictions may have spurred him to treat the Christians
with exemplary cruelty (Rives 1996). As is clear from the other evidence cited above, the *iudex*, wherever he appears in a literary source,
is designed to further the rhetorical purpose of the author. Urbanus
may indeed have been an enthusiastic supporter of his friend
Maximinus' policy of persecution (Mitchell 1988) and a harsh
judge; whatever the reality behind the portrait, his demonisation
by Eusebius served the historian's rhetorical purpose, of conveying,
to a readership not conditioned to understatement, the horror of
Christians' suffering and the courage with which they endured it.
Hierocles may or may not have been corrupt; but his attacks on
Christians at a sensitive time ensured that he would be pictured as
such. More important for the future of the Persecuting Judge in
the fourth century and later is that Eusebius, in particular, shaped
both the perception of persecution and the rhetoric to be applied
henceforward to the agent of the (pagan) persecuting state.
Unbridled rage, sadistic inventiveness, the readiness to inflict every
form of torture and pain, would henceforth be the hallmarks of
Urbanus' literary siblings (cf. Augustine, *Sermon* 276.3 (Datianus,

persecutor of Vincent of Saragossa); Zeno of Verona, *Tractatus* 18.3 = PL 11.453).

Image and accountability

The influence of Eusebius' depiction of martyrdom and persecution reflected in the hagiography to come was also a by-product of a more significant development in the Roman attitude to authority. late antique autocracy, Janus-like, faced two ways. On the one hand the period from Diocletian onwards witnessed the development and elaboration of court ceremonial, ritualised acclamations for emperors and other rulers, and the evolution of complex strategies for the assertion and expression of power. On the other, emperors repeatedly stressed the accountability of their officials and openly acknowledged, in the rhetoric of their laws, that there did (in theory) exist lazy, incompetent, corrupt and venal servants of the state, whose crimes the emperor would severely punish (if he found out). Thus, while asserting his own authority, the emperor, through the language of his laws, encouraged a culture of criticism. Moreover, he also reflected it. The emperor issued most of his laws in response to formal approaches from influential and articulate groups within and far beyond his court and, although drafted by court officials, their content and justification depended, to a great extent, on the representations received (Harries and Wood 1993: 8–14). As the texts of many laws reveal, those representations were often highly critical of the emperor's men in the provinces and, in the dialogue between emperor and empire, expressed, albeit one-sidely, in the constitutions of emperors, the emperor's *iudex* was often the agreed scapegoat.

Conversely, in the cities of the empire, Christian readers of Eusebius were further conditioned to scepticism of the agents of the state, through the annual readings at their festivals of the gory *Passiones* of martyrs. In their daily lives they interacted with others, Christian and pagan alike, who, for various reasons, felt free to deploy standard rhetorical attacks on corruption to discredit imperial officials of whom they disapproved. Skilled in *eloquentia* and the cultivation of the powerful, local *potentes*, however subservient to his face, had the reputation of the *iudex* – and perhaps also his career – at their mercy. Thus the literary representation of the Judge and the frequency of the attacks launched by ancient writers on the arrogance, venality and cruelty of *iudices* in late antiquity do not indicate, by themselves, that corruption or the abuse of power (cf. Bagnall 1989: 212) were rife in the system (or that they were not). The reality of the late Roman judicial system cannot be properly analysed by uncritical acceptance of a rhetoric designed to construct a figure to fit the purposes of authors or perceptions of their audiences, or by the uncritical deployment of anecdotes about individual judges, who may, or may not, be representative of the whole. The different faces of the *iudex* constructed by the literary sources reflect, not fact, but the perceptions of a critical age, an age conditioned by imperially inspired notions of accountability and the pervasive impact of the rhetorical culture of late antiquity.

Acknowledgement

This chapter was composed while I was a Visiting Fellow at All Souls College, Oxford. I am grateful to the Warden and Fellows for their hospitality and support.

Bibliography

Bagnall, R.S. (1989) 'Official and Private Violence in Roman Egypt', *BASP* 26: 201–16.
—— (1993) *Egypt in Late Antiquity*, Princeton NJ: Princeton University Press.
Barnes, T.D. (1981) *Constantine and Eusebius*, Cambridge MA: Harvard University Press.
Coles, R.A. (1966) *Reports of Proceedings in Papyri*, Brussels: Papyrologica Bruxellensia 4.
de Ste Croix, G.E.M. (1954) 'Aspects of the "Great Persecution"', *HTR* 47: 75–109.
Dionisotti, A.C. (1982) 'From Ausonius' Schooldays? A Schoolbook and its Relations', *JRS* 72: 83–105.
Duncan Jones, R. (1974) 'An African Saint and his Interrogator', *JTS* 25: 106–10.
Eusebius (1912) 'Against Hierocles' in *Philostrati Opera*, ed. F.C. Conybeare, Loeb Classical Library, Cambridge, MA: Harvard University Press.
Harries, J. and Wood, I. (eds) (1993) *The Theodosian Code*, London: Duckworth.
Katzoff, R. (1982) 'Sources of Law in Roman Egypt: the Role of the Prefect', *ANRW* II.13: 807–44.
MacCormack, G. (1982) 'The Liability of the Judge', *ANRW* II.14: 3–28.
MacMullen, R. (1986/90) 'Judicial Savagery in the Roman Empire', *Chiron* 16: 147–66 = (1990) in id. *Changes in the Roman Empire. Essays in the Ordinary*, Princeton NJ: Princeton University Press: 67–77.
Mitchell, S. (1988) 'Maximinus and the Christians in AD 312: A New Latin Inscription', *JRS* 78: 105–24.

Pearl, O.M. (1971) 'Excerpts from the Minutes of Judicial Proceedings', *ZPE* 6: 271–7.

Rives, J. (1996) 'The Piety of a Persecutor', *JECS* 4: 1–25.

Skeat, T.C. and Wegener, E.P. (1935) 'A Trial before the Prefect of Egypt Appius Sabinus c. 250 AD (P. Lond. Inv. 2565)', *JEA* 21: 224–47.

Teitler, H. (1985) *Notarii and Exceptores*, Amsterdam: J.C. Gieben.

11

THE BARBARIAN IN LATE ANTIQUITY

Image, reality, and transformation

Peter Heather

In AD 370, a group of Saxon raiders advanced by boat onto Roman territory and proceeded to create mayhem. Eventually, a show of Roman force led them to make a truce, whose terms allowed the Saxons to return home. The truce was no more than a front, however, to allow Roman troops to set up an ambush, in which the Saxons were wiped out (AM 28.5.1–7). Ammianus Marcellinus comments that an impartial judge (*iustus quidam arbiter*) might condemn the ambush as 'treacherous' (*perfidum*) and 'degraded' (*deforme*), 'but on careful consideration of the matter, he will not think it improper (*indigne*) that a destructive band of brigands was destroyed when opportunity arose' (28.5.7).

Ideology and practice thus met in the field of foreign policy, or, at least, in Ammianus' response to that policy. Because the Saxons are not to be treated as equals but as a 'destructive band of brigands', it is perfectly proper to destroy them, even at the cost of breaking agreements. The passage defines the area I wish briefly to investigate in this chapter. How did fourth-century Romans construct their image of the barbarian, and how did it impinge upon policy-making? More than that, what happened to these old images in the face of the new realities of the fifth century, when barbarians conquered the western half of the Roman state?

Image and reality in the fourth century

'The only good barbarian is a dead barbarian' would be no unfair summary of Ammianus' attitude, and his general vision of those living beyond the frontier finds strong echoes in a wide variety of other late imperial authors and contexts. No Roman victory was complete without its supporting cast of subservient barbarians. In 383, Symmachus wrote to the emperor Valentinian II to say how reassured the populace of Rome had been of the prospects of long-term imperial prosperity by the sight of some hapless Sarmatians being fed to wild beasts in the course of celebratory games (*Rel.* 47). This, of course, was in the aftermath of Hadrianople when Roman populations were in particular need of such reassurance, but there is no reason to suppose this demonstration a one-off or even unusual event. Seventy years earlier, the emperor Constantine's well-publicised gibbeting of two Frankish kings had been used to make the point that he was far from soft on the barbarian issue (*Pan. Lat.* 7.[6].10.1–7). More generally, the building of fortresses, bridges over the Danube, and a host of Roman victories were customarily celebrated with coin issues showing defeated, recumbent barbarians at the bottom of the pictorial space (e.g. Calo Levi 1952). Less durable pictorial propaganda in the form of large posters displayed in circuses was also used to illustrate victorious imperial battles (Themistius *Or.* 16.199c–d; Eunapius ed. Blockley fr. 68). As the fate of the Sarmatians or ambushed Saxons makes clear, such pictorial topoi were far from empty images. A whole host of means were used to create, reinforce and fulfil the expectation, among the Roman population at large, that the imperial ship of state would cut a triumphant and bloody swathe through the waves of barbarians which broke against it (cf. McCormick 1986, chs 1–3). Sometimes, of course, barbarians could be a bit annoying in how they reacted to such treatment. Symmachus' plans for his son's Praetorian Games were briefly interrupted by the mass suicide of a group of Saxon prisoners who were supposed to immolate themselves, this time as gladiators, on the pyre of Roman senatorial greatness; he replaced them with Libyan antelopes (*Ep.* 2.46).

It was thus the fate of many outsiders – 'barbarians' as the Romans would call them – to die for the empire, both so that its frontiers could be preserved intact, and to reinforce the ideologies which gave the empire internal coherence. For, as in most empires, the assertion of power to sustain, reinforce, and extend existing patterns of wealth required ideological justification. Educated elites, no matter how much they may benefit materially from the aggression of the political structures to which they belong, like to be reassured that this aggression is in a teleologically good cause. It is no surprise, therefore, that the more precise connotations of the image of the barbarian, as it had evolved by late antiquity, served to underline what was good and important about being Roman.

Ideas of what it meant to be properly Roman were in many ways surprisingly specific. As the philosopher and political propagandist Themistius put it, significantly enough, in a speech celebrating the deal struck between the emperor Valens and some Goths in 370, 'There is in each of us a barbarian tribe, extremely overbearing and intractable – I mean temper and those insatiable desires, which stand opposed to rationality as Scythians and Germans do to the Romans' (Themistius, Or. 10.131b–c, trans. Moncur in Heather and Matthews, 1991, 38–9). Themistius is referring here to a central contention of the self-image of the Roman elite; namely, that its members were actually more rational than barbarians from beyond the frontier. In this context, rationality meant, after Stoic patterns, the individual's ability to control bodily passions by exercise of the intellect. This rather extraordinary claim was justified via a series of related ideas. First, classical literature, in which this elite was customarily educated, played a central role. Immersion in classical literature exposed the individual to accumulated *exempla* of human virtue and vice, which, if properly digested, enabled the powers of the mind to be extended, as reflected in an individual's character, to control bodily, fleshly impulses (see e.g. Kaster 1988, esp. 12–19). As Themistius continued, 'it is virtue's task to render [the passions] submissive and amenable to the dictates of the intelligence', and literary *exempla* generated virtue. Second, the greater rationality of its individual members meant that Roman society as a whole was prepared to subordinate its immediate desires to the rule of written law: the guarantee of an ordered society. Thus for Romans the rule of written law – encapsulated, in the late imperial concept of *civilitas* – was the great distinguishing feature of their society.

Third, the official conversion of the empire to Christianity added a further dimension to this sense of superiority. The Roman educated elite identified an underlying order in the cosmos, whose structure reflected, throughout, the one organising principle which had shaped it from primeval chaos (Sorabji 1983, esp. chs 13, 20). The Christian Roman empire, following the strong lead of pagan emperors, claimed that there was a political dimension to cosmological order. No earthly ruler could hold power unless the Divinity so ordered. This basic idea was developed still further into the claim that the Roman empire was the particular agent of Divine power for perfecting humanity. Hence Eusebius of Caesarea argued that it was no accident that Christ should have been born in the reign of Augustus; it was part of the Divine Plan that the founders of Christianity and the Roman empire had coexisted. More generally, Christian emperors arrogated for themselves the role of Christ's vice-gerent on earth. Imperial ceremonial was held to echo the majesty of heaven, and an aura of Christian sacrality surrounded the imperial person and his officers (Dvornik 1966, chs 8, 10–12; MacCormack 1981). A proper classical education thus led the individual to appreciate the benefits of the Roman way of life, and its historical importance within the Divine scheme of things: to spread Christianity and bring individuals to their teleological maximum (on all these ideas, see further Heather 1993, 1994).

Barbarians, by contrast, having not studied Latin, were prey to their every passion. 'Faithlessness', for instance, was, as far as Romans were concerned, of the essence of the barbarian in political relations. In other words, barbarians were quite unable to formulate sensible, consistent policies, with a tendency to give way to unjustified joy or despair according to circumstance. They were also particularly given to gratifying the desires of the flesh. Ammianus was being in no sense complimentary when noting the vigorous interest taken by nomadic Arabs in matters sexual (14.4.4). Barbarians likewise tended to drink. In his famous article on Cassiodorus and the literary culture of his day, Momigliano picked out the telling phrase from an Italian saint's life, *biberunt ut Gothi*: drinking like Goths (Momigliano 1955, 208). Written law, likewise, figures centrally in famous Late Antique contexts where barbarian and Roman societies are being compared. Orosius claims that Athaulf decided to support *Romania*, rather than replace it with *Gothia*, because his Goths were unable to obey written laws (*Hist. ad Pag.* 7.43.2–3). The famous and no doubt largely fictional conversation between Priscus and a Roman merchant turned Hun in the camp of Attila also eventually turned to law. Commonly cited are the merchant's criticisms of Roman society, acknowledged by Priscus to be largely just. Almost totally ignored is the story's punchline. When Priscus brings up the written laws of the Romans, the ex-merchant bursts into tears and agrees that they make Roman society superior (ed. Blockley fr. 11.2, esp. 272, 508–10). Overall, indeed, the natural state of barbarians, who were prisoners of their bodily lusts and unfortunately lacking in knowledge of Sallust and Virgil, could be considered – on a number of levels – as slavery (e.g. Libanius, *Orr.* 19.16, 20.14; Synesius, *De Regno* 21: both discussing Goths). Living under good laws, on the other hand, brought the

Romans true freedom: *libertas*. Thus the Roman image of the barbarian was intimately linked to – being exactly the mirror image of – the image they wished to assert of themselves (cf., with further refs, Dauge 1981, esp. pt. ii, chs 3, 7–8).

The relationship of this coherent and carefully structured image to reality was multifarious. In some contexts, the correspondence to reality was minimal or even non-existent. By the fourth century, Germanic societies beyond the empire's European frontiers had changed beyond recognition from the time of Augustus. Demographic and economic expansion had been matched by social and political transformation. None of these processes had entirely worked themselves out, nor had they proceeded in the same way everywhere at the same speed. Nonetheless, in strategic terms, they had had an overall tendency to generate larger and more coherent political entities beyond the Roman frontier (see e.g. Hedeager 1987, 1988, 1992; Heather 1996, ch. 3; Whittaker 1994). These required a much more varied and subtle foreign policy than the outright military domination which was part of the general Roman image of superiority, and whose continuation was deliberately suggested by such carefully orchestrated acts of brutality as gibbeting captured kings or feeding prisoners to wild beasts in front of admiring audiences.

For much of the fourth century, peace was actually maintained on the frontier not by slaughtering inferiors, but through diplomatic alliances with a series of essentially client kingdoms. Relations with Alamanni and Gothic Tervingi are best documented, but Sarmatian and Taifali leaders on the Danube were also under the Roman thumb, and this may well have been true in the cases of others (Franks etc.) about whom we have less information (on the theory and reality of these treaties and their historical development, see now Heather 1997; Wirth 1997). In certain circumstances, these clients could even extract more equal treatment from the Roman state than was ordinarily the case. In the early 370s, Roman policy in the Upper Rhine and Danube region was directed towards destroying Macrianus, an Alamannic leader of such pre-eminent prestige that his power threatened frontier security. After three attempts at removing him failed, however, the emperor Valentinian I found himself pressed by events on the Middle Danube. In consequence, he decided that peace had to be made with Macrianus, largely on the Alaman's own terms. The two met in a boat on the river, a setting which recognised different zones of influence, and Macrianus was duly placated (AM 28.5; 29.4; 30.3). I have also argued that this is the right way to read the similarly waterborne summit of 369 between Athanaric, leader of the Tervingi, and Valentinian's brother Valens, which ended three years of warfare between them. The similarity of the sequences of events is striking, and, again, it was pressing events elsewhere – Persian moves into Iberia and Armenia – which forced Valens' hand, not simply the power of the Goths (AM 27.5; Themistius, *Orr.* 8 and 10; cf. Heather 1991, 115–21; Heather and Matthews 1991, ch. 2).

The frontier neighbours of the Roman empire in the fourth century were not limitlessly powerful, but they could be formidable, extracting, in the right circumstances, some degree of compromise from the Roman state. The gap between Roman image and frontier reality could, on occasion, be even greater. Ammianus reports that, in 361, troops of the emperor Julian captured the secretary of the Alamannic king Vadomarius. On his person were letters from Julian's uncle, the emperor Constantius II, to Vadomarius, encouraging him to cause periodic trouble on the frontier to keep Julian occupied and prevent him from hatching ambitious schemes against his uncle's interests (21.3.4–5). On the face of it, this shows us a Roman emperor perferring to be in alliance, if covertly, with a so-called barbarian against a fellow Roman emperor. However, the secretary was captured after the outbreak of Julian's revolt against Constantius, and it was one of the central conceits of Julian's propaganda that Constantius' jealousy had prevented his nephew from defeating the barbarians as thoroughly as he could otherwise have done. Showing Constantius contravening the generally accepted image of Roman/barbarian relations right at the moment of Julian's revolt, therefore, seems just a bit too convenient. I do hesitate, therefore, to take this incident entirely at face value.

There is a whole series of other, less problematic, incidents from the fourth century, however, where the realities of strategy and diplomacy departed in slightly less dramatic ways from the natural order of relations dictated by inherited images of Roman and barbarian. The military power of its barbarian clients was certainly made use of by the empire in the fourth century. On three occasions after 332, Gothic troops from beyond the Danube marched across Asia Minor to fight in Roman campaigns against Persia (348: Libanius, *Or.* 59.89; 360: AM 20.8.1; 363: AM 23.2.7). This was one barbarian being used to fight another, and hence merited no adverse comment. Barbarian contingents – by natural extension – thus also found themselves fighting in Roman civil wars. Gothic Tervingi fought with Licinius against Constantine and with Procopius against Valens

(*Anon. Val.* 5.27; AM 26.10.3), Franks, Saxons, and Alamanni with the usurper Magnentius against Constantius II (Julian, *Or.* 1.36c, cf. 34b–35c). Such incidents – Romans and barbarians fighting together against other Romans – clearly contravened the image. It is striking, however, that the contingents we hear about in these circumstances were always on the side of the 'usurper'; i.e. the emperor who eventually lost. I suspect that this is no accident. Foreign contingents were probably in quite general use in the Roman army of the fourth century, and hence found themselves periodically involved, as circumstance dictated, in wars against other barbarians or in Roman civil wars. Because of the inherited stereotypes, however, their presence in civil wars was an extremely useful stick with which to beat defeated opponents, and history is always written by the victors.

Image and reality could also collide in more subtle ways. The emperor Valentinian I, for instance, liked to present his regime as tough on barbarians. One symbol of this popular with taxpayers – to judge, at least, by the *De Rebus Bellicis* – was fortress-building, and Valentinian undertook plenty of defensive works on the Rhine and Upper Danube (AM 28.2.1; cf. *De Rebus Bellicis* 20.1, *praef.* 7). Over-enthusiastic fortification, however, might cause trouble. In the Neckar region, Valentinian decided that he needed to build beyond the river, but this move broke existing agreements with the Alamanni of the area, and drove them to revolt (AM 28.2.5– 10). According to inherited imagery, fortresses could only be a good thing for controlling savage outsiders. In certain areas, however, peace was actually maintained not by fortresses but by peace agreements, which fortress-building contravened. Frontier-management could thus demand a more sophisticated approach than inherited stereotypes notionally allowed, and the need to impress taxpayers might override local best practice.

Even so, up to the last quarter of the fourth century, the new, more sophisticated reality did not depart so far from inherited imagery that established rhetorical categories could not for the most part be deployed to describe – if a little selectively – events on the ground. The reality of the fourth century, everywhere but the Persian front at least, was that Roman armies did usually defeat outsiders in armed confrontations. Before he reaches Hadrianople, the pages of Ammianus are full of Romans massacring Alamanni, Franks, Sarmatians, and Quadi. Such groups were now effectively part of a Roman imperial system, enjoying a more structured role, which allowed them to make some demands of, and impose some limits on, Roman emperors. It was, however, a *Roman* imperial system, built on Roman military hegemony, and even acknowledged allies held only subordinate, satellite status, the origin of which – whenever we have any information – was Roman military victory. On the Lower Danube, thirty-odd years of close relations between the empire and the Gothic Tervingi were inaugurated by Constantine's great victory of 332. Likewise, both Constantine and Constantius II used victory to reorder – to their own liking – the tribal groups of the Middle Danube, and Julian's victories occasioned similar activities on the Rhine (Heather 1991, 107ff; Heather 1997). Any immigration of outsiders into the empire, similarly, was controlled according to well-established practice: militarily subdued groups under a variety of regimes (sometimes involving military service on their part, sometimes not) being dispersed widely across the imperial landscape, to minimise the possibility of revolt and maximise the pressure towards full integration (Heather 1991, 128–31).

The inherited rhetoric was flexible enough, moreover, to encompass a variety of situations. There was no overriding ethnic content, for instance, to concepts of *Romanitas*: 'Romanness'. Through education it was, notionally at least, available to all, many provincials had themselves by the fourth century graduated from barbarism to *Romanitas*, and any particular barbarian individual might, through virtue, rise above the general state of the society which produced him. Thus Gregory Nazianzus could congratulate Modares, a renegade leader of the Tervingi, who had been fighting for the Romans against his compatriots, for his honesty, which stood in stark contrast to usual Gothic faithlessness (*Ep.* 136). And as long as Roman armies had not actually been defeated, a clever spin doctor could usually find some way of presenting a sequence of events as being somehow to Roman advantage. In 370, Themistius appealed to the sensitivities of taxpayers when the emperor Valens, because of events in Armenia, was forced to abandon his attempt to reassert close diplomatic hegemony over the Gothic Tervingi. The end of diplomatic subsidies would save money, Themistius stressed, and so too would the end of expensive campaigning on the Danube which benefited only local landowners, but which was paid for by everyone. Themistius also devoted much space, however, to showing both that Valens had not been forced into a course of action by outside constraint – something not in tune with the prime virtue of victoriousness required of emperors (cf. McCormick 1986) – and that he was taking proper care of the frontier. New forts – built where no one had been able to build them before – would prevent Gothic raiders

241

from hiding in Danube marshes and ambushing the unwary, while tighter controls on cross-border trade (now confined to only two points) would prevent unlicensed flows of population. Value for money could thus be combined with enough lip-service to the vision of foreign affairs demanded by traditional stereotypes to sell what was actually a diplomatic setback (Themistius, *Or.* 10; trans. with commentary in Heather and Matthews 1991, ch. 2). Two contemporary commentators, interestingly, were happy enough to buy this presentation of these events (AM 27.5.8; Zosimus 4.11.4: the opinion, no doubt, of Eunapius).

Despite considerable changes on the ground, the traditional image of the barbarian continued to hold sway in the fourth century. Peter Brown has talked of the 'osmosis' which allowed ideas to move across the Mediterranean landscape and generate from it a surprising degree of cultural unity (Brown 1976). The image of the barbarian was one such idea; it can be found in both Greek and Latin authors, on display in the rhetoric deployed at court, and in the letters of private individuals. It was so widespread, of course, because it said as much about Romans as it did about barbarians. Indeed, I strongly suspect that it was part of the value-system transmitted within Mediterranean elites by the grammarians, to whom their education was entrusted (see further Kaster 1988). This, after all, was a value-system which stressed the importance of text-derived moral *exempla*, and it seems appropriate to situate such an ideology among the textual guardians of the Graeco-Roman world. What I would stress above all, however, is that we must take seriously the 'Latin-speaker's burden'. It gave unity to a landowning class dispersed between Hadrian's Wall and the Euphrates, and was part and parcel of the political miracle involved in generating any sense of unity over such an area using pre-industrial communications. It also constrained foreign policy. Its straitjacket was not so tight as always to dictate a policy of confrontation on the frontier. It did, however, demand that policies *be shown* to be in accord with certain norms, and could lead to tensions between the management of reasonably sophisticated client kingships – the stuff of the fourth-century frontier – and an inherited need to be seen to be tough on barbarians.

Image and reality transformed

From the last quarter of the fourth century, the gap between rhetoric and reality was stretched seemingly to breaking-point as Roman hegemony in Europe was overthrown in a number of distinct phases. First, the Roman state was forced to accept the presence within its frontiers of militarily unsubdued, and politically at least semi-autonomous, groups of outsiders. Starting with the Goths who crossed the Danube in 376 and with whom a peace treaty was eventually made in 382, this represented a major break with established diplomatic precedent. Second, further groups of entirely unsubdued outsiders followed in the Goths' wake, removing large tracts of western Europe permanently or temporarily from Roman control (Vandals, Suevi, Anglo-Saxons, etc.). Third, as the loss of territory diminished Roman revenues and hence undermined the power of the state, these groups – both those officially tolerated and those not – proceeded more and less quickly to carve out independent kingdoms for themselves from within the former body politic of the western Roman state. This political revolution was accomplished neither quickly nor peacefully. The west Roman state, with periodic but significant help from the East, fought tooth and nail for life in the fifth century, and not without success. Matters rarely proceeded – from the outsiders' point of view – in a straight line from original barbarian settlement to independent kingdom (for an overview, see Heather 1995a).

For this reason, the fifth century saw not only the end of the western Roman empire, but a further revolution in the history of the barbarian groups involved in its dismemberment. Gothic, Frankish, Vandalic and Suevic groups, for instance, were all forced to operate in larger numbers to survive and prosper (Heather 1996, pt. ii). The death struggles of the Roman state thus generated a further stage in the processes of state formation which had been working themselves out in the Germanic world for four hundred years (p. 238). Nonetheless, the disjuncture between observable events on the ground, at any point after 406, and traditional expectations of Roman victory was immense. It continued to grow until the successor states were created and the western Roman empire ceased to exist.

Surviving elements of the old Roman landowning elite – and outside central and eastern Britain and northern Gaul considerable numbers did survive – were faced, therefore, with a considerable problem. Their ideological heritage taught them that they were superior to barbarians; indeed, barbarians who were inferior in every conceivable way were necessary to their own self-image. Before their very eyes, however, Roman power ebbed away, and 'barbarian' groups remade the map of western Europe.

Not surprisingly, our sources reflect a range of responses to this collapse of inherited ideological certainty. One famous and well-explored rejection of the old vision of the world, directly inspired by fifth-century events, is Salvian of Marseilles' tract for his times: *On the Government of God*. Here we encounter virtuous, if simple and occasionally ignorant, barbarians and vicious Romans: the success of the former stemming directly from their relative virtue and God's determination to punish the latter for their wickedness (cf. Courcelle 1964, 146–55). Indeed, given their religious belief in the soteriological equality of all men and the immediacy of God's power in the world, Christian writers could not but tend to revise inherited Roman world views as the empire collapsed. The collapse of the empire and triumph of the barbarians had to represent God's will, so that the relationship between God's plans for the universe and the Roman empire could not be quite as close as fourth-century propaganda liked to pretend (see pp. 2136–7). A more radical strand of Christian opinion had never bought fully into the ideology of the Christian empire, and more mainstream Christians of a thoughtful disposition were quickly led by events to rethink basic assumptions, some coming to more substantial conclusions than the theoretical and rather optimistic Salvian. As early as the 410s, Alaric's sack of Rome led Augustine to reject the central tenet of Christianised imperial propaganda: that the Roman empire was God's special tool for spreading right, Christian, religion to the entire world (*The City of God* 1; *De Urbis Excidio*; cf. Courcelle 1964, 70–7).

By implication, although we hear little in detail, some very secular members of the Roman elite, similarly faced with the decline of Roman power, likewise abandoned the old ideologies, joining themselves unreservedly to the new barbarian powers in the land, at a point when the empire, or parts of it, still continued to exist. Four Hispano-Romans, prominent enough to merit individual mention, for instance, joined the Vandals, probably in the 420s (Arcadius, Eutychius 2, Paschasius 1, Probus 3: Prosper *s.a.* 437, cf. Honoratus, *Epistula Consolatoria*). These men had quickly overcome, it would seem, any inherited scruples they may have had about their own superiority and working with barbarians. Their circumstances are not known in detail, however, and it is possible that, rather than having become convinced that the old order was simply wrong, they had lost out in some political struggle within the Roman world and been forced to join the barbarians. This was certainly true of Sebastianus, son-in-law of the African army commander

Boniface, who eventually made his way to Vandal Carthage after he had lost out to Aetius, been expelled from Constantinople, and no other Roman refuge was left to him (refs as *PLRE* 2, 983–4). Some of the groups labelled *Bacaudae* in our sources may also fall into the category of those rejecting *Romanitas* at the earliest opportunity. Again, however, it may also have been the brute impact of events – the need to preserve one's position in drastically changed circumstances – rather than any looseness of attachment to the old ideologies that really explains such behaviour (contrast the interpretations of Thompson 1963 with those of Van Dam 1985, chs 2–3 and Drinkwater 1992). Unfortunately, no *apologia* from a Roman-turned-barbarian has come down to us from the early period. Sidonius' letters suggest something about the motives of leading Gallo-Romans from his circle who abandoned a Roman allegiance. But this evidence relates to a point after the deaths of Aetius and Valentinian III, when the edifice of empire was clearly crumbling, so that the motive need not have been more than self-preservation. We are left to judge the internal ideological readjustments made by early barbarophiles from the external evidence of their behaviour.

Perhaps more striking than these explicit and implicit rejections of established images, however, is the extent to which the old vision of Romans and barbarians continued to exercise a hold on men's minds, among the elite at least, both in the period of imperial collapse, and well into the period of the successor states. Not even every Christian, particularly those living alongside them, was ready to draw the same conclusions as Salvian of Marseilles from the triumphal progress through North Africa of the Vandals. In his *History of the Vandal Persecution*, Victor of Vita used an account of present and past events to establish two opposed sets of categories: 'Roman = Catholic = Civilised' and 'Vandal = Arian = Barbarian'. The essence of his argument is that the two groups can never intersect or mingle. The Vandal king Huneric, it seems clear, was trying to establish a uniform religious settlement within his kingdom, and Victor reasserts traditional distinctions to prevent any accommodation, i.e. backsliding on the part of Catholic Christians (esp. 3.62–70). In this case, heresy has merely been added to the traditional list of distinctions between Roman and barbarian.

Even where surviving authors were advocating accommodation with the new powers in the land, the old ghosts still had to be exorcised. A striking case in point is provided by works of Sidonius Apollinaris from the mid-450s. By this date, the Visigoths of Aquitaine were a permanent feature of the political landscape of southern Gaul, and, by extension, of the rump western empire. They had recently participated in the great alliance which had repulsed Attila from Gaul, and, following the death of Valentinian III, had been immediately courted by his would-be successor, Petronius Maximus. Maximus sent the Patrician Avitus to Toulouse to canvass their support, but, while Avitus was still in Toulouse, news came through that Maximus had been killed in the Vandal sack of Rome. In response, the Visigothic king Theoderic II had Avitus declared emperor, and only later, on 9 July 455, was the elevation ratified by a meeting of the Gallo-Roman council at Arles. In a striking development, Gothic military power and a faction of the Gallo-Roman aristocracy had come together to launch an imperial regime (cf. Heather 1995a).

It was at precisely at this point that Sidonius penned a lengthy description of the court of Theoderic II. The whole deserves close attention, but let me quote from the dinner scene:

> When one joins him at dinner . . . there is no unpolished conglomeration of discoloured old silver set by panting attendants on sagging tables; the weightiest thing on these occasions is the conversation, for there are either no stories or only serious ones . . . The viands attract by their skilful cookery, not by their costliness, the platters by their brightness, not by their weight. Replenishment of the goblets or wine-bowls comes at such long intervals that there is more reason for the thirsty to complain than for the intoxicated to refrain. To sum up: you can find there Greek elegance, Gallic plenty, Italian briskness; the dignity of state, the attentiveness of a private home, the ordered discipline of royalty.
>
> (*Ep.* 1.2.6 Loeb trans.)

Parts of the letter still seem condescending, particularly Sidonius' assertion that, if you can let the king win at games in an unobvious manner, you have a very good chance of getting him to grant your requests. Nonetheless, Theoderic's court and his routine, as portrayed by Sidonius, bear a striking similarity to what we know of the Roman imperial ideal. That this is hardly accidental is confirmed by the dinner scene, which deliberately and pointedly refutes the traditional Roman stereotypes of barbarians. Contrary to expectation, you find at Theoderic's court no drunkenness, no greed, and only serious conversation. In the quoted remarks about ostentatious silver plate and slightly later references to unseemly 'light' post-prandial entertainments, Sidonius would also appear to be making flattering comparisons of the Gothic king with lifestyles of the Roman rich and famous (compare Ammianus' famous Roman digressions: 14.6; 28.4). Set in the context of the radical political initiative represented by the alliance of Goth and aristocratic Roman which was Avitus' regime, there seems no doubting Sidonius' message. Far from being a barbarian, the Gothic king was a worthy political ally who had firmly entered the world of Roman civilisation. Moreover, as Sidonius' panegyric on Avitus from the same period informs us, Theoderic had studied Virgil and Roman law (at Avitus' instigation: *Carm.* 7.495ff). Hence the Gothic king had indeed followed the traditionally prescribed path to rationality and an appreciation of the Roman way. I have not the slightest idea from all this what the Gothic king and his court were 'really' like, but there is likewise not the slightest doubt what Sidonius was trying to say about him. Presumably to comfort and attract Roman landowners, somewhat perturbed at sleeping with the enemy, Sidonius was rallying the doubters. Theoderic and his Goths were no longer barbarians, but, in the proper sense of the word, Romans.

In Sidonius' circles at least, then, the response to a developing clash between image and reality was, in a sense, to change reality. The power of the inherited stereotypes remained strong enough that political cooperation with barbarians had to be justified on the grounds that the particular group involved – here Goths – were no longer barbarians. They might wear skins rather than togas (*Carm.* 7), but, in the development of their minds and character, they – or, at least, their king – had passed onto the higher level of Romanness through proper appreciation of Latin literature and Roman law. In defence of Sidonius' grasp of reality, it is worth noting that Theoderic II does seem to have accepted the basic existence of the western Roman empire and sought to maximise his position within its surviving structures. When his brother Euric murdered and replaced him, matters changed. Perceiving that the power of the empire had almost totally ebbed away, Euric launched a series of campaigns entirely on his own initiative. Sidonius immediately ceased to cooperate with the Goths, and, with a group of friends, he attempted to raise troops to resist Gothic expansion by force. In this context, Theoderic's 'Romanness' had an important kernel of meaning: a declaration of willingness to work alongside the empire (on this important contrast between Theoderic and Euric, see further, e.g., Heather 1992, 1996). It was

PETER HEATHER

this basic political stance, perhaps, that Sidonius was trying to communicate to his Gallo-Roman peers through these Romanising characterisations of the king.

Even after the western empire had disappeared completely, we still find very much the same strategy of ideological adjustment being pursued. Outside of Anglo-Saxon England, the world of the successor states is littered with parvenu kings of non-Roman origins striking decidedly Roman poses in all kinds of ideologically significant areas. Burgundian kings are famous for continuing to hold on to Roman titulature as *Magistri Militum per Gallias*, their subservient attitude to Constantinople, and for the brief summary of Roman law – the *Lex Romana Burgundionum* – which seems to have been issued under their aegis (the first two are best evidenced in Avitus *Epp.* 78, 93–4). The Visigothic king Alaric II, although an Arian Christian, called councils of Catholic bishops, in which they dutifully prayed for his welfare (most recently Klingshirn 1994, ch. 4), and issued his famous *Breviary* (the *Lex Romana Visigothorum*): a lengthy summary of Roman law based on the *Theodosian Code* and other important Roman legal sources. Clovis, likewise, initiated a series of Gallic councils, perhaps issued the first written Frankish law code, and is famous, after Gregory of Tours' description, for his consul-like ceremonial procession in Tours after defeating the Visigoths. His familial successors were customarily educated in Latin, one even writing poetry and attempting a reform of the alphabet (Wood 1990; 1994, ch. 7). Even the Vandals, generally considered, in the wake of Victor of Vita, to be the most anti-Roman of them all, structured their authority to a significant extent after a Roman imperial model. Court hierarchies and titles maintained some Roman traditions; we know, thanks to the *Tablettes Albertini*, that elements of Roman land law continued to apply, and even the Vandals' persecution of Catholics followed Roman example. With a nice, if rather alarming, sense of humour, Huneric's persecuting edict ordered that the penalties which late fourth-century emperors had heaped upon Arians should now be applied to Catholics (Victor of Vita 3.3–14). Victor's whole response to the religious crisis in which he found himself – arguing vigorously, along traditional lines, that Roman and barbarian were totally distinct and could never intermingle (see, p. 245) – actually suggests that boundaries were beginning to disintegrate even in Vandal Africa. If that were not the case, why did Victor work so hard to reassert their validity?

Pride of place among the Romano-barbarian kings of the successor states must be reserved, however, for Theoderic the Ostrogoth. His regime seized upon every facet of traditional visions of *Romanitas*, not least the claim to be part of a divinely inspired order for the world. In his letter to Anastasius, Theoderic noted that it was God's help which allowed him to rule Romans properly (*Variae* 1.1). Likewise, the mosaics of S. Apollinare Nuovo originally portrayed him enthroned in majesty, surrounded by his court in the new palace in Ravenna. Opposite him was displayed Christ the Pantocrator and the majesty of heaven. The greater authority (Heaven) was shown directly sustaining the lesser (Theoderic) (MacCormack 1981, 236–9). Theoderic's Italian palaces (that of Ravenna is best known, but two others were built at Pavia and Verona) imitated the architecture of the imperial palace in Constantinople, and, within them, Theoderic deployed the imperial cult of the sacred ruler. Great public occasions, such as his *adventus* into Rome in the year 500, were designed to proclaim, after the Constantinopolitan pattern, the sanctity and divinely inspired nature of his rule (Johnson 1988; cf., more generally, Ward-Perkins 1984).

Theoderic was also aware of the ideological importance of written law, and of being seen to further individual human rationality via education in the classics. Ennodius' panegyric observed that *ius* and *civilitas* presided in Theoderic's palace: *ius* designating the fundamentals of Roman law (Barnish 1992, pp. xxiv–xxv; cf. *Variae* 1.27; 2.24; 6.5; 8.33; 9.18). Closely related to this was the concept of true freedom (*libertas*), attained by those who obeyed this law (*Variae* 12.5; cf. 11.13). Many of the letters written for Theoderic by Cassiodorus demanded respect for Roman law, reflected upon its fundamental correctness, or even cited it (e.g. *Variae* 2.7; 3.17 (cf. 18); 4.22; 5.40; 10.5). For the king's recognition of the importance of education, Ennodius' panegyric is again a prime piece of evidence. Amongst other things, it stressed the importance of the Greek education Theoderic had received in Constantinople (ed. Hartel, pp. 264.13ff). In his letter to Anastasius, Theoderic also claimed that it was precisely this education which had taught him to govern Romans. Through a classical education, therefore, Theoderic claimed to have grasped the importance of doing things the divinely-ordained Roman way, and a number of *Variae* underline the attention he devoted to it. He proclaimed education the key to morality. Through it, he noted, the individual learns the self-control without which obedience to Roman law is impossible. Likewise, the individual who lacks self-control cannot be trusted to govern others. For the maintenance of good social order – *civilitas* – education had to function properly (e.g. *Variae* 3.13, 8.15, 8.31).

Every trick in the book was deployed, then, to get over the central message that Theoderic's regime was 'Roman' and in tune with God's plans (see further Heather 1993). The evidence suggests, however, that, leaving aside Anglo-Saxon England, any differences between Ostrogothic Italy and the other western successor states were no more than ones of degree. If we had a set of administrative letters from Clovis' reign, rather than Gregory of Tours' highly partial and posterior account of it, I am quite sure that Theoderic and Clovis would not look so very different (in some ways also the drift of Daly 1994, although I see no reason to think that Clovis was not both Romanising and a personally violent warrior king; cf. Heather 1995b on Theoderic). Across former Roman Europe, successor-state rulers responded to the potency of inherited images of 'barbarian' and 'Roman' by ruling in a style which made the claim that they had crossed the boundary into civilisation.

Why was this? The somewhat later Arab take-over of the eastern empire, for instance, provides an illuminatingly contrary model of possible historical development. Here again former Roman clients, but this time armed with a profoundly alternative ideology, generated a cultural as well as political revolution: the Islamicisation of the eastern and southern Mediterranean. In striking contrast, the Germanic take-over of the West was, in the first instance at least, limited to politics. Several levels of explanation are required, I think, to account for the inherent limitations of this earlier revolution.

First, there was a basic admiration of things Roman on the part of the rulers of the new kingdoms. The Roman empire had existed for as long as anyone could remember and was associated with political-cum-military potency and advanced technologies of striking kinds. Being seen as smaller versions of the Roman state, adopting all the paraphernalia of its civilisation, then, had its attractions for Germanic kings and nobles. A nice testimony to this is the career of Venantius Fortunatus. In the later sixth century, Gallic nobles of both Roman and Frankish origin continued to have a taste for classicising Roman poetry celebrating everything from their careers to their dinner tables (George 1992). And here, I suspect, the adoption of Christianity on the part of the invaders was a crucial cultural conduit. Some more radically ascetic strands of Christianity had rejected classical culture (cf. p. 244), but most embraced it. Indeed, the *technê* of the grammarian, guardian of the Graeco-Roman heritage, fundamentally shaped the late antique and early medieval versions of Christianity passed down to the successor states. It has become increasingly clear, for instance, that educated Christians (even while sometimes denying it) merely redeployed on the Bible everything the grammarians had previously done with Virgil and Homer (e.g. Oberhelman 1991, with refs). As late as the eighth century, Christian missionaries could be urged to use the clinching argument that God's power was visible in the greatness of the Christian Roman world and the fact that Christians enjoyed the wine, olive oil and sun of the Mediterranean, while pagans were freezing their rear ends off in northern Europe (Daniel of Winchester to Boniface, *Ep.* 23).

Second, there were some extremely practical reasons for successor-state kings to dress up their power in Roman forms. Where Roman landowning elites continued to exist, they remained structurally central to the exercise of power. These landowning families controlled important reservoirs of financial power in the new kingdoms (e.g. Barnish 1988; Schäfer 1991). They dominated local administration and landowning, and their willingness to pay and raise taxation sustained the whole edifice (Wickham 1984). A militarily dominant ruler could of course compel payment to some extent, but taxation is a political issue, and successful taxation requires an element of consent. The presentation of the new order in the clothes of the old empire helped to render it acceptable, and encouraged the participation in the new world of those who had dominated the old. This was a basic advantage to the new kings, because it brought within the web of their control areas of the kingdoms – often substantial – where few of their original followers had settled. Frankish settlement seems to have been confined to north-east Gaul, for instance, Ostrogothic to northern Italy and the north-east Adriatic coast (respectively James 1988, 108ff; Heather 1996, 237–9). It also put new levers of power into their hands. There is no evidence for the existence of centralised legal structures or of large-scale redistributive taxation powers among Germanic kingdoms outside of former imperial territory. Inherited Roman wealth and models of ruling, like inherited ideologies, could thus be deployed by the new kings of western Europe to strengthen their own position, not least *vis-à-vis* their own followers. A good case in point is the patronage structure to reward loyal Goths which Theoderic was able to finance using the wealth of Italy (Heather 1995b). By the early sixth century,

Roman populations were also becoming militarised (although this is a subject awaiting comprehensive treatment), which provided a further important reason for kings to attract their support.

In this context, promising to maintain Roman legal structures had a very particular point. In ideological contexts, Roman law was equated, as we have seen, generally with civilisation. Occasionally, however, the mask slips, and it emerges clearly that one very important significance of the rule of law to Roman landowning elites was secure tenure of their properties and the right to pass them on to the heir(s) of their choice:

> Amongst the Romans there are many ways of giving free-dom. Not only the living but also the dead bestow it lavishly, arranging their estates as they wish; and whatever a man has willed for his possessions at his death is legally binding.
>
> (Priscus ed. Blockley fr. 11.2, p. 273.504–7)

This, of course, makes perfect sense. Landownership and its con-tinuity was the basis of elite status and its maintainance in the later empire. Successor-state kings who promoted the continuation of Roman law were guaranteeing to Roman elites that their basic pattern of life and their landed fortunes would survive intact into the new era, that political revolution would not be accompanied by social revolution. Such policies were, at least in some cases, deliberate, and not the result of mere inertia. During his struggle with Odovacar, for instance, Theoderic the Ostrogoth threatened to cancel the testamentary powers of all Roman landowners who had not actively supported his cause. Pushed through, such a policy would have meant social revolution. Theoderic acceded, how-ever, to the request of an embassy, led by Bishop Epiphanius of Milan, to cancel the order (*Life of Epiphanius* 122–35). I doubt that Theoderic ever really meant to implement the policy, but making and then withdrawing the threat would have made crystal clear to Italian landowners the substantial virtues of the Ostrogothic regime, and of active participation in its structures.

The boot could, of course, sometimes be on the other foot. We have already encountered the *Breviary* of Roman law issued by the Visigothic king Alaric II. This text was put out in the middle of an extended conflict between Alaric and the Frankish king Clovis, which had already seen Clovis attempt to woo Gallo-Romans away from their Gothic king (most recently, Heather 1996, ch. 7). If one checks what Alaric included and omitted in the *Breviary*, the wholesale inclusion of books 2–4 of the *Theodosian Code* is very striking. The contents of these books reconfirmed stability in such basic points of Roman elite life as property and testamentary rights, and the legal procedures relating to them. At certain points, therefore, the Romanness of successor-state kings was an attempt to outbid rivals for much-needed support from the landowners of western Europe.

Third, on perhaps a less structural note, Romanness could also be a weapon for furthering the ambitions of the first-division powers of the new world order. At first sight, for instance, Theoderic's attitude to Constantinople seems highly deferential, not least as reflected in the first letter of the *Variae* collection to the emperor Anastasius. The deference is superficial. An iron fist is evident within the letter's velvet glove:

> Our royalty is an imitation of yours, modelled on your good purpose, a copy of the only Empire; and in so far as we follow you do we excel all other nations. . . .We think you will not suffer that any discord should remain between two Republics, which are declared to have ever formed one body under their ancient princes, and which ought not to be joined by a mere sentiment of love, but actively to aid one another with all their powers. Let there be always one will, one purpose in the Roman Kingdom.
>
> (*Variae* 1.1.2–5; trans. Hodgkin)

The letter was written in 508, when 8,000 east Roman troops in 100 warships and 100 troopships were harrying (or about to harry) the coast of Italy. They were acting on an alliance which the eastern emperor had forged with the Frankish king Clovis. In this context, the letter is actually a demand note, in which Theoderic used his own assumed Romanness to rebuke Anastasius on two counts. First, there should be peace, not conflict, between the two Roman states. Second, since Ostrogothic Italy is the only legitimately Roman state in the West ('in so far as we follow you do we excel all other nations'), Anastasius should not be concocting alliances with other powers. Theoderic obviously has the Franks in mind. A further sting in the letter's seemingly respectful tail is its allusion to the 'Divine help' (see p. 249), which had sustained Theoderic's attempts to govern Romans. This amounted to a claim that Theoderic's 'Romanness' was as much part of God's order as the eastern 'Romanness' of Constantinople. It had, therefore, its own, separate, legitimacy (cf. Claude 1978, 42–4). Beneath the surface deference, Theoderic used his own Romanness to claim virtual parity of status with the eastern empire.

This claim to quasi-imperial status also appears in some of Theoderic's communications to other western successor states. A good example is his letter to King Gundobad of the Burgundians (like Anastasius an ally of the Franks), on the eve of the same crisis. Again, but superficially, the letter suggests friendship, since Theoderic sent Gundobad two timepieces (a sundial, and a water-clock). But the letter presented these offerings as gifts from Graeco-Roman civilisation to help bring the Burgundians to a more rational, fully human way of life (*Variae* 1.46, trans. Barnish):

> [2] Under your [Gundobad's] rule, let Burgundy learn to scrutinise devices of the highest ingenuity, and to praise the inventions of the ancients. Through you it lays aside its tribal way of life. . . . Let it [by the clocks] fix the hours with precision. [3] The order of life (*Ordo vitae*) becomes confused if this separation is not truly known. Indeed, it is the habit of beasts to feel the hours by their bellies' hunger, and to be unsure of something obviously granted for human purposes.

Theoderic thus presented himself as controlling the monopoly of surviving Roman wisdom in western Europe, with rights to distribute the benefits of classical civilisation as he saw fit. The Burgundians, by contrast, are placed on a much lower level of human evolution, still closer to beasts than rational human beings. And alongside this total assumption of Roman ideology, there arguably went a sustained attempt to re-create the western empire in practice (Heather 1996, ch. 8).

On close inspection, therefore, what seems striking about the stereotyped views of Roman and barbarian of late imperial ideology is the extent to which they emerged unscathed from the political revolution of the fifth century. Outside a limited number of Christian writers, the intrusion of outsiders and destruction of the western Roman empire did not see the collapse of traditional notions of 'Roman' and 'barbarian'. Individuals and groups were recategorised, or recategorised themselves, for a variety of purposes. Many former barbarians became Roman to justify political accommodation on the part of Romans, to attract the support of locally dominant Roman landowners, or to justify grabbing the reins of imperial power. The actual categories, however, remained the same. The later Roman empire, even as it failed politically, succeeded in setting an ideological agenda for post-Roman Europe. There can be no greater tribute to the prevalence and power of the self-definition which had united Roman elites from Hadrian's Wall to the Euphrates.

Bibliography

Primary sources

Ammianus Marcellinus, ed. and trans. J.C. Rolfe, Loeb, 3 vols (London, 1950–2).
Anonymus de rebus bellicis ed. and trans. E.A. Thompson, A Roman Inventor and Reformer (Oxford: Oxford University Press, 1952).
Anonymus Valesianus, ed. and trans. J.C. Rolfe in vol. 3 of his Loeb Ammianus.
Augustine of Hippo, The City of God, ed. C.C.S.L. 47–8; Eng. trans. H. Bettenson, Harmondsworth, 1972; De urbis excidio PL 40, coll. 715–24.
Avitus of Vienne, Opera, ed. R. Peiper, M.G.H., A.A., 6.2 (Berlin, 1883).
Boniface, Letters, ed. W. Tangl, Die Briefe des heiligen Bonifatius und Lulles (Berlin, 1916); Eng. trans. E. Emerton, The Letters of St. Boniface, New York: Columbia University Press, 1940.
Ennodius, Opera, ed. W. Hartel, C.S.E.L, 6; Life of Epiphanius, trans. Fathers of the Church, vol. 15.
Eunapius, ed. and trans., Blockley 1983.
Gregory Nazianzus, Letters, ed. and trans. P. Gallay, Budé, 2 vols (Paris, 1964–7).
Honoratus, Epistula Consolatoria ad Arcadium actum in exsilum a Genserico rege Vandalorum (PL 50, 567–70).
Julian, Works, ed. and trans. W.C. Wright, Loeb, 3 vols (London, 1913–23).
Leges Burgundionum, ed. L.R. de Salis, M.G.H., Leges I, vol. 2 (Berlin, 1892).
Lex Romana Visigothorum, ed. G. Haenel (Berlin, 1849).
Libanius, Opera, ed. R. Foerster, Teubner, 12 vols (Leipzig 1903–27). Orr. 19. and 20 trans. in A.F. Norman, Libanius: Selected Works, Loeb, 2 vols (London, 1969–77).
Panegyrici Latini, ed. and trans. E. Galletier, 3 vols, Budé (Paris, 1955).
Paulus Orosius, History Against the Pagans, ed. K. Zangmeister, C.S.E.L. (1882); Eng. trans. Fathers of the Church, vol. 50.
Priscus of Panium, ed. and trans. Blockley 1983.
Prosper Tiro, Chronicon, ed. Th. Mommsen, M.G.H., A.A.9, Ch. 1 (Berlin, 1892).
Salvian, On the Government of God, ed. C. Halm, M.G.H., A.A.1 (Berlin, 1872); Eng. trans. E.M. Sanford (New York, 1966).
Sidonius Apollinaris, Poems and Letters, ed. and trans. W.B. Anderson, Loeb, 2 vols (London, 1935, 1965).

Symmachus, *Relationes* ed. and trans. R.H. Barrow, *Prefect and Emperor: The Relationes of Symmachus AD 384*, Oxford: Oxford University Press, 1973.

Synesius, *De Regno*, ed. N. Terzaghi, *Synesii Cyrenensis Opuscula* (Rome, 1944); Eng. trans. A. Fitzgerald (London, 1930).

Tablettes Albertini: Actes Privées de l'Epoque Vandale (fin du v siècle), ed. C. Courtois et al., Arts et métiers graphiques (Paris, 1952).

Themistius, *Orationes*, ed. G. Downey and A.F. Norman, 3 vols, Teubner (1965–74). Orations 8 and 10 trans. in Heather and Matthews 1991; Oration 16 trans. in Heather and Moncur forthcoming (1999).

Theodosian Code, ed. Th. Mommsen and P.M. Meyer, Weidmann, 3rd edn (Berlin, 1962); Eng. trans. C. Pharr (New York, 1952).

Venantius Fortunatus, *Opera Poetica* ed. F. Leo, M.G.H., A.A., 4.1 (Berlin, 1881); selected works in Eng. trans. J. George, *Venantius Fortunatus: Personal and Political Poems*, Translated Texts for Historians, Liverpool: Liverpool University Press, 1995.

Victor of Vita, *History of the Vandal Persecution*, ed. C. Halm, M.G.H., A.A.2 (Berlin, 1879); Eng. trans. J. Moorhead (Liverpool, 1992).

Secondary sources

Barnish, S.J.B. (1988) 'Transformation and Survival in the Western Senatorial Aristocracy, *c.* AD 400–700', *PBSR* 65: 120–55.

—— (1992) *Cassiodorus: Variae*, Translated Texts for Historians, Liverpool: Liverpool University Press.

Blockley, R.C. (1983) *The Fragmentary Classicising Historians of the Later Roman Empire: Eunapius, Olympiodorus, Priscus and Malchus*, vol. 2, Liverpool: Francis Cairns.

Brown, P.R.L. (1976) 'Eastern and Western Christendom in Late Antiquity: A Parting of the Ways', in D. Wood (ed.) *The Orthodox Churches and the West*, Studies in Church History XIII, Oxford: Oxford University Press.

Calo Levi, A. (1952) *Barbarians on Roman Imperial Coins and Sculpture*, Numismatic Notes and Monographs 123, New York: The American Numismatic Society.

Claude, D. (1978) 'Universale und partikulare Züge in der Politik Theoderichs', *Francia* 6: 19–58.

Courcelle, P. (1964) *Histoire littéraire des grandes invasions germaniques*, 3rd edn, Paris: CNRS.

Daly, W.M. (1994) 'Clovis: How Barbaric, How Pagan?', *Speculum* 69: 619–64.

Dauge, Y.A. (1981) *Le Barbare. Recherches sur la conception romaine de la barbarie et de la civilisation*, Brussels: Collection Latomus.

Drinkwater, J. (1992) 'The Bacaudae of Fifth-Century Gaul', in Drinkwater and Elton 1992.

Drinkwater, J., and Elton, H. (eds) (1992) *Fifth-Century Gaul: A Crisis of Identity*, Cambridge: Cambridge University Press.

Dvornik, F. (1966) *Early Christian and Byzantine Political Philosophy: Origins and Background*, Washington D.C.: The Dumbarton Oaks Center for Byzantine Studies.

George, J. (1992) *Venantius Fortunatus: A Latin Poet in Merovingian Gaul*, Oxford: Oxford University Press.

Heather, P.J. (1991) *Goths and Romans 332–489*, Oxford: Oxford University Press.

—— (1992) 'The Emergence of the Visigothic Kingdom', in Drinkwater and Elton 1992.

—— (1993) 'The Historical Culture of Ostrogothic Italy', in *Teodorico il Grande e i Goti d'Italia, Atti del XIII Congresso internazionale di studi sull'alto medioevo*, Spoleto: Centro italiano di studi sull'alto medioevo.

—— (1994) 'Literacy and Power in the Migration Period', in A.K. Bowman and G. Woolf (eds) *Literacy and Power in the Ancient World*, Cambridge: Cambridge University Press.

—— (1995a) 'The Huns and the End of the Roman Empire in Western Europe', *English Historical Review* 110: 4–41.

—— (1995b) 'Theoderic King of the Goths', *Early Medieval Europe* 4.2: 145–73.

—— (1996) *The Goths*, Oxford: Blackwell.

—— (1997) '*Foedera* and *Foederati* of the Fourth Century', in Pohl 1997.

Heather, P.J., and Matthews, J.F. (1991) *The Goths in the Fourth Century*, Translated Texts for Historians, Liverpool: Liverpool University Press.

Heather, P.J., and Moncur, D. (forthcoming 1999) *Themistius: Select Orations*, Translated Texts for Historians, Liverpool: Liverpool University Press.

Hedeager, L. (1987) 'Empire, Frontier and the Barbarian Hinterland. Rome and Northern Europe from AD 1–400', in K. Kristiansen et al. (eds), *Centre and Periphery in the Ancient World*, Cambridge: Cambridge University Press.

—— (1988) 'The Evolution of Germanic Society 1–400 AD', in R.F.J. Jones et al. (eds), *First Millennium Papers: Western Europe in the First Millennium*, Oxford: British Archaeological Reports IS 401.

—— (1992) *Iron Age Societies. From Tribe to State in Northern Europe 500 BC to AD 700*, trans. J. Hines, Oxford: Oxford University Press.

James, E. (1988) *The Franks*, Oxford: Blackwell.

Johnson, M.J. (1988) 'Towards a History of Theoderic's Building Programme', *DOP* 42: 73–96.

Kaster, R.A. (1988) *Guardians of the Language: The Grammarian and Society in Late Antiquity*, Berkeley: California University Press.

Klingshirn, W.E. (1994) *Caesarius of Arles. The Making of a Christian Community in Late Antique Arles*, Cambridge: Cambridge University Press.

MacCormack, S. (1981) *Art and Ceremony in Late Antiquity*, Berkeley: California University Press.

McCormick, M. (1986) *Eternal Victory: Triumphal Rulership in Late Antiquity, Byzantium and the Early Medieval West*, Cambridge: Cambridge University Press.

Momigliano, A. (1955) 'Cassiodorus and the Italian Culture of his Time', *Proceedings of the British Academy* 4: 207–45.

Oberhelman, S. (1991) *Rhetoric and Homiletics in Fourth-Century Christian Literature*, Atlanta, GA: Scholars Press.

Pohl, W. (1997) *Kingdoms of the Empire: The Integration of Barbarians in Late Antiquity*, Leiden: Brill.

Prosopography of the Later Roman Empire (1980) vol. 2: AD 395–527, ed. J.R. Martindale, Cambridge: Cambridge University Press.

Schäfer, C. (1991) *Der weströmische Senat als Träger antiker Kontinuität unter den Ostgotenkönigen (490–540 n. Chr.)*, St. Katharinen: Scripta Mercaturae.

Sorabji, R. (1983) *Time, Creation and the Continuum: Theories in Antiquity and the Early Middle Ages*, London: Duckworth.

Thompson, E.A. (1963) 'The Visigoths from Fritigern to Euric', *Historia* 12: 105–26.

Van Dam, R. (1985) *Leadership and Community in Late Antique Gaul*, Berkeley: California University Press.

Ward-Perkins, B. (1984) *From Classical Antiquity to the Middle Ages: Urban Public Building in Northern and Central Italy AD 300–850*, Oxford: Oxford University Press.

Whittaker, C.R. (1994) *Frontiers of the Roman Empire*, Baltimore: Johns Hopkins University Press.

Wickham, C. (1984), 'The Other Transition: From the Ancient World to Feudalism', *Past and Present* 103: 3–36.

Wirth, G. (1997) 'Rome and its Germanic Partners in the Fourth Century', in Pohl 1997.

Wood, I.N. (1990) 'Administration, Law and Culture in Merovingian Gaul', in R. McKitterick (ed.) *The Uses of Literacy in Early Medieval Europe*, Cambridge: Cambridge University Press, 63–81.

—— (1994) *The Merovingian Kingdoms 450–751*, London: Longman.

INDEX

INDEX

Clement of Alexandria 86, 104
Clovis 250, 253
Cobain, Kurt 65
Colluthus 43
Constantine 10, 163, 168, 170, 172, 173,
  177, 179, 220–1, 222–3, 224, 229, 235,
  239, 241
Constantius II 239, 240, 241
Cooper, Kate 64
Crucifixion, the 169
culture 8, 12, 23, 32, 95–6, 126, 129;
  continuity of 160, 182–3; 'high' 100,
  107; intellectual 208; and identity *see*
  identity
Cyprian 226–7

Damnatio memoriae 161–3, 177–9, 183
Delphic Oracle 128
De Rossi G.B. 173, 175
Descartes 150, 153–4
dialogue, structure of 138–40, 145–6
Dictys the Cretan 122
Didymus the Blind, 128
Dio 164, 165
Dio Chrysostom 30, 105
Diocletian 112, 160, 218, 231
Diogenes Laertius 31, 115
discourse 126
Domitian 181, 183
Domitianus 165, 166
Dunn (& Jones) 44

elite 10, 105–6; Roman 114, 254, 255
Ennodius 249
Epictetus 133
Epiphanius of Milan 252
epistemology 151
ethnography 123
Eunapius of Sardis 101, 116, 242
Euric 247–8
Euripides 20, 101, 103, 105; *Andromeda* 20,
  101, 102; *Bacchae* 104; *Phoenician Women*
  103
Eusebius 11, 127, 128, 166, 172, 173, 177,
  229, 230, 231, 236; *Historia Ecclesiae*
  177; *Triennal Ortation* 179; *Vita
  Constantini* 179–9
Eutropius 161
Evagrius 228
Evodius of Uzalis 134, 137–8, 141–2,
  143–4, 145–9

fatherland 129–30
Favorinus, sophist 168
Felix, Bishop of Aptungi 220

Felix of Corsica 223
Felix of Thibiuca 230
Foucault, Michel 17

Galerius Maximus 226
Gallienus 114
Gelzer, Thomas 60, 61,
gender 49, 53, 55, 190, 207, 210
geography 7–8, 27–30
Georgius, Bishop 165, 166
Gibbon, Edward 95
Gleason, Maud 45, 195
Gnostics 129
Goldhill, Simon 56
Grant, Michael 42
Gregory, Andrew 167
Gregory of Nazianzus 103, 241
Gregory of Tours 248
Gunderson 73
Gundobad, King 254

Hall, Edith 57
Haworth 79
Heliodorus 6, 8, 9, 16–33; *Aethiopica* 4, 9,
  16–33
Hellenism 100, 102, 107
Hellenocentrism 23, 32
Hermes Trismegistus 123
Hermetic Corpus, the 125–6
Hermias of Alexandria 61
Herodotus 25, 120, 122
Hierocles 229–30
Hilarianus 230
Homer 22, 23, 42, 105, 128, 251; *Odyssey*
  21–23, 27, 47, 52, 57–8
Hopkins, Keith 170
Hopkinson, Neil 41, 43, 59
Horace 18
Huneric 248
Hunter, Richard 50
Hutchence, Michael 65

Iamblichus 116, 117–18, 123, 124, 125,
  126
iconoclasm 159–84
iconography 173–5
identity 1–2, 8–11, 22; barbarian 245; civic
  44, 62, 99–100; construction of 4, 5–6,
  134–5, 137, 154, 155; crisis of 1;
  cultural 18, 32–3, 112, 155, 160, 190,
  207; sexual 44; of speaker 44, 138–45,
  155; vocalising 44–5, 50–1; of women
  190–210
ideology 1, 5, 43, 191–2, 234, 244–5,
  254–5

260

INDEX

image, imperial 164, 170, 182; women
192–200, 208–9; barbarian 7–8, 238
imagery, Christian 75, 200–3
initiation 20, 26, 30–31
intellectualism 11, 193–7, 201–6, 208
Ioannes Eugenikos 61
iudex 7, 8, 214–32
Iunilius Africanus 140

Jacob of Saroug 172, 179
Jerome 159, 169, 170, 171, 180–1, 182,
228–9
John of Stobi 105
Jones 98
Jones A.H.M. 159
Julian 239
Juvenal 169

Kampen 192, 207
Kost, Karl-heinz 43

Lactantius 160, 182, 183, 229, 230;
De Mortibus Persecutorum 181
Lamberton, Robert 61
language 10, 48, 54, 73–4, 118–21, 124,
160
Lascaris, Janus 60
de Lauretis, Teresa 45
law-courts 216, 218
Lewis, C.S., 70
Libanius 97, 102, 160, 165, 168, 223
libertas 238
Licinius 239
logos 119, 121, 126
Longinus 120
Longus 23
Lucian 102

Macrianus 238
Magnentius 240
maiestas 160
Malamud 73, 76, 78, 88
Manichees 143
Manutius, Aldus 60
Marius Victorinus 116
marriage 44, 48–9, 63–4
Martial 43, 87; *Species De Spectaculis* 87
Marlowe, Christopher 41, 42, 60; *Hero and
Leander* 41
Marrou 193
Maximian 181
Maximus 168
Menander 105
Merkelbach 19
Merrifield, Ralph 177

Miller, Jane 46, 60
mob violence 167, 168
Momigliano 237
Montius 165, 166
Muses, the 192
Musaeus 41–65; *Hero and Leander* 3, 9,
41–65
mutilation (of statues) 165

Nabokov, Vladimir
Navigius 141
Nazarius 168
necessity 149–50
neoplatonism 123, 124
Nero 74, 122, 164
Nicomachus 127, 168–9
Nippel 164
nomen 165
nomos 128
Nonnus 42, 43; *Dionysiaca* 42; *Paraphrase of
St John* 42
Novation 99
Nugent 76, 78, 80, 84
Numa, King 115
Numenius 123, 127, 128

Odyssey see Homer
O'Donnell 142–3
oecumenism 128
Old Testament, *see* Bible
Orientalism 6, 118, 123
Origen 62, 127
Ovid 43, 44, 54–5, 74, 84–86; *Amores* 43;
Ars Amatoria 43; *Heriodes* 43, 44;
Metamorphoses 74, 84–6

paideia 5, 100, 102, 103, 105, 105
paganism 72–3, 75, 76, 89, 98, 99, 103,
106–7, 160, 172, 175, 181, 182–3
Palmer 73
pantomime *see* theatre
parthenia 48, 50, 53, 56, 57, 58–9, 60
paterfamilias 215, 216
Paulinus of Nola 137
Pausanius 59
Pelagius 137, 155
periodisation 2–4
Perkins, Judith 64
Philip Philagathos 61
Philo of Bylos 121
philosophy 116–18, 128, 129, 133, 152,
155
Philostratus 24–5; *Life of Apollonius* 24
Plato 31, 43, 117, 123, 124, 126, 127,
129, 136, 145, 151; *Phaedra* 43;

261

—